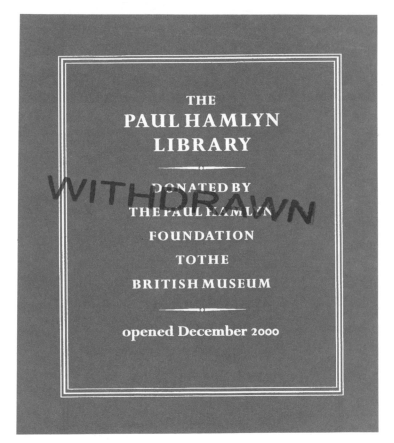

History Curatorship

Leicester Museum Studies Series
General Editor: Dr Susan Pearce

History Curatorship

by

Gaynor Kavanagh

Leicester University Press
(A division of Pinter Publishers)
Leicester, London

First published in Great Britain in 1990 by Leicester University Press
(a division of Pinter Publishers Limited)

Editorial Offices
Fielding Johnson Building, University of Leicester
University Road, Leicester, LE1 7RH

Trade and other enquiries
25 Floral Street, London, WC2E 9DS

British Library Cataloguing in Publication Data
A CIP cataloguing record for this book is available
from the British Library
ISBN 0-7185-1305-3

Typeset by GCS, Leighton Buzzard, Beds.
Printed and bound in Great Britain by Billings and Son Ltd, Worcester

Written in memory of Harry and Mary Ann Tudgay
who made history for me.

Contents

General preface to series

Museums are an international growth area. The number of museums in the world is now very large, embracing some 13,500 in Europe, of which 2,300 are in the United Kingdom; some 7,000 in North America; 2,800 in Australasia and Asia; and perhaps 2,000 in the rest of the world. The range of museum orientation is correspondingly varied and covers all aspects of the natural and the human heritage. Paralleling the growth in numbers, comes a major development in the opportunities open to museums to play an important part in shaping cultural perceptions within their communities, as people everywhere become more aware of themselves and their surroundings.

Accordingly, museums are now reviewing and rethinking their role as the storehouses of knowledge and as the presenters to people of their relationship to their own environment and past and to those of others. Traditional concepts of what a museum is, and how it should operate, are confronted by contemporary intellectual, social and political concerns which deal with questions like the validity of value judgments, bias in collecting and display, the de-mystifying of specialized knowledge, the protection of the environment, and the nature of our place in history.

These are all large and important areas and the debate is an international one. The series *Leicester Museum Studies* is designed to make a significant contribution to the development of new theory and practice across the broad range of the museum operation. Individual volumes in the series will consider in depth particular museum areas, defined either by disciplinary field or by function. Many strands of opinion will be represented, but the series as a whole will present a body of discussion and ideas which should help to redress both the present poverty of theory and the absence of a reference collection of substantial published material, which curators everywhere currently see as a fundamental lack. The community, quite rightly, is now asking more of its museums. More must be given, and to achieve this, new directions and new perspectives must be generated. In this project, *Leicester Museum Studies* is designed to play its part.

SUSAN M. PEARCE
Department of Museum Studies
University of Leicester

Preface

Few towns and cities are without museums. It is not known for certain how many museums currently exist, although the Museums Association cites 2400 as a guide figure for the UK. The rate of growth in museum provision has been spectacular. Throughout the 1980s it was claimed that on average a new museum opened in Britain every fortnight. In 1984 the Museums and Galleries Commission estimated that museums were being opened at the rate of 30 a year. Much of this expansion relates to museums dealing with some aspect of recent human history.

Visitor figures can be equally spectacular. It is believed that at least 73 million visits are made to British museums each year, with the expectation that in Museums Year, 1989, this number will have risen to 100 million. In effect, more people visit museums than attend football matches. Popular interest in the recent past has never been greater, nor more democratically based than at present. History museums have been a key agency in promoting understanding of the past through the development of exhibitions and services of a quality not previously associated with museum provision. It is clearly evident that the better the standard of museum provision, the greater the public response.

Broadly categorized as a service industry, museums are classified as part of tourist and arts provision. In 1987 the Policy Studies Institute calculated that collectively the arts in Britain for the year 1985–6 had a turnover of £230 million. Once considered as small beer in terms of local government funding, museums are beginning to be thought of as viable propositions, especially within the contexts of urban regeneration and tourist development. But, like the arts, their potential appears to be considerably underestimated by government. The initiative has passed instead to those museum bodies able to develop successfully all opportunities for plural-funding and support. Such is the commercial potential of the popular interest in history that private trusts and heritage companies are also growing in number and scale. Eager to capture a market share, they have moved away from the idea of the museum as a public institution, charged with long-term research and communication functions and instead developed the high-cost, short-term commercial heritage exhibition, resplendent with replicas, noises and smells, which visitors 'experience' from mobile cars.

In the face of this mounting commercial competition, established museums are having to emphasize that their potential lies not only in their contribution to the local economy, which can be considerable. They are also having to make their case for survival and continued support on what they offer to the quality of life in Britain, in particular their social and cultural worth and the specific contribution they can make to education, especially life-long learning.

In such a competitive and increasingly crowded market-place, history museums are under constant scrutiny from many quarters, not least from an informed public, academics and journalists in the cultural studies field, and all bodies that contribute financially to their growth. The arguments for museums, the ideas that underpin them and the methods that create and sustain them have to be not only well understood but also well developed. Much depends upon the quality of curatorship, since it is curators, both through their actions and their attitudes, who shape arguments for museums. They have an influence on both the present and future of museums that should not be underestimated, least of all by themselves.

This book is written for graduates training for the museums profession, but it is hoped that history curators and people with an interest in museums will also find it helpful. It is the first attempt since 1963 and J. W. Y. Higg's booklet *Folk Life Collection and Classification* to present a theoretical and methodological framework for professional history curatorship. This in itself is indicative of the nature of museum development in Britain. It has not been supported either by a body of theoretical argument or, until 1980, a formal means of training curators in the ideas and skills relevant to history in museums. The growth has instead been sustained by a highly talented generation of curators who, in their various ways, have learnt through practice and through example.

It has not been the author's intention to present a manual of curatorship or to provide some kind of recipe book for museum practice. Instead the aim has been to explore the background to curatorship and the ideas which do, or could, inform museum work. In this a wide range of museum theory and practice is drawn upon. Some of the exhibitions and museum activities referred to may be discontinued or substantially altered by the time the book is in print: such is the rapid rate of change in the museum world. However, it should be understood that such examples have been selected for the ideas and methods they represent. Their relevance to museum practice as a whole is not diminished by their departure.

Although it is appreciated that many curators are eager to discuss the nature and direction of current professional practice and will use this book as one aspect of an ongoing debate, it is also recognized that some curators will reject much of what is contained here in preference for curatorial practice based on instinct and inclination. It is hoped that in their disassociation from these ideas, they may pause to consider what it is that informs the choices they make in their own work and in that way discover the theory which underpins it.

The central point of this book is that history museums are essential in modern life. But that this depends upon recognition and development of museum practice that is socially and intellectually relevant. In the very broad use of the word 'history' in this book, a perspective is adopted. It is this: the history museum exists to record and interpret ways of living and working through evidence derived from objects, oral testimony, music and sounds. The history museum can trace the configurations of cultural

Figure 1. People are the essential subject of any history museum.

Figure 2. Evidence of their lives is revealed in objects, images, memories and sounds.

definition and social change and reveal its understanding of these to a wide audience in ways that promote discussion and awareness. The central concern is not 'Great Men' or even 'Man', but people—men, women and children, in all their complexities of class, gender and cultural expression. It is their social experiences and ways of being and becoming to which museums should direct their attention.

Research for this book has been greatly assisted by grant aid from the Research Board of the University of Leicester, the British Council and the Swedish Institute, which has enabled me to visit museums in Britain and Sweden and talk to curators about their ideas and methods. I am pleased to acknowledge the generosity of the following museums in allowing publication of photographs: Sheffield City Museums; Stockholm City Museum; Bohusläns Museum, Uddevalla; Museum of the Moving Image, London; Plimoth Plantation, Massachusetts; Quarry Bank Mill Museum, Styal; Glasgow City Museums; Edinburgh City Museums; Nordiska Museet, Stockholm; and Västerbottens Museum, Umeå.

I am indebted to a large number of people who have supplied me with information, given me their time and their thoughts, and generally kept me going. They include: Dr Geraint Jenkins, Welsh Folk Museum; Dr Alan Gailey, Ulster Folk and Transport Museum; the Society for Folk Life Studies; Christine Stephens and Bill Jones, the National Museum of Wales; Peter Brears, Leeds City Museum; John Gall and Rosemary Allen, the North of England Open Air Museum, Beamish; Elspeth King and Michael O'Donell, People's Palace Museum, Glasgow; Mark O'Neill, Springburn Museum, Glasgow; David Anderson, the National Maritime Museum, London; Mary Gryspeerdt, the Somerset Rural Life Museum; Steph

Mastoris, Harborough Museum, Leicestershire; Timothy Ambrose, the Scottish Museums Council; Roy Brigden, the Museum of English Rural Life; Dr John Shaw, the National Museum of Scotland; Helen Clarke, the People's Story, Edinburgh; Katarina Ågren and Göran Carlsson, formerly at Västerbottens Museum, Umeå; Gunilla Cedrenius and Hans Medelius, Nordiska Museet, Stockholm; Per-Uno Ågren, the University of Umeå, and Britta Lundgren. I especially appreciate the assistance received from a large number of curators in Britain who took part in a questionnaire survey which provided guidance in the direction this book has taken.

Thanks go particularly to David Bostwick of Sheffield City Museums for reading the text and to all history option students past and present who collectively have enabled this work. As ever, I am indebted to the wisdom, sanity and friendship of my colleagues at the Department of Museum Studies, Dr Susan Pearce and Dr Eilean Hooper-Greenhill. And of course my special thanks to the Coles and Kavanagh families.

GAYNOR KAVANAGH
Leicester
November 1989

Part one. History museums:
past and present

1. History Museums

Definitions of the term 'history museum' are somewhat elusive; even more so coherent definitions of the nature and configuration of 'history' in museums. In a major survey of museums in Britain, published in 1987, David Prince and Bernadette Higgins-McLoughlin catergorized the types of material forming founding collections (1987: 49). They used 14 designations, twelve of which can be considered broadly historical: fine art, decorative art, science, industrial archaeology, technology and transport, maritime history, rural social history, urban social history, archaeology and ethnology, music, architecture, military and service. The shift in museum provision since the 1970s towards the foundation of museums based on social history, industrial archaeology and technology collections is noted, and is given some measure in the statistics that reveal that 817 of the 1750 museums surveyed held social history collections, 464 museums held industrial archaeology collections and 542 technology and transport.

The very fact that Prince and Higgins-McLoughlin had to use so many categories and that the museums surveyed separated social history collections from those of decorative art (middle and upper-middle class material culture which draws on working-class craft skills), industrial archaeology and technology (frequently evidence of work and relations of production) and transport (indicative of the changing nature of travel and communication) is significant. It demonstrates the division and variety of orientation within those museums that lay some claim to the past. Even if a common definition could be found, the different approaches to collections and the sheer variety of current museum provision represent forces that will not be bound by simple formulas.

Beyond their specialist collections, history museums are distinguished by their diversity of size, corporate organization and commitment. The comparison of a national museum (for example, the Imperial War Museum) with a local museum (such as that in Wells) or of an independent museum (such as the Ironbridge Gorge Museum) with a major city museum (such as the Museum of London) requires careful adjustment and many caveats. Yet they all exist within a broad philosophical framework through recognition that objects have value as evidence, that their retention and care are significant social and intellectual acts, and that their explanation through the medium of exhibition has genuine value.

In the absence of intellectual unity about the nature of history in the museum, or convenient definitions of the 'history museum', the concept of a museum devoted to the history of a person, place, process or people can be more fruitfully explored by tracing the main factors that create and shape it. These are the ideological circumstances in which it develops; current configurations of popular interest in history; and the character and direction of professional curatorship.

A product of social need

Historians have sought to examine the place of history within society and its uses (for example, Bloch 1954; Carr 1964; Elton 1968; Burke 1981; Tosh 1984). Most have argued that history is an essential point of reference within any society. Arthur Marwick observed 'quite simply human society needs history: the sophisticated societies of our own day need a lot of history' (1981: 14). To service such needs, societies gather together the dross and detritus of human activity and experience. These become primary tools in re-casting the events of the past into a pattern that makes some sense today. This pattern is crafted—sometimes carefully and critically, sometimes crudely—into forms conducive for contemporary need and understanding.

Therefore, in a bid for self-knowledge or justification, formal and informal histories are created. This process is not confined to national histories. Many sectors of society, as well as individuals, deeply need to find self-definition and explanation through the cognition of a past in which their part is duly recorded. As women, indigenous and migrant peoples have known, to be without history is to be outside the prescribed view of the world, to be deleted from the human picture, to be the ignored and forgotten. A recognized place in history is a means of finding self-esteem and social value.

Because societies need specific and apposite views of the past, and as there is no such thing as an organic memory, a pure knowledge that is innocently passed on, a group of functionaries or an apparatus has to be developed to serve. So there are remembrancers, priests and bards in some societies, as well as archivists, historians and museum curators in others. They exist to equip the need for memory, recall and recognition. Their methods involve the careful arrangement and interpretation of pieces of information and images left over from life in the past.

But because society needs histories, this does not necessarily mean, as Dellheim reminds us, that *any history* will do and that there can be an inviolable integrity in its production, even professionally (1982: 24–7). The themes and narratives of any society's history are the ones that are consistent with its current ways of believing in itself. Moreover, the loss of evidence and the inability to cope with discordant images of the past rob histories of proximity to past episodes. Inevitably, the past becomes a contemporary construction, built out of present-day interests with the materials that immediately come to hand. This holds risks. History can become many things: a political tool, an escape route from present realities or the key to liberation. At its most superficial, it is transformed into a 'gloss, as a light touch of a dab hand, an impression of pastness which is caught at a glance' (Wright 1985: 69).

It is in this immediate context of social need for the past that the history museum exists. It plays its part alongside a host of other agencies and social activities. The family, history books, television drama and documentaries, historic buildings and sites, and formal education collectively contribute to social awareness of the past. The contribution made by the history museum will vary. An idealist view is offered by the American historian Thomas Schlereth, who has drawn a parallel between the family photographs, attic trunks and objects that are kept and valued during individual and private lives with history books and history museums that reveal a similar, though more formal and public, attempt to collect, keep and interpret communal memory (1981:255).

Just as there are different social needs for history within any society, so there are different forms of history in museums and different roles for them to play. At one level they can provide emotional and social refuges where the past is rearranged to suit the needs of the moment. In this they become salves to the problems and pressures of modern living by suggesting that there were better and other times and places. Alternatively, they can be a candid witness of social change, expressing common humanity and errors. Either way, the histories in museums are neither innocent nor pure. They are created using current mind-maps and express dominant ideologies, in essence our beliefs about ourselves and the world. As a result, they reveal the traditions of history-telling that are prioritized in contemporary life.

The form of histories in museums particularly reveals their social and politicial constructions. For example in the USA, in the state of Virginia, a substantial number of the buildings in Colonial Williamsburg were restored in the mid–1930s to create an image of a clean and tasteful eighteenth-century town, with an investment of around $79 million from John D. Rockerfeller Junior. The town was then made available to the public as a commemoration of the planter elite and the cradle of Americanism, of which men like Rockerfeller were seen as the inheritors. At the time, in its celebration of genteel Virginian life, there was no reference to the fact that over half of the eighteenth-century population would have been black slaves. It took the political and emotional force of the civil rights movement to create change: in the 1970s slavery was discovered at Williamsburg (Wallace 1981).

There are similar instances of exclusion in British museums. The omission of organized labour from a significant proportion of history museums has created a demand in some quarters for the establishment of separate and specialist labour history museums to rectify some of the balance (Knowles 1987). The social experience of work and changing patterns of skill has yet to be dealt with by museums of technology and industry. The exclusion of women (Porter 1987), post-war immigration and the cultural development of local ethnic communities from many of the histories offered by museums has yet to be set right.

In some situations the political context may have a more direct, significantly less subtle and perhaps more urgent, bearing on museums. In the emergent nations, particularly in Africa, the history museum has become one of the means of demonstrating and confirming liberation from colonial experience, and an instrument in the consolidation of national consciousness. The new African histories stress the historical evidence of African creativity and the richness of African culture (Tosh 1984:4). Museums have been founded to stress these points. In so doing the call has gone out for the return of African cultural property from the colonial and imperial nations where they have been employed to illustrate the otherness of the African cultures. As George Thompson, former Curator of the Ulster Folk and Transport Museum, has pointed out, the anthropological curio of the imperialist is now being recognized as the folk artefact of the new nationalist (Thompson 1985).

At a different level, economic and political changes have altered the idea of museums in Britian. During the past half century far-reaching changes have occurred in the industrial structure and in the geography of manufacturing industry. The view is now offered that Britain, having been the first nation to industrialize, now appears to be the first major economy to *de-industrialize* (Dickens 1982:171). Service industries have been seen as the motive force for post-industrial growth (Dawson 1982:203). Museums are part of this, and in the last 20 years have been conspicuously occupying the sites of Britain's late nineteenth-century industrial base.

Many museums have prospered by being part of initiatives aimed at promoting tourism, especially in areas where traditional industries have been in rapid decline. But the fudging of boundaries between museums as part of social provision, that is as a focus of local interest, recovery or self-discovery, and the museum as tourist provision, from which a regeneration of the local economy is primarily sought, has brought a cynical edge to museum development. This twist is noted by the Curator of the Welsh Folk Museum, Geraint Jenkins, who has observed 'there is a grave danger in saying "we have a site and since we are in the middle of a tourist area, let us interpret it", rather than saying "we have a theme that is of vital importance in the story of our people, let us find the best possible site where this can be done"' (Jenkins 1987:9).

This has been well illustrated in the mining valleys of Wales, in particular in the proposals for a mining museum on the site of the Ty Mawr-Lewis Merthyr Colliery. In 1983 the closure of the colliery was the subject of a bitter dispute involving a sit-down strike and a national ballot of all NUM members for an all-out strike to support their cause. The national ballot failed, although it was followed not long after by the longest and most bitter miners' strike ever, over just the situation that prevailed at Lewis Merthyr: the closing of collieries and the destruction of the communities that supported them. Eventually the colliery did close and in the spring of 1984 proposals were made public for a 'museum village'.

The *South Wales Echo* (12 March 1984) described how the aim of the museum 'would be to create "a mining community" complete with replica buildings and costumed demonstrators showing as many aspects of Valleys life as possible'. It aimed to cover the transition of the valley's 'rural communities' in the nineteenth century to the boom mining town of the 1920s. The emphasis would be on people and activities, with visitors being encouraged to join in the life of the times. The central irony that a community denied its continued existence was to be replaced by one artifically created appears not to have gone unnoticed by local people.

Clearly, the social need to remember, and, by implication, to forget, determines much of our public histories. This is evident in history museums where discussion of past experiences and activities is found neutered of references to social and political challenges to established order, forms of class distinction and conflict, and alternative ways of being and believing. History in museums can frequently be observed avoiding evidence of rupture and rapid social change preferring a more palatable version of past life in Britain. But where this is so, forces far greater than professional curatorship are in play. Instead, what is evident is the social need for historical myth being served.

Popular interest

Popular enthusiasm for history has grown significantly since the 1960s and has taken many forms. In 1979 Lord Blake suggested that the growth of interest in local history was due to social and psychological needs arising from attacks on traditional landscape by such developments as intensive farming, motorway construction and the building of urban tower blocks. In contrast, social history has been described as being derived from the cultural revolutions of the 1960s, when efforts to 'modernise' history took place against a background of rapid social change.

The essential characteristic of modern social history is its accessibility. It focuses on issues that are still current and has the capacity to 'mobilise enthusiasms and popular passions'. Raphael Samuel considers its practitioners to be counted in thousands rather than in hundreds. Included in these are 'those who fill the search rooms of the Record Offices, and the local history rooms of public libraries, documenting family "roots"; the volunteer guides at the open-air museums; or the thousands of railway fanatics who spend their summer holidays acting as guards or station staff on the narrow gauge lines of the Pennines and North Wales'. If to the list of practitioners we add all those who read, write, think and talk about the past, whether as part of a voluntary project, school exercise, family conversation or museum visit, the number would be not thousands but millions. The historiographic process is now one that many encounter firsthand: history no longer belongs to the academic historians. Samuel considers that 'social history does not only reflect public interest, it also prefigures and perhaps helps to create it' (1988). Thus, the study of social history has established its own momentum.

Popular interest in the past is stimulated and developed by a variety of media, principally television, but also films, radio and publications. This may, in part, account for its configuration and some of the areas of interest. The commemoration of events and anniversaries also has a particularly powerful effect, the result of which is relatively short-term, although often intense, concern with specific periods or phenomenon from the past, with some long-term implications. For example, the bicentennial celebrations in the USA, in 1976, precipitated a massive industry devoted to the rediscovery of a positive, pioneering and successful American past: a significant number of new local museums resulted (Schlereth 1980: 130–42). Similarly, the bicentennial celebrations in Australia, in 1988, provided an opportunity for museum enterprises addressing early settlement and local history to prove their worth.

Likewise, in Britain the fortieth anniversary of the end of the Second World War gave the opportunity for public exploration of war memories, selected experiences of which are enshrined in a series of specialist museums from the Imperial War Museum to the D-Day Museum, Portsmouth. These museums and the commemorative exhibitions they provided became set-pieces in the memorializing of the war's events. Similarly, the four hundredth anniversary of the defeat of the Spanish Armada was celebrated in 1988, but in this instance with a degree of re-interpretation, principally at the National Maritime Museum, that quite ruffled popular and nationalist preconceptions of the defeat of the Armada as a glorious English victory.

However significant such celebrations may be, varying periods of grace need elapse before they become proper and popular forms for the recognition of past events. What becomes central to such occasions is the spirit in which the event is perceived to have occurred and the part its remembrance now plays. The anniversaries of the end of the Vietnam War and the Falklands conflict will take more decades before they can be commemorated with any form of emotional detachment or popular acclaim, in museums or out of them.

Other forms of popular interest may be stimulated by television drama. The family dramas that spread more than one generation, such as *Roots* and *The Forsyte Saga* and of late *A Woman of Substance*, or set-piece dramas dealing with specific periods and places, such as mid-Wales in the 1930s in *The District Nurse* or the industrial North-east in the 1920s in *When the Boat Comes In*, place before large audiences very visual, personable references to human change and experience. These are explored through characters and situations vividly presented for the viewer to em-pathize within the intimacy and comfort of the living-room. The nuclear group extends itself into a television-provided family with many members. Thus the history of the dramatic character is joined to that of a nationwide audience, which connects through varying degrees of personal or cultural identification.

The relationship of commemoration and historical drama to museums is both direct and indirect. Museums often adopt similar themes for exhibitions and publicity, using current media images as points of reference. For the viewer, commemorations and historical dramas stir consciousness and create opportunities for conversation about the past. They create, in turn, a relatively informed and often receptive museum audience. The museum can service and expand its awareness by supplying alternative views, local memories and material evidence; elements which television can only provide in generality and in two dimensions. In effect, museums can enhance historical knowledge stimulated by external other media, and also have the opportunity to challenge received truths, by dealing in solid evidence of an experienced, and not just make-believe past.

A special kind of industry has grown up dependent on the ability to touch popular sentiment and the very human proclivity for nostalgia. Called the 'heritage industry', this now offers opportunities and initiatives that need only be loosely connected to the past to qualify. The definition of heritage is somewhat difficult to pin down, and in a perverse way this is what has given it such a pliable usage. The term became particularly common after the passing of the National Heritage Act in 1980, although it had some currency before this time. 'Heritage' soon came to be used for anything that has connection to the past which is commercially viable. The niceties of the difference between heritage and inheritance have largely been avoided. As one museum observer remarked: 'The right have heritage, the rest of us—history.' Inheritances are not always about good and acceptable things, neither is history: but heritage certainly is.

The high public profile of enterprises within the 'heritage industry' has now reached the point where it is open to criticism (Wright 1985; Hewison 1987). Much of this has been thoughtful and timely. However, the dominant images of 'the heritage industry' mask a separate and growing movement that may be found to employ the term heritage but thinks of it and needs it in a very different way. This movement encompasses all efforts currently being made to record and value individual and community memory. The boundaries of its activities have been determined by the needs and opportunities that prevail.

A significant number of museums foster and promote such activity, and by so doing explore and extend the museum's social role. Beyond this there is a host of small, voluntary projects, set up predominantly by, or within, self-defined communities in varying stages of change, growth or stagnation. Local history libraries have often played their part here, as have community centres and caring organizations such as Age Concern. Many of these initiatives have used photography and oral history to reclaim and explore identity, shared values and a communally experienced past. As a result, alongside museums and local libraries, reminiscence centres, oral history groups and local history projects have flourished. Most have aimed at recovering a past that other forms of history production and representation, including many public museums, have ignored. This has then been communicated to wide, and sometimes new, audiences through exhibitions, publications and audio-visual work.

It is as if the concept of the museum (and the ideas of the past within it) is a wide-swinging pendulum. If it sweeps in one direction, it plays to tourism and leisure provision, and presents a past which is marketable and carefully sanitized of jarring or unproven images and themes. If the pendulum swings in the other direction, it locates itself within social provision and seeks to find and present the past through direct human experiences.

In the absence of a coherent and guaranteed view of the museum, a tentative conclusion may be drawn. History museums operate in the context of the social need for history, which is formed by the dominant political views and textured by current historical interests. Each of these important forces adds to the idea of the history museum. There are two other factors which must be considered: current convictions about what a 'museum' actually is; and the nature and substance of curatorship.

The curatorship factor

In 1984 the Museums Association agreed that the museum should be defined as 'an institution which collects, preserves, exhibits and interprets material evidence and associated information for the benefit of the public'. This is the most recent of a series of attempts over the last century to say what a museum is, and by implication, what it is not. A definition of a history museum needs further qualification. It is not only a keeping place for *material* evidence, but also for *non-material* evidence, including records of oral testimony, dialect, song and stories. The museum's clear and specific role is to record and explain the cultural whole through the interplay of this material. This wide cultural interest, coupled with the commitment to retain such information as archives of value, not just for today but for future generations, differentiates the museum from other institutions.

The central position of objects and archives and long-term commitments to the public, in whose name the museum operates, are the principal characteristics of the museum. Beyond this the history museum has become anything that the public and the curator's imagination can make it, given the media at its disposal. The museum seen as a dimly lit building in which warders sleep over their charge of object-filled glass cases, although deeply embedded in some aspects of curatorial attitude and popular definition of the museum, is now neither fair nor accurate. The form a museum takes may not necessarily be determined by whether it is constitutionally independent, municipal or national. More relevant will be the museum's perceptions of its audience and the compass of its curatorial interests.

History museums need not be housed in the traditional museum building, coolly colonnaded and quietly intimidating. Substantial progress has been made in the forms museums can take. The open-air museum, with its reconstructions, recreated environments or resited buildings; the site museum, exploiting a historic environment or situation; the specialist museum, with its in-depth studies; the community museum, with its network of contracts and participants; and the eco-museum, with its presence through, as well as in, a place—have each opened up new possibilities for the exploration of the recent past.

Indeed, the hybridization does not stop with these forms but gives way to specific spheres of professional interest, each dominated by some spirit of established practice. Thus, curators can specialize in technology, costume, rural life or numismatics, rather than in broader, more-integrated approaches. In essence, the museum form has given rise to various means of codifying the past, of organizing the physical evidence of human existence and experience into set, tried and tested forms. The classification systems used to order collection records have come, in turn, to tidy the past into categories suitable for these hybrid types of museums and curatorship. These buttress specialist views and can deny social contradiction and change, dismissing them as inconveniences to the curatorial art.

In Britain there are many hundreds of curators working in what might be termed history museums. However, whether there is a collective notion and common approach that might be defined as 'history curatorship' is open to question. The comparison with practice in Scandinavia, especially Sweden, is interesting. In Sweden most curators working in cultural history museums have studied ethnology (cultural history), often to higher degree level. Although there may be areas of dispute, the study of cultural history through the agency of Swedish museums has an essential degree of theoretical and practical unity. The confidence that this gives has facilitated important and wide-ranging discussions about curatorial theory and method that are significantly ahead of other countries.

In Britain curators working in the history field need not necessarily have a history or social science background, do not receive any required training in the theories or methodologies of history curatorship practice (unless they take the University Diploma or Masters Degree in Museum Studies at the University of Leicester) and have a very limited museum literature on which to draw. This is a mixed blessing: on the one hand, curatorship does not lie in the hands of a privileged, specialized elite. Non-professionals and non-historians have often brought fresh and interesting views of history to the museum. On the other hand, there is no strong central core of theory and there has been little, if any, rigorous consideration of history practice, let alone challenge to it. As a result, it might be said that this area of museum practice is more self-conscious than self-confident. Indeed, as museums become more closely identified as part of the 'heritage industry' rather than a direct part of social or community provision, aptitudes and skills other than those within the appropriate disciplines are looked for, specifically in the fields of commerce and management.

The strength of history curatorial practice is that there are, and have been, curators with clear ideas about people, objects and the potential of history in the museum who, through their museum work and publications, have broken new bounds and stimulated much interest. In a sense, their work has helped to indicate and reveal the potential of the museum and the nature of historical studies that can take place within it. Even though curatorial practice is much more than a set of individual initiatives, a number of curators stand out and have to take credit for the intellectual and professional contributions they have brought to the idea and purpose of the history museum. Their work will be a recurrent touchstone of this text.

In sum then, the history museum is more or less defined in the set of circumstances and ideas that create and foster it. It does not exist in glorious innocence, defended by the sanctity of professional practice. Instead, the museum is used to service society's need for history. In this it is moulded by dominant political views; textured by popular interest and attitudes to the past; re-cast according to current ideas and opportunities of what a history museum should be, whether within leisure or social provision; and then finely tuned and patterned by the diverse and, at times, discordant practice of curatorship.

2. *History and the Public Museum: 1850-1930*

In recent years the history of museums has been attracting an increasing amount of scholarly attention (Wallace 1981; Van Keuren 1984; Skinner 1986; Hopkin 1987; Marsh 1987). These and awaited studies are laying the foundations for a more critical understanding of museums, not as institutions that are created in a moment of intellectual purity and professional worthiness but as forms of remembrance shaped, enabled or stunted by a range of intellectual and social forces. Curatorship in this new reading is not the instigator as much as an instrument of dominant trends.

Several texts on the history of history museums exist. Perhaps the best summary to date is provided by J. W. Y. Higgs (1963). But recent works by Marsh and Wallace, on the history of history museums in England and the USA respectively, have shown that new ground can be broken by bringing new questions and more thorough research techniques to bear. In different ways they have opened up the history museum to detailed scrutiny, and attempt to see it in its social and political contexts. Further, Dieter Hopkin's important study of railway museums has indicated how the histories of museums are curiously intertwined, yet in many key respects are separate and subject to individual circumstances. Thus there is not one story, one history of history museums, but many. Therefore, alongside Hopkin's work, we need similarly detailed, analytical studies of museums devoted to science, technology, education, costume, city history, rural life and regiments if we are to grasp the range and import of museum provision, past and present.

Clearly, the history of the social history museum cannot be served by a gentle genealogy. There has been no smooth incremental passage from crude beginnings to a modern form. Instead, the history museum's own history is dominated by ideas about the past and its value to the present which change through pressures outside the direct influence of curatorship. This brief survey aims to highlight some of the principal moments in the history of those museums that exist to provide a record of recent popular experience.

Public museums 1850-1920

The public museum in Britain is essentially a creation of the second half of the nineteenth century. The earlier precedents, particularly the Ashmolean

Museum in Oxford 1683) and the British Museum (1759), were a world away from the Victorian museums in both their intent and purpose. Born of a new civic and national consciousness, and funded by the heaviest of the fruits from Britain's industrial growth, the nineteenth-century museum became a credential of urban sophistication, the cultural goal of a rapidly expanding industrial nation.

The Victorian idea of history was reflected in the National Portrait Gallery, which opened in London in 1856. This aimed to assemble a national history of Britain through portraiture. A portrait was to be included in the collections if its sitter was a person distinguished by intellectual or political achievement, active or heroic actions, or moral deeds either in the fields of religion or philanthropy. Most of the portraits selected were of men and were exhibited with the expressed motive that gallery visitors might be led to a higher social order through contemplating, and even imitating, these historic figures (Hooper-Greenhill 1980: 39).

In the provinces the trappings of the new museums, from Leicester to Liverpool, were formed more in response to the great museums in London and the ideas they represented than to local needs. Colonnaded exteriors, natural science and archaeology collections with imperial rather than regional boundaries, art collections selected for scale and grandeur, and an odd corner filled with 'curiosities' and even freaks of nature such as two-headed calves, became well-established ingredients of a provincial museum. The foundation of the civic museum on the amassed collections and good intentions of philosophical and literary societies gave them a flying start. Packaged and presented as being vital to the self-improvement of the rising artisan and middle classes, they met an enthusiastic, popular reaction. For example, in 1851, its first year and open only for four days a week, Liverpool Museum attracted almost a quarter of a million visitors.

In themselves, the Victorian museums were arguably reflex reactions in an age when middle- and upper-class opinion sought to dissociate itself from innovation and expansion, preferring the ancient and peculiarly stable (Weiner 1981: 42-6). Practically, they were one of the initiatives taken by the emerging urban authorities to distance themselves from the chaotic conditions that prevailed in their growing towns and cities in the first half of the nineteenth century. Museums were founded alongside concert halls, public parks, libraries and, the most potent indicator of urban self-consciousness, the municipal building or town hall.

In their focus on the classic disciplines, many museums in Victorian Britain became part of a host of mechanisms that demonstrated the tension between the relative dynamism of an industrial, urban and palpably unequal state, and a forceful social elitism that favoured a rising myth of a distinguished rural (that is non-industrial) past. This myth was imaginatively extended by notions of an established order selected from the histories of ancient civilizations, and further buttressed by righteous convictions in the ennobling process of imperialism.

Thus, the new museums rarely reflected the worlds of commerce and industry that had created and funded them. Admittedly, a small number of museums drew together minor collections of objects from local manufacturing industries. But these were often inconsistent. The lives and experiences of ordinary people in a rapidly changing industrial age were far removed from the ideas that informed their collection (Brown Goode 1895; Baldwin-Brown 1901; Kusamitsu 1980).

One of the exceptions to this pattern was the museum at Farnham, Dorset, established in 1880 by Augustus Pitt-Rivers. With collections of local material organised along typological lines, and with bands and pleasure gardens for popular amusement, the museum was seen by Pitt-Rivers as a means of edifying and instructing the masses:

> If no more good come of it than to create other interests, which would draw men's minds away from politics, that greatest of all curses in a country district, good would be done. [Van Keuren 1984: 185]

The significance of the museum at Farnham lies in Pitt-River's conviction that a properly organized museum could teach history and, if successful, would have measurable political and social consequences. The popular approach adopted, appealing to the sense of enjoyment, was possibly influenced by the obvious success of the Earls Court exhibitions, presented on a hugh scale and with great flamboyance by Imre Kiralfi (1845-1919) (Marsh 1987: 31-3, i-xviii; Greenhalgh 1988) and an awareness of, and regard for, the work of Arthur Hazelius in Sweden.

But in the general intellectual confusion and contradiction that arose from a newly self-defined curatorial profession composed of an incongruous group of academics, pseudo-academics, committed museum enthusiasts and elevated town hall clerks, the development of museums into a form that had coherence and social relevance had become a problem by the last two decades of the nineteenth century. As a result, by the early years of the twentieth century museums were in a state of stagnation. This is to a degree surprising because the Victorian museums existed in a period when there was a wealth of potential influences which could have strengthened museums and curatorial practice in such a critical moment of their development.

Throughout the second half of the nineteenth century, there was growing social and commercial interest in recent British objects, both as curiosities and as antiquities. In 1840-41 Charles Dickens wrote *The Old Curiosity Shop*, describing the shop as 'one of those receptacles for old and curious things which seem to crouch in odd corners of this town and hide their musty treasures from the public eye in jealousy and distrust'. By the end of the nineteenth century, antique shops were well established, but even so museums were only beginning to take interest in the objects Dickens had described: 'suits of mail standing like ghosts in armour... fantastic carvings brought from monkish cloisters, rusty weapons of various kinds, distorted figures in china and wood and ivory: tapestry and strange furniture that might have been described in dreams'.

A strengthening folk life studies movement existed outside museums. It was evident on the fringes of scholarly middle-class activity, in remote corners of 'antiquarianism' and even remoter corners of evolutionary or colonial anthropology. A minor industry developed in which notably vicars and retired country gentlemen published their research findings in parish histories, county glossaries and *Notes and Queries*. Interest in orally transmitted tradition was such that the English Dialect Society was founded in 1873. *Folk Lore Record* was first published in 1878. Individual initiatives also came to the fore, one of the most important being J. R. Green's *Short History of the English People* (1877).

Museums might also have taken impetus from the massively successful trade fairs and grand exhibitions that so graphically demonstrated means which could be adopted to enliven museum displays and develop collections (Greenhalgh 1988). But largely they did not, a fact that met with disappointment amongst more foresighted curators in the years immediately before the First World War, when they saw the need to articulate radical and socially relevant arguments for the continued presence of museums.

The reasons why history in museums failed to prosper in these obviously propitious times are open to question. It may have been something to do with the calibre of person attracted to museum work, the pressure from the municipal authorities for classical disciplines rather than local human interest and the relative buoyancy of imperialism, which kept attention away from local studies. It may also have been due to the lack of a charismatic figure who could provide both inspiration and example. In Sweden such a figure emerged: Artur Hazelius (1833–1901). If there has to be a beginning for history museums and curatorship, then it is to his work that we must turn.

Hazelius, Nordiska Museet and Sweden

Sweden experienced rapid economic growth in the second half of the nineteenth century. In the 1860s demand for its grain, timber and iron grew, and led in turn to industrialization and much social change. Such swift changes and the wealth generated by them affected much which had remained unaltered for generations. Artur Hazelius was a witness to these changes (Alexander 1983). Son of a Swedish army officer, Hazelius was a romantic and a committed patriot, who, in his student days, had identified himself with the Pan-Scandinavian movement.

His interest in folk ways was prompted by a visit to Dalarna province in 1872, when he was moved by the changes he saw around him. Alexander describes Hazelius as being

> distressed to find the pleasant, coherent, and highly individualized way of living he had known as a schoolboy and had observed in Dalarna on trips, before his marriage, was beginning to disappear. The industrial revolution, he feared, was bringing about a stifling and tasteless uniformity and threatening the natural beauty of the environment and the cultural variety of Swedish life. The booming grain market was making farmers prosperous, tempting them to buy luxury goods, and changing traditional ways of dress, food and even religion [Alexander 1983: 243]

Hazelius's view was inevitably influenced by his own romanticism about the old ways and his patriotic fervour. It led him to the decision to form a record of the Sweden he thought was disappearing through the collection of objects and information. He was also prepared to collect like material from Norway, Denmark and Finland.

He began collecting material in 1872-3, taking meticulous care to keep full records of what he acquired, which was not just material culture—old clothes, furniture, furnishings, tools and paintings—but also notes on music, dance, stories and sayings. His collections were first opened to public view in 1873: he called them the Museum of Scandinavian Ethnology. His methods of displaying material in small 'scenes' were striking: the closest museum development to this approach was the display of habitat groups in natural history displays.

Hazelius built 'living pictures', or tableaux, using wax figures, such as the 'Lapp encampment' he exhibited, along with other scenes, at the Universal Exhibition in Paris in 1878. Perhaps the most famous and earliest of his 'pictures' was that based on the painting *The Little Girl's Death Bed* by Amelia Linegren. The parallel between the display of natural history 'specimens' in diorama and Hazelius's 'folk specimens' in diorama was easily drawn. He was, however, using a method that was more popularly known, that of the travelling waxworks shows. This was a medium through which he could engage Swedish popular interest and curiosity. At a point of considerable social and political change, Hazelius alerted Swedish national consciousness to some of the effects of industrialization.

The work of recording and collecting continued to the point where Hazelius's personal resources were nearly exhausted and the buildings he had available at bursting point. In 1875 the Swedish government agreed to grand aid the museum, and in the late 1870s the King gave a piece of land on which a permanent museum building could be erected. Plans were drawn up for the museum, which was to be called Nordiska Museet. It was to have the motto 'Know thyself', and in its form and architecture was to embody and symbolize Hazelius's view of the value and purpose of the study of the Swedish past. Thus, it was to be fostered as a means of stimulating self-awareness, imagination, Swedish style and nationalism. The museum building, completed in 1907, six years after Hazelius's death, has a central hall with proportions and atmosphere not unlike a cathedral. Twenty-eight side display areas framed by arches were incorporated for more 'living pictures'. Rooms on the first and second floor were provided for reconstructed interiors.

Nordiska Museet was intended to be a powerhouse of research and scholarship, a place where material could be properly processed and understood. Hazelius ensured there was an excellent library, a commitment to publication (the first yearbook came out in 1881), and a staff of skilled and accomplished scholars. The museum was to allow the exploration not only of regional and cultural diversity within Sweden but also an examination of social contrast. There was no division of material indicative of richer life-styles into 'fine and decorative art': all material was to be evidence of ways of life in Sweden.

But Hazelius's vision went beyond this. In 1891, on a hill called Skansen overlooking Stockholm and close to where Nordiska Museet was being built, Hazelius opened the first 'open-air museum'. With selected buildings from all over Sweden erected on the site, appropriately furnished and sited with gardens, enclosures and out-buildings, Hazelius intended to show in Stockholm, Sweden in miniature. Skansen was developed to be the focus of national identity and inspiration. Costumed guides, music, dance, demonstrations of craft techniques, anniversaries, concerts, restaurants and festivities were planned to bring Skansen to life. Popular education particularly relying on sensory perception—sight, sound, smell, touch— was developed to help visitors 'glimpse the past' and to be pleasantly entertained while so doing. Serious concepts of popular education and patriotism underlay the activities at Skansen and were planned to be received through recreation.

Hazelius died before the museums were fully developed. Subsequent generations of curators have fulfilled and extended his original ideas. The influence of Hazelius, not only in terms of the museums in Sweden but also worldwide has been considerable. First, his insistence on detail and high standards in recording and collecting ensured that there was a firm and coherent base from which curatorial practice could develop intellectually,

Figure 3.   Construction of Nordiska Museet in Stockholm began in 1888 and was completed in 1907. The central, cathedral-like hall was intended by Hazelius to house great festivals. It is now used for temporary exhibitions, such as *Modell Sverige*.

and could provide a museum service that had strength, depth and interest. His purpose throughout and the path he set for the museums was the recording and comprehension of cultural definition and contrast: this could be achieved only through comprehensive fieldwork and directed acquisition. Largely as a result of his work, ethnology, or folk life, as an academic discipline emerged in Sweden. The impetus Hazelius gave was such that in 1918 an Institute of Ethnology was established in Stockholm, with joint staff positions with the university and Nordiska Museet. The institute still enjoys a close relationship with the museum and it provides useful intellectual impetus for ethnology in Sweden.

Secondly, the creation of both the Nordiska Museet and Skansen, the one a centre for research, the other a popular 'show', demonstrated that the history and cultural experiences of people could be made accessible to all and not just to the scholar and enthusiast. His work demonstrated that a firm intellectual and methodological foundation was essential, and that it was possible to convey information in ways that were educational and moving. Moreover, the work of the museum was not simply to put on exhibitions but to create a social and cultural record for the long term.

Thirdly, Skansen became a blueprint for subsequent 'open-air' museums and 'reconstruction' forms of exhibition in other parts of the world, just as the 'living pictures' and period rooms were adopted elsewhere, too. Few folk museums or open-air museums have developed this century in Europe and the USA without some reference to Skansen. The work in Sweden prompted other countries to establish folk museums or open-air museums. Most notably in the pre-war years, the Danish Folk Museum came into being in 1881, the Norsk Folkemuseum in 1887, the Sandvigske Samlinger in Lillehammer in 1887, and Den Gamble By in Denmark in 1909.

In contrast, and in spite of conditions that might have suggested that it would be possible for a centre for the study of British ethnology or a national folk museum to be established in England, no such institution developed. Imaginative but unsuccessful proposals were made for an Imperial Bureau of Ethnology to be established at the British Museum. Similarly, an active campaign led by F. A. Bather of the Natural History Museum and Henry Balfour of the Pitt-Rivers Museum found little support and was lost in the years of the First World War (Marsh 1987: 30–48).

The First World War

During the war many museums, including the nationals, were closed, ostensibly as an economy measure. In those that remained open, curators had the challenge of producing exhibitions and providing services relevant to the home front and the war effort. Some of these challenges were met with flair; many more were lost. The circumstances of the war itself led to the establishment of a National War Museum in March 1917 (called the Imperial War Museum from 1918). Born out of a propaganda initiative, but led by a group of people anxious for the museum to hold a full record of the experience of the war, it developed a radically different approach to collecting and recording (Condell 1985; Kavanagh 1985,1988).

The museum's committee divided the responsibility for collecting between subcommittees, each consisting of specialists who were both well informed in their fields of interest and well placed to gather material. There was a precedent for this approach in a short-lived initiative taken by the Science Museum in 1912, to keep itself in touch with changes in industry and science. The Imperial War Museum's subcommittees, including those for the Admiralty, the Red Cross, Women's Work, Records and Literature, Air Services and Munitions, brought together a quality and range of material that is now fundamental to our understanding of the war. The process of delegated, contemporary collecting was quite extraordinary and in its scale and scope is unrivalled in museum projects before or since.

The closest parallel to it is the work of Swedish curators and their co-operative efforts since the late 1970s to create a record of contemporary Swedish life through the organization SAMDOK (Rosander 1980). But in the post-war years in Britain all interest was lost and the notion that museums could be archives of contemporary or recent experience was abandoned or passed over. The methods of contemporary recording and collecting employed at the Imperial War Museum found no sympathetic adherents in the ranks of curators or politicians.

At the end of the war provincial museum collections relating to local or regional human history were clearly little more than jumbles of oddments, frequently called 'bygones'. In 1916 the British Association, in a survey of 134 museums, revealed that 60 laid claim to having sections dealing with archaeology and antiquities, 22 industrial art and 20 history. The research showed that these subject definitions were very confused and at one point stated that 'far too much prominence is given to specimens that are the easiest to acquire, and that museums depend too largely on the force of circumstances' (3067: Haddon papers: University of Cambridge). Material was being collected not as part of any great plan but because it 'drifts into the museum'. There was relatively little on which to build public confidence in the museum as a positive social, educational or intellectual institution.

The situation had hardly changed by 1928 when Sir Henry Miers published his report on provincial museums in Britain for the Carnegie United Kingdom Trustees. The *Miers Report* was an indictment of poor standards of curatorship and the lack of initiative in museum development. Miers drew a sketch of one museum 'by no means the worst', in which a small case held a saxon brooch, a few feathers, several geological specimens and a couple of fossils nestling side by side. By the fireplace were two beautifully carved wooden stairheads; on the top of one 'reposed' a Russian helmet and on the other a Roundhead casque. There were only a few labels, some illegible. He observed: 'it may be questionable whether such a museum, and there are many similar, serves any useful purpose whatever, and whether it should continue to exist' (Miers 1928: 39–40).

Miers fostered interests in local history and folk life. He regretted the lack of any folk museum in Britain, calling it 'a serious reproach'. He was also concerned that museums had largely failed to develop coherently the local material available:

> There is a great difference between the acquisition of material for a definite purpose, and the acceptance or purchase of miscellaneous objects. For example, there is every reason why a local museum should possess a large collection of objects of local interest, provided that the exhibited portion is carefully selected and devoted to the elucidation of the history and resources of the locality, or of its industry as has been successfully done at Huddersfield, Warrington, Ipswich and elsewhere. [Miers 1928: 43]

Miers's essential argument for museums was that they could be one of the best recognized forms of public service, which should attract the enthusiastic support of the whole community. In this, he held that museums were failing very badly indeed through lack of purpose, resources, and skilled and enthusiastic staff. To this analysis has to be added an observation made in a Board of Education pamphlet on *Museums and the Schools* (1931), that the museums in Britain were carrying the legacies of muddled ideas about museums and about museum collections left over from the nineteenth century. The conclusion to be drawn from both reports is that extreme and radical revision was needed if museums were to find a role and purpose in recording and representing with any dignity or relevance the lives of ordinary people.

3. Folk Life Museums: The Inter-War Years

Between the wars there was an appreciable expansion in the number of museums devoted to folk life, especially in the 1930s, when a new generation of curators was at last able to influence change. This took place in a social climate that attempted to put behind it, or at least out of its mind, the war, the depression, social division, industrial strife and the frightening changes taking place in Nazi Germany. The circumstances were conducive for the establishment of museums that recorded and celebrated ways of living in what were thought to be less threatening and more secure times, before the advent of the Industrial Revolution.

The time was ripe for folk museums, but not sufficiently so that government would sponsor them. Proposals made to the Ministry of Works by a special working party looking at a possible National Folk Museum for England failed to capture the political imagination (Wheeler 1934). Instead, individual initiatives developed: Iorwerth Peate at the National Museum of Wales (Stevens 1986); William Cubbon and the founding of Cregneash and the Folk Life Survey on the Isle of Man (Harrison 1986); and the gathering of collections for a Highland Folk Museum by Dr I. Grant (Cheape 1986; Noble 1977). Their collective work did much to lay the foundations of folk life studies and professional curatorship.

Iorwerth Peate and the Welsh Folk Museum

Iorwerth Peate (1901–82) was one of the founding figures of the folk life movement in Britain. He trained as a geographer at University College, Aberystwyth, where he was greatly influenced by his tutor Dr H. J. Fleure. As a consequence, Peate developed broad interests in historical geography, archaeology, anthropology, dialect studies, history and literature. But these were not his sole influences. He drew greatly on his home background, which was rural, independent, pacifist, craft-centred and traditional.

His biographer, Catrin Stevens, describes his romantic preference for 'the glorious ability of ordinary men to create every day, ordinary objects . . . wedding beauty of form and excellence of shape with practical usefulness, of making necessary everyday objects both handsome and functional' (Stevens 1986: 18). Peate was conscious of the criticism this approach attracted, conceding that 'it would be totally unprofitable to paint every aspect of the old way of life in beautiful hues'. However, his work contained little to indicate poverty amongst the craftsmen or examples of poor workmanship which, as Stevens has pointed out, must undoubtedly have existed.

He joined the National Museum of Wales in 1927 to work in the Department of Archaeology, which had a collection of 'bygones'. Peate worked carefully and enthusiastically on this collection, examining, measuring, dating and locating each object. He wrote labels in both Welsh and English and, in 1929, produced a bilingual *Guide to the Collection of Welsh Bygones*. This publication was a landmark both for the collections in Wales and for folk life studies in Britain.

The first part of the *Guide* was a descriptive account of 'old-fashioned life in Wales', through which Peate was able to outline a historic and cultural context in which the collection could be understood. By moving away from the objects, looking at their origins and considering their relevance, Peate was effectively drafting an agenda for folk life study in Wales, drawing attention not just to material culture but, also to oral traditions, customs and folk lore. The second part of the *Guide* was a detailed catalogue of the 1294 objects on exhibition. Although museum catalogues, as lists of objects, were by no means new, Peate's approach was different. The material in Peate's care was to him manifestly far more than an appendage to archaeology, or groups of objects that could be found to be relevant only if studied in type or evolutionary sequence. He lifted 'bygones' out of a rut of casual interest and proposed that through objects the cultural whole should be seen, studied and understood.

His perseverance was rewarded in 1932: a Sub-Department of Folk Culture and Industries was set up, the collections reorganized in new galleries and recognized as the National Folk Collections. By 1936 Peate was in charge of a fully fledged department. In ten years he had taken a significant collection of objects, annexed to the archaeology collections, and through them and his well-articulated yet developing beliefs in folk life studies, created a tantalizing case for folk life to be taken seriously both as an academic approach and a legitimate area for a museum department. Nowhere else in Britain had this occurred.

Peate's achievements were hard earnt, through dedicated work and much application. The period from the late 1920s to the war years was one of fevered activity for him. Catrin Stevens describes how he travelled the length and breadth of Wales, gathering material, furthering research, addressing specialist societies and lecturing to every interested party. Much of this effort was devoted to developing and broadcasting his ideas of the role of the National Museum of Wales and the potential of folk life studies as a scholarly discipline.

His vision of a Welsh Folk Museum was not very far removed from that which had originally inspired Artur Hazelius, although he appeared to lack a sense of what a Welsh Folk Museum could do in a practical way for the principality. In 1938 he wrote that the museum should be

a home for a new life and not a collection of dry bones, since there will be

gathered together in it every national virtue until it becomes in Welsh History . . .
the heart of Welsh Life . . . a means of uniting every movement in our land into
national identity . . . so that we may, by drinking of its living well, quench our
thirst ready for our national purpose in the future. [Quoted in translation in
Stevens 1986: 56]

But his romanticism, so evident in this almost fanatical view of a Welsh
Folk Museum, was tempered by a deep seam of humanism and by a
passionate concern for old ways of life rapidly disappearing in the rural
areas of Wales. His own background and understanding of the nature of
change in Wales led him to feel a strong empathy with the people whose
lives and ways of working he sought to record. But his studies were centred
on just a portion of Wales. He paid limited attention to industrial Wales,
where the extent of social change and the influences of England and
English consumerism had been greatest.

It is significant and a measure of his influence that for the next thirty-five
years his adopted term 'folk life' predominated in museum practice, and
similarly concentrated on the rural rather than the urban experience.
Ultimately, perhaps the most important point about his work was that he
was the first curator in Britain to demonstrate effectively that the lives of
ordinary people and the objects and oral traditions that gave their lives
meaning were a legitimate area of study and museum activity.

Dr I. F. Grant and Kingussie, Cubbon and Cregneash

Parallel to Peate's work in Wales, was that of Dr I. F. Grant in Scotland. A
significant difference was that where Peate was able carefully to develop his
ideas and collections within the relative security of a national museum,
Elsie Grant's work sprang entirely from her own initiative and resources.
In many ways this makes her achievement even more remarkable.

Born of a privileged background, in Edinburgh in 1887, Dr Grant
developed a strong personal identification with the Highlands, where some
of her childhood was spent. In her twenties she began writing about
Highland traditions and industries, and in 1924 published her first book,
Everyday Life on an Old Highland Farm 1769–1787. The extent and depth
of her research and interest in the Highlands is well reflected in this and
subsequent publications, of which there were many. Dr Grant was
enterprising and astute in her research, using a range of fieldwork and
source material, including archives, oral testimony and material evidence.
An interest in objects and illustrations associated with the subjects she
recorded and wrote about developed. She began collecting the material she
studied and in time this collection formed the basis of the museum she
founded, the Highland Folk Museum.

Her views about the 'folk' and about the 'folk museum' were in some part
influenced by her first-hand knowledge of the museums in Lillehammer
and Stockholm, and by her visit, in 1912, to the Rijksmuseum in
Amsterdam. She was struck by the inadequacy and problems of the term

'folk'. She felt it was used too readily to describe 'the peasant culture of an unsophisticated country people'. It was not an adequate term for what she wanted to see: a museum of wide-ranging social history that could tell the story of the life and work of the people of the Highlands and Islands. However, it was the term which, like Peate, she found herself using. Her biographer, Hugh Cheape, sums up her underlying thesis of the 'folk culture':

> this was no 'peasant' culture but an ancient and an aristocratic culture. Highland society, though hierarchical, was well integrated and adhered to the values of an aristocracy whose values had a long pedigree. These values were adopted, imitated and reflected on by all levels of society as, for example, Gaelic song and story clearly indicated. Every member of the Highland community looked to an aristocratic and heroic past and understood its conventions and metaphors. [Cheape 1986: 115]

Her idea of a folk museum was very distinct from the general view of her day. She saw the need for contemporary curatorial concerns to lie not with rare and the curious objects but with those which were familiar and the workaday, and with the life of a people within an ancient and aristocratic culture.

Cheape described the springboard for the museum as being Dr. Grant's involvement with the Highland Exhibition, held in Inverness in 1930. Material was brought together and exhibited under a number of headings including 'folk life'. The latter was a large category which included material that was intended to illustrate regional variation: in its content it was astonishingly rich and informative. Through the catalogue, to this day an invaluable research tool, Dr. Grant was able to articulate her hopes for the Highland Folk Museum, which she believed should develop from the exhibition. She was explicit in the arguments she used to support her idea: the present generation was faced with the opportunity of preserving a past that was slipping away without recall; this was the 'last chance' to record it; and there were proven examples of such work in the Scandinavian countries. The exhibition was well received: it was seen by about 20 000 visitors in seven weeks.

It did not, however, generate sufficient public or political interest in a folk museum. In spite of the fact that Dr Grant believed that such a venture should be a national enterprise, such as was beginning to develop in Wales, she found herself continually having to take the initiative. In 1935 she set up her collections in the United Reform Church building on the island of Iona as the 'Highland Folk Museum', *Am Fasgadh*. The inadequacies of the site and the island location led her to look for a mainland home for the museum. After several years of being beset by considerable difficulties, in 1944 she was able to reopen her museum in a more permanent site, Kingussie.

There are many aspects of Dr Grant's work and attitudes that are common with those of Iorwerth Peate in Wales: a scholarly attention to detail; a willingness to go outside predominating academic and museum conventions and to strike new ground; a personal identification with a distinct region and a depth of knowledge and empathy with its people and characteristics; consciousness of public and political opinion and its role in enabling their ideas of national folk museums to be fulfilled; and, more than anything, a romantic, nationalist and anti-modern view. Peate's work was to succeed largely because it was fostered within the framework of a national museum and because he was able to tap into a deep well of Welsh nationalism, convulsively redefining itself once again in the face of industrial uncertainty and decline. Grant had no such buffer. Moreover, the Highlands were sufficiently separate from the political consciousness to make her personal initiatives laudable but, especially while the museums in Edinburgh staked some claim, not sufficiently inviting for political and crucial financial support.

While Peate and Grant were in the course of developing their ideas of folk museums to an amalgam of national cultural centre and open-air museum as seen at Nordiska Museet and Skansen in Stockholm, plans for an open-air museum were underway on the Isle of Man. In 1886 the Museum and Ancient Monument Trustees had been established by Act of Tywald to preserve the relics of the Island's cultural past and, as a consequence, to found a museum. After difficult years in which some collections were amassed and finance sought, the Manx Museum was opened in 1922.

In 1932 William Cubbon became its curator, having for ten years occupied the post of Secretary and Librarian. Cubbon was an experienced journalist, from 1900 joint owner of the *Manx Sun*, and librarian. He was an active supporter of Manx studies and co-operated with researchers and writers alike, impressing upon them the need to formalize and publish their work. Throughout his professional life Cubbon appeared to follow the ideals his paper espoused in the announcement of his takeover, which were 'to promote Manx National interests, to create a higher ideal among the people as to their duty to the country, and to influence a higher degree of patriotism' (quoted in Harrison 1986: 17).

His contributions to the development of the Manx Museum were many, not the least being the formation of the Museum's National Reference Library containing almost every printed work ever published concerning the Isle of Man. Cubbon did much to encourage Manx studies both on the island and from overseas scholars. Along with other colleagues, he contributed linguistic and historical information to Professor Carl Marstrander, a scholar in Celtic studies at the University of Oslo who was studying the Manx language.

Marstrander's work had taken him to the village of Cregneash, a typical upland crofting village, or *clachan*, relatively isolated from modern developments on the rest of the island. The Manx language, *y ghailck*, had been spoken there by all the inhabitants within living memory. One of the people with whom Marstrander had worked was a man called Harry Kelly, whose Manx speech he recorded on wax cylinder. After his death, Harry Kelly's cottage was donated by his family to the Museum Trustees. Marstrander was instrumental in this decision.

Cubbon, who had visited Oslo and was interested in the ideas of folk museums developed in Scandinavia, was swift to grasp the potential of this gift. At the formal opening of Kelly's cottage to the public in 1938, Cubbon reflected on the spirit of the crofting communities living on there and 'dedicated the house as a memorial to them and as a reminder of the environment in which they lived and worked' (Harrison: 58). The opportunity that the gift of Harry Kelly's cottage provided was not lost either on the Museum Trustees. Harrison describes how the Trustees were conscious of the relationship the Manx Museum should have with the community it served, and that it should not be confined to a formal museum in the island's capital.

The Trustees had hoped for a branch museum which could provide a fuller and more effective picture of traditional Manx life. This intention was to seem even more crucial as social change on the island accelerated in the face of the increasing demands of a thriving tourist industry and the changing structure of the Manx economy. These, Harrison explains, presented a considerable threat to the customary life-style of the Manx countryside, which, it was felt, had contributed so much to the development of the national character. Cubbon's astute curatorship, with Marstrander's encouragement, led them to the founding of what is considered to be the first public open-air museum in Britain. Manx Museum interest in Cregneash was to be considerably enlarged by his successors, 'providing the island with one of its most prized conservation projects'.

The opening of Harry Kelly's cottage to the public once more focused attention on the fragile evidence that remained of the traditions, craft, skills and outlook of the people of these rural communities. At the opening ceremony Cubbon, in conversation with an invited delegation from Ireland, learnt of the work of the Irish Folklore Commission. Established in 1935, the Commission was concerning itself with recording the material and non-material aspects of Irish folk tradition: customs, beliefs and folk narrative were given equal attention, in so far as was possible, as were folk song and music. This, too, took its inspiration from developments in ethnography in Sweden (Almqvist 1979). Seizing on the relevance of the Commission's approach and purpose, Cubbon set in motion the development of a similarly comprehensive record of folk life on the Isle of Man. A number of difficulties prevailed, but with the encouragement and assistance of Eamon De Valera, Taoiseach of Ireland and the assistance of Basil Megaw, Deputy Director of the museum, the survey began in 1948. The Isle of Man folk life Survey now represents an astonishingly rich and important archive: 'the voice of the people' of the Isle of Man.

The work of Peate, Grant and those involved with the beginnings of Cregneash, but particularly William Cubbon, have much in common. Sound scholarship, a consciousness of changing ways of life and strong senses of regional identity underlay their work. There was as well a clear commitment to pass on a full and detailed archive of information to future generations, in which material and non-material culture were parts and evidence of a larger cultural whole. These initiatives were also outside England, in areas where some form of Celtic identity held strong. Museum developments in England were far less well developed.

Folk Museums in England

Museum developments in England between the war lacked both the scale
and intellectual integrity of much that was happening elsewhere in the
folk life movement. In England museum developments at this time were
dominated by generous private collectors, anxious to find a home and
public purpose for their collections. The most celebrated, and perhaps
misunderstood, of these was Dr John Kirk, upon whose collections the
Castle Museum at York, opened in 1938, was based.

Although often treated as a significant landmark in the evolution of
history museums, the Castle Museum owed very little to the philosophies
that underpinned those described above. Moreover, there was little, if any,
intellectual or methodological foundation to Kirk's work. Indeed, J. W. Y.
Higgs identified Kirk as one of 'a number of important enthusiasts who
did much good work but failed to understand the essential difference
between simply collecting specimens and making a record of daily life and
work' (Higgs 1963: 24). This assessment is not far removed from the truth.

Kirk was a physician who, in his tastes and approach, owed much to the
amateur and eclectic traditions of late-Victorian antiquarianism. In the
early 1890s, when he was living in London, he began to collect 'bygones'.
Over the years his collection grew to extraordinary proportions. The
material he amassed was selected very much at random and gathered
together with enthusiasm, to the point of obsession. Kirk purchased much
of his material from antique shops and dealers, allowing his natural
curiosity to dictate the choices made. He was quite prepared to buy objects
in 'sets', exchange material if necessary and purchase from as far afield as
Dundee and Weston super Mare. Kirk advertised in publications such as the
Exchange and Mart and in various ways established trade contacts
throughout England and Scotland. His collecting activities had no
geographic boundaries and no cultural purpose, other than apparently to
satisfy his personal need to acquire. In this he was happy to take over whole
collections: in 1925 he bought a collection of 'bygones' from Darlington
Library; and in 1933 the collections of the Greenland Fishery Museum,
Kings Lynn (York Castle Museum Archives).

In 1898 he took up a medical practice in Pickering, in the North Riding
of Yorkshire. He developed a strong interest in the 'bygones' of the area and
the changing ways of life he saw around him. As a consequence, he took the
opportunity to accumulate objects on his rounds. Whatever Kirk's interest
might have been in the lives and histories of the people he met through his
work, or the cultural significance of the material he gathered, little, if
anything, was committed to paper. It is remarkable that with the
documentation that survives with the collections now housed at York there
is little except lists of the names of objects. No notebooks, fieldnotes,
observations or publications appear to exist. His activity was personal
collecting rather than an extension of painstaking, in-depth scholarly
curatorship.

Kirk's private collection was made public out of personal generosity and
the pressing need to find some home for all he had amassed. But this was no

easy task. Although he had managed to persuade Pickering Urban District Council to make the Memorial Hall available as a museum for his collections in 1922, it was an unhappy partnership from which he withdrew in 1931. After several years of extreme difficulties, Kirk came to an agreement with York City Council, which made available to him the Female Prison near York Castle. With the able assistance of G. Bernard Wood, Kirk moved his collections into the prison, and displayed them as he saw fit.

He chose a mixture of methods in the displays he created. Some of the material was organized in type series for example, the Hearth Gallery, to demonstrate how the hearth had evolved—an approach that was the legacy of Kirk's Victorian antiquarianism. Where series were not possible, an attractive pattern was attempted instead: for example, 200 police truncheons and tipstaffs were arranged in geometric rhythms. He organized other material into 'room settings', including a late-Victorian parlour and a moorland cottage. But much of the collection went into a celebrated street scene, Kirkgate and Alderman's Walk. The display and interpretation of material through the re-creation of a life-size street was an approach that had not been tried before to any great extent in England, and certainly not to these proportions.

The origins of his ideas for the York 'streets' are open to question. Brears points out that Kirk had visited Sweden in 1910 and that he was much impressed by what he saw of the museums there (1980: 90). But the connection between the museum work underway in Stockholm and what Kirk was attempting to achieve at York is somewhat tenuous. The scholarship and fieldwork that were fundamental to Skansen and Nordiska Museet were not readily, if at all, evident in Kirk's work. He appears to have employed instead his own interests and judgement, partly born of observation and a lifetime of curiosity-driven collecting. The idea of the street scene may not have been totally original to Kirk. It was also pursued by Thomas Sheppard, Curator of Hull Museum, who, in 1931, had entered into negotiations with Kirk about the creation of such a street at Hull employing Kirk's collections. In spite of the negotiations failing, Sheppard did achieve the creation of his street scene (Sheppard 1935). (It was destroyed by enemy bombing during the war). Exactly which man had the idea first is open to question.

The popular success of the museum contrasts sharply with the professional criticisms made of Kirk's methods. Higgs commented that it was

> unfortunate that Kirk despite his energy and enthusiasms did not take more pains to relate his material to the sources from which it was obtained. As a result the staff of the Castle Museum have been continually troubled by their inability to catalogue the Kirk collection effectively and to use it for anything more than public display. [Higgs 1963: 24]

In this a little sympathy is due to Kirk, who amassed his collection not as a curator but as a private individual, and who donated his collection to the public in the face of official indifference and cynicism. As a dying man he supervised the formation of the York Castle Museum, giving it a scale that no other curator or museum authority in England, with the exception of Thomas Sheppard at Hull, had attempted. The museum opened in April 1938. Regrettably, the museum and its collection, in the absence of their originator, who died in February 1940, lost whatever purpose it might have had, and in the years to date has failed to find a central philosophy or direction other than entertaining the public with a mixture of myth and theme park.

The legacy of Kirk's work to museum practice in England has been the continuation of an eclectic, erratic, 'bygone' approach. The shallow material view, where the visual image—the object itself—obscures consideration of the deep and varied textures of cultural and historic meanings goes on. The mesh and interweave of material and non-material culture that were central to the work of Peate, Grant and Cubbon, and that of many others, appear not to have taken a ready hold in England before the war. The other Kirk legacy has been the acceptance that collections can be organized regardless of relevance and significance. Incongruous street scenes and meaningless, unresearched reconstructions of domestic and workplace interiors are, in part at least, direct consequences of the early years at the Castle Museum York.

The growing interest in England in folk life museums, which the developments at Castle Museum York encouraged, involved little in terms of dialogue or commitment which could shake it into *bona fide* folk life studies. Arguably, one of the stumbling-blocks was a recurrent obsession with folk museums as essentially 'open-air' museums with reconstructed buildings. This neglected a far more important view of a folk museum as an institution devoted to the study and explanation of past ways of life, of which an open-air museum might be one element (see, for example, Fox 1934).

When Mortimer Wheeler, then Keeper of the London Museum and an enthusiast for folk museums, came to discuss his idea of what an English Folk Museum should look like, he revealed a remarkably stunted vision. Expressing the quite valid opinion that the structural antiquities of England belonged in their own environments, he went on to say: 'although I deplore the sentiment—the English country side may be described as one vast folk museum'. He further suggested that, instead, museums should join forces with the various preservation movements (Wheeler 1934: 192-3).

Wheeler served on a committee established by the Ministry of Works to consider how an English Folk Museum might be set up and what form it should take. It was a subject that had obviously given those involved a great deal of trouble. Their conclusion was that if there had to be such a thing then it should consist of: (*a*) a building containing museum-collections of folk material, and (*b*) a small, coherent village group representing the principal phases of English life before the Industrial Revolution and covering a space of from 10 to 15 acres of ground' (*Museums Journal* 34: 195). Their plan, which drew on Home Counties examples, where it drew on any at all, was a remarkable piece of nonsense which showed no evidence of understanding the nature and purpose of folk life studies as pursued not only in Scandinavia but also, with growing awareness, in Wales, Scotland and Ireland. As could have been expected, the committee's report made no headway.

The mid-war years were of critical importance to the development of professional curatorship: the new folk life specialists laid the foundation for an academically respectable and socially relevant museum discipline. However, radical revision of ideas about folk life museums was still awaited in England, where amateurism, with much good intent, prevailed. But, like all else, this was interrupted and turned around by the outbreak of war in 1939.

4. History Museums: Post-War

The Second World War occasioned few significant museum developments. Many museum collections were removed from their premises to places of safety: a wise precaution as a number of museum buildings (some with their collections) were destroyed in bombing raids. Buildings that remained intact were used for other wartime purposes, the most celebrated being the concerts given at the National Gallery in London. But, in the main, these alternative uses had more to do with the central location and size of the buildings than with the fact that they were museums.

One of the ironies of war is that it creates a period in which unprecedented consideration and forward planning are given to the sort of society and economy a country wants when peace returns. In the war years, thought was given to established institutions, services and facilities and the role they might play in peacetime. Museum curators, and others with an interest in museums, were just one of the interested groups who took part.

Throughout the war the *Museums Journal* published reflective and forward-looking articles on folk museums and 'period museums'. Not least of these was a paper by Dr D. A. Allen, delivered as his presidential address to the Museums Association in August 1943. Allen argued the case for period museums 'not sited with regard to present day needs but unique in retaining—not recreating the setting of our national history'. This discernable change of attitude no doubt was a reflection of wartime national unity and heightened patriotism which had been built, in part at least, on heroic images of the national (often English) past. The *Museums Journal* published articles and reviews of museum ventures abroad: for example, on Colonial Williamsburg, Virginia (Brown 1942), as a means of focusing interest on possible future developments.

Folk museums for Wales and Scotland

The war was a traumatic period for Peate, but a crucial one in securing a Welsh Folk Museum. Peate was a committed pacifist, a member of both the Peace Pledge Union and the Fellowship of Reconciliation. In the last months of 1940 he was called before the South Wales Tribunal to defend his stand as a conscientious objector. As a result, he was dismissed from the National Museum of Wales. After what he described as 'eight quite nightmarish months', he was reinstated fully as a Keeper at the Museum: his pacifist views still firmly intact.

From the early 1930s Peate had been building and strengthening his arguments for a Welsh Folk Museum. One of the key people he needed to convince was Cyril Fox, Director of the National Museum. Some ground had been won in 1930, when Fox and two members of the National Museum's Council visited Scandinavia. In 1934 three of Europe's leading folk life scholars visited the Sub-Department at Cardiff. Dr Ake Campbell of Uppsala University, Professor C. W. von Sydow of Lund University and Dr Seamus O. Duilearga of the Irish Folklore Commission were able to impress upon Fox the importance of promoting folk life studies. Fox became a convert.

With formal support from the Director of the National Museum, what was needed was full political support. This came in mid-war, in 1943, when the Welsh Reconstruction Advisory Committee proposed 'that an open-air museum was an essential auxiliary to the National Museum of Wales'. As Catrin Stevens points out: 'it is one of the cruellest ironies that a pacifist's ideals should have received such a boost through the demand and necessity for reconstruction and rejuvenation during the post-war years' (1986:64). In 1946 the Earl of Plymouth offered the National Museum of Wales the castle at St Fagans, 4 miles outside Cardiff; 18 acres of land were part of the original offer, but when this was considered too small a further 80 acres were forthcoming. Peate was conscious that he had a site 'comparable with the great Scandinavian museums' and hoped that in the next forty years St Fagans could be developed at least as extensively as Skansen (Peate: 1949).

With a loyal and dedicated group of assistants, technicians and craftsmen, Peate set about creating the Welsh Folk Museum. A new central building would provide a number of facilities including galleries housing material illustrating 'all aspects of Welsh life'. Museum offices, workrooms, reserve collections and archives, and, most important of all research facilities including a library, would also be accommodated in this building. As with the Swedish Folk Museum models, this was to be the academic powerhouse for the whole museum: a national centre for teaching as well as research.

The castle was to be developed to illustrate 'the spaciousness of the life of the landed classes'. In the grounds various buildings removed from different parts of Wales would be erected with their outbuildings. They would be suitably furnished; outside Welsh black cattle and sheep would run. Traditional crafts would be demonstrated and fostered—wood-turning, textiles, carpentry, smithying, pottery and so on, as well as 'impermanent' crafts such as hedging and rick-thatching. A tea-room was to be provided for visitors. A charge would be levied for entrance to the museum and capital raised for some of the developments through subscription—and so it was. By 1949 the work was well underway and the museum opened. Peate was buoyant, and confident that

such museums will strengthen and deepen the best in national life and will serve to reinvigorate many aspects of our social life, the texture of which has suffered so greatly in the dark periods of this century. The folk museum is not only a re-creation of a picture of the past: it is also an experiment in social regeneration'. [1949: 804]

Such experiments did not meet with strong political support elsewhere. Dr Grant had managed to move her collection to a Georgian house in Kingussie, which she opened as the 'Highland Folk Museum'. This had some land on which she planned to reconstruct nine cottages to illustrate 'local types of buildings and could also illustrate different stages in the evolution of the fireplace' (quoted in Noble 1977: 144). Four buildings were constructed for her by two elderly craftsmen: a Lewis 'black house', a traditional Inverness cottage, an example of the 'improved' cottage and a water-mill. The fact that these were not originals met with Peate's disapproval (1949: 797). However, they were furnished with material from the collections and 'enlivened by having Soay sheep and cattle grazing about them'. But the lack of official status and recognition was a significant handicap to the museum's development. When Dr Grant retired in 1954, the museum was purchased by the Pilgrim Trust and presented to the four Scottish universities. Its subsequent development, over the next twenty years or so, appears to have lacked the vigour and commitment evident elsewhere. In 1959 the National Museum of Antiquities appointed an Assistant Keeper with the task of studying Scottish folk life and collecting material for an open-air museum with a rural theme. It ended any expectations that the Highland Folk Museum would develop into a national museum and cultural centre, other than by the efforts of those directly involved.

A national museum for England

In England the cautious interest in a national folk museum eventually gave way to a number of formal proposals, which conspicuously lacked much of the nationalist and romantic rhetoric and illusions of the pre-war discussions. In 1949 the Royal Anthropological Institute's British Ethnology Committee put forward a scheme for the development of a Museum of English Life and Traditions, to be called 'the English Museum', the central purpose of which would be the study of 'English culture'. However, there was an alternative 'English Museum' already under consideration.

The University of Reading had well-established academic interests in agricultural studies. There were a number of individuals at the university who were highly conscious of the ways in which much of rural England was being changed in what has been called the 'Second Agricultural Revolution'. They saw the need to record established practices and the social changes being experienced. From the first they conceived of the museum as a library of records, in which objects would be a part. In 1951 the university formally established the Museum of English Rural Life (MERL) 'to serve as a national centre for material connected with the history of the English countryside' (Higgs 1963: 27). But more than anything it would be a centre of research, 'a genuine University institution' (Museum of English Rural Life 1954: 5). Significantly, the first Keeper was also a lecturer in agricultural history, J. W. Y. Higgs, MA. In the spring of

1953 two Assistant Curators were appointed, one of them was a young Welshman, J. Geraint Jenkins, MA.

MERL was able to build its collections and archives through a number of means. Donations were important and included a number of private collections. H. J. Massington gave his collection of old tools and implements and a large collection of rural material acquired by Miss Lavinia Smith was also made available. The Victoria and Albert Museum donated material including domestic and agricultural metalwork. However, although donations were encouraged, fieldwork and research-aided acquisition were the central activities in building the collections. Yet, in spite of having a brief that covered 'England', much of this collecting activity appears to have taken place in the South. Perhaps this was inevitable: but it certainly was of concern to Higgs (Museum of English Rural Life 1954: 9). MERL systematized its approach by electing to collect and view material under four main headings: agriculture, rural life, domestic material and village life. These groupings formed the rudiments of the classification system and underpinned curatorial activities.

In the early years there was considerable consciousness of how much had been swept away in radical changes of farming practice. This, coupled with a growing awareness that the task should have begun twenty years before and that the disinterest of many museums across England had exacerbated the loss of significant material, gave the early collecting a sense of urgency: it was in a sense a 'rescue' mission. Additional pressure was created when commercial interest raised the financial value of old rural objects.

In the light of the obvious difficulties and to ensure that the collections gathered would be worthy and relevant, careful thought was given to the material acquired, its condition and its information value. But objects were only part of the archive. There was a strong commitment to record the non-material aspects of rural life, particularly oral testimony. In the early days shortage of staff prevented as much fieldwork developing as Higgs would have liked. However, the importance of such work was well recognized and opportunities were grasped whenever possible. The urgency felt was expressed by Higgs when he wrote: 'there is no time to be lost for every rural octogenarian that dies carries with him to the grave a wealth of useful information about the life of the last century' (Museum of English Rural Life 1954: 11).

Therefore, from the beginning great stress was laid upon proper documentation and an adequate recording system. The potential future use of this information by students and researchers was a guiding influence on the systems developed. Acquiring a tool, for example, was perceived of very limited value unless certain questions were asked and the answers recorded. Higgs identified some of the more relevant of these as: 'Where was it made? Who made it? Who used it? How was it used? In what farming system was it used? For what type of crops? and so on, (Museum of English Rural Life 1954: 9).

The organization of this material into a system for ordering and retrieving information led to the examination of approaches adopted by other museums in Britain and in Scandinavia. In time MERL developed its own systems: a new form of catalogue card, a classification system and a topographical index. This became the standard for many museums working in this field at regional level. For example, the Museum of Lincolnshire Life, founded in 1969, developed the MERL system for the needs of its collections. In this MERL contributed a framework of museum practice which could constantly remind curators that the object was only a part of their recording task and that the essence of all collecting and fieldwork activity was the creation of a databank of in-depth information about their subject.

MERL not only established standards of acquisition, research and documentation which influenced other museums, it also developed procedures for the careful conservation of the material in its care and initiated investigations into the treatment of what they chose to call 'folk life material'. This was to have significant bearing on how museums in Britain cared for their collections. Arguably, MERL was also instrumental in forming opinion about folk life or rural life museums in general amongst the people who, in terms of getting such projects off the ground, mattered: rural politicians and local societies. It did this through a number of ways including its connections with the Royal Agricultural Society of England, and (given that in the early years MERL did not have its own exhibition facilities) by staging displays of material at the Royal Shows, for example at Cambridge in 1951 and Newton Abbot in 1952. Moreover, MERL involved itself with the press and television, opening relationships with the media that have been a definite contributing factor to museum development.

Growth and development

The 1950s were very much times of consolidation for those museums already underway. MERL strengthened its position and developed archives, collections and a considerable awareness of its purpose. The movement of collections and buildings to the Welsh Folk Museum at St Fagans continued, with Peate seeing many of his ideas being put into practice. In 1957 the recording of information from ordinary people, *y werin*, began. These developments in time led to the division of the interests of the Welsh Folk Museum into two separate departments: material culture, under the direction of F. G. Payne, and oral traditions and dialects, under V. H. Phillips. As Peate was to point out: 'it is not enough to have a plough without also knowing the dialect names for all its parts' (quoted in Stevens 1986: 70). On the Isle of Man, the Manx folk life Survey continued apace with a degree of success which must have outstripped expectations. Meanwhile opportunities were being presented to develop and extend Cregneash as a folk museum.

Interest in folk life was also being indicated by two universities in England. In the 1950s the Department of English Language at the University of Leeds began the New English Dialect Survey; and the English Folklore Survey was initiated by the English Department of University

College London. A School of Scottish Studies was set up at the University of Edinburgh, and was housed next door to the Linguistic Survey of Scotland. There was some discussion about forming a Scottish National Folk Museum to work alongside the School of Scottish Studies and the National Museum of Antiquities.

In 1955 proposals were made for creating a folk museum for Ulster. This was realized in 1958, when legislation empowered that the museum be 'established for the purposes of illustrating the way of life, past and present and the traditions of people of Northern Ireland'. The Trustees of the museum were charged 'to take such other actions ... proper for the purpose of acquiring or disseminating knowledge of such ways of life and traditions' (quoted in Gailey 1906. 51). Development of the Ulster Folk Museum required that broad contexts be addressed, in cultural-geographical terms, wider than Ulster itself. The early years were hampered by the lack of a site, although collecting and research activities continued nevertheless. In the middle of 1961 the Trustees purchased the Cultra Manor Estate of 136 acres and provided the museum with a superb site on which to develop. In its form and intent the museum drew on the experiences of Scandinavian museums and also on the work in hand at the Welsh Folk Museum. The Ulster Folk Museum developed an ethnological research unit, an indoor museum with formal exhibition galleries and an outdoor museum consisting of re-erected buildings.

The Welsh Folk Museum, the Manx Museum, the Highland Folk Museum, the Museum of English Rural Life and the Ulster Folk Museum at this time had a number of factors in common. These included a commitment to recording and explaining the historic and cultural contexts of their distinct areas, and an academic interest in rural life. Considerable support and encouragement were given to their work through the spirit of co-operation that existed between the museums. Mutual interests were strengthened through the publication *Gwerin*, which first appeared in 1956 and which aimed to be an international platform for all those who studied Celtic and English folk life, and were further enhanced by formation of the Society of Folk Life Studies in 1961.

But it would be far from fair to portray these as the only museum developments in the early post-war years. Many local museums and departments within museums were founded or were emerging during this time, sometimes from 'bygone' collections already in existence, sometimes from local society collections. For example, Blaise Castle Museum, Bristol, was opened in 1949 with a declared interest in 'West of England folk material'. The West Yorkshire Folk Museum, a branch of the Halifax Museum, was opened at Shibden Hall in 1953. Abbey House Museum, Kirkstall, which was opened in 1928, had developed a town and crafts museum with reconstructed shops. In fact, since the street scenes at York and Hull this form of display became very popular, being copied at a number of museums including Newarke Houses in Leicester and Salford Museum.

Through the late 1950s, and particularly in the 1960s, more and more material became available to museums willing to collect. These were yielded through cycles of economic and social redundancy which rendered whole ranges of objects useless in their original surroundings: for example, tools from common craft practices, such as wheelwrights, saddlers, blacksmiths and cobblers; and wagons and ploughs no longer required on farms shifting from horses to tractors. For those museums committed to recording, the easy availability of material linked directly with the people who had used it and knew its meaning was a critical moment in their work. It inevitably resulted in a great deal of fieldwork and directed acquisition, leading to records and collections that are now the main evidence available of ways of living and working that have already begun to move beyond popular memory.

But many museums applied a far more pragmatic approach: whatever theory and justification applied to their tasks emerged, if at all, after the event. For them there was a conspicuous lack of clear ideas about the nature and purpose of collecting much of this redundant material. There was a far greater lack of clearly defined objectives for folk museums locally and the role of objects within them. Such museums collected whatever was available, regardless of its degree of relevance locally, any oral traditions associated with it, or its condition. In the meantime, more fundamental local changes were taking place, to which such institutions turned a blind eye and collected nothing. As interesting as some of the material later proved to be, undirected acquisition substantially weakened the legitimate case for some folk museums. Many curators today find themselves with large amounts of material gathered during this period, the documentation of which could be politely called rudimentary, and the relevance of which to the local community remains in some question. They also find themselves with a legacy of received and stunted views of what such museums should be.

Many folk life curators, particularly if part of a larger museum with traditional collections of art, ethnography and natural history, found themselves marginalized and treated with a degree of condescension. It was (and to some extent still is) as if art, archaeology and the accepted disciplines were perceived as 'intellectual' and 'credible', while folk life or social history were for those curators and visitors who could not quite stretch themselves to the academic demands of the proven collections. Regardless of the fact that several decades had passed in which the strongest of arguments for the intellectual and social worth of folk life studies had been repeatedly aired, these appear to have fallen on deaf ears in many quarters of museum opinion. The term 'folk museum' gradually became used for a history museum that lacked depth and sense of intellectual purpose.

The *Survey of Provincial Museum and Galleries*, undertaken by the Standing Commission on Museums and Galleries in 1963, exemplifies this. Folk museums received only the minimum of note, in which it is quite clear that they were perceived by the Commission as being collections of 'tools and products', rather than as a developing record of local ways of life (Rosse 1963: 27). Moreover, museums of local interest were seen to be warranted only if the place was sufficiently interesting or there was a 'focus . . . some picturesque local hero, natural feature, historic event or industry' (1963: 29).

5. History Museums Since the 1960s

The present pattern of history museum provision in Britain owes much to developments that have occurred, both in museums and out of them, since the early 1960s. This is not to dismiss the importance of the early initiatives described in the previous chapters. But history in the museum, and particularly social history, has come into its own in the last 30 years, to the point where there are now more museums devoted to history than to any other museum-centred discipline. This period has been propitious for history in museums for a number of reasons. Curatorship has matured and has developed more viable methods and attitudes. This is particularly evident in a new generation of museum curators who came into museum work in the 1970s and 1980s. Popular interest in history has heightened in response to educational interests, a changing social and economic environment, and intensive media interest in the past. Objects and sites have become available at key moments. Museums have benefited through access to these and to that element of the past to which they refer. But, most significantly, museums now figure in leisure and tourist industries in ways that the early curators could not have imagined. In this context the past seen as something which, through participation, social strength and cultural understanding can be derived has begun to give way to the idea of the past as a commodity, a product to be consumed.

Scientific, industrial and technology museums

A distinct element of post-war museum development has been a growing concern for urban and industrial history. This gathered momentum in the 1960s and brought with it a particular approach to the interpretation of industrial and technological collections that was often different from the field of social history. The view that developed is perhaps best summed up in the introduction of a Standing Commission report on the *Preservation of Technological Material*, published in 1971:

> Britain started to make her outstanding contribution to the industrial development of Europe and the world in the early eighteenth century. There is a growing recognition of the need to record and preserve the best of the industrial relics which remain, but the modernization of plant and the development of cities is leading to accelerated destruction of important material every year. [1971: 2]

This statement sums up many of the attitudes held by the industrial preservation movement: an unshakeable conviction in the superiority of British design, implicitly devoid of lack of innovation or failure; a total all-consuming concern for the 'relic'; and an inability to grasp the fact that what was being lost was far, far more than 'relics' but whole ways of life, complex yet integrated ways of living and working which had been created and shaped by specific modes of production in which 'relics' were just one operating part.

But the 1960s were by no means the beginning of museum interest in industry, technology or science. Indeed, the position of scientific material within museums has a lengthy pedigree. Scientific instruments, evidence of ever-enlarging understanding of the universe, featured frequently in the cabinets of curiosities formed by European princes during the sixteenth and seventeenth centuries. One of the earliest surviving museums in Britain is the Museum of the History of Science in the Old Ashmolean at Oxford (Impey and Macgregor 1985).

From quite an early date, exhibitions of art and industry were held in England, although some of them were quite modest by later standards. The Society for the Encouragement of Arts, Manufacturers and Commerce was a prime force. Founded in 1754 by William Shipley, the Society was more commonly known as the Society of Arts, and, after 1847, as the Royal Society of Arts. Shipley's aim was to give rewards to worthwhile ventures in the liberal arts where they could be shown to have beneficial effects upon commerce and industry (Greenhalgh 1988). The exhibitions organized by the Mechanics' Institutes, the first in Manchester in 1837, widened the scope of English exhibitions. The Mechanics' Institutes were situated in the industrial North and the English Midlands, and were concerned with the education and leisure of the working classes, aiming to stimulate working-class consciousness and generally advance industrial culture.

This exhibition movement, encouraged and supported by 'the flourishing bourgeois culture of the provincial manufacturing towns' (Kusamitsu 1980: 71) provided opportunities for the working classes to have access to fine art and to study technical innovation. In many respects it was a popular movement which captured the imagination of many, not least because the exhibitions included up-to-date, even new, pieces of machinery. Kusamitsu comments on how textile machinery was displayed in the exhibitions held in the Midlands. In spite of the memory of the Luddites in the 1810s and 1820s, which must have been still firsthand in the 1830s and 1840s, there was little evidence of hostility towards the machinery, particularly the weaving and printing machinery, on exhibition. The rationale Kusamitsu gives for this is that manufacturers would have wanted their workmen to see new machinery, to learn from it and so break the resistance to new technology. In time artisans and mechanics contributed exhibits 'in which they proudly showed their skill and craft pride' (Kusamitsu: 87).

These exhibitions contributed some momentum to the establishment of local, provincial museums, especially in their expanding industrial areas. They contributed also to the spirit in which plans were developed for the

Great Exhibition of 1851, although the main impetus was the success of the French exhibitions, especially the Paris Exhibition of 1849. As is well known, one of the consequences of the Great Exhibition was a train of events that led to the founding of the South Kensington Museum in 1857 and eventually the Science Museum, which adopted the aim of increasing 'the means of industrial education and to extend the influences of science and art on productive industry' (quoted in Day 1987: 14). The lessons of the Science Museum, therefore, were about achievement, innovation and technical developments.

During the second half of the nineteenth century some museums in the provinces collected material from local industries, in the main their products rather than their technology. Not until the 1920s and 1930s did collections of industrial technology develop with any degree of coherence. Some of these were specialized collections, for example the remarkable transport collection amassed by Thomas Sheppard, Curator of the museums in Hull, which first opened to the public as the Museum of Commerce and Transport in 1925 (Hopkin 1987: 21-2). In 1934 the Museum of Science and Industry was founded in Newcastle, specializing in engineering and applied sciences. But these were fairly isolated initiatives, even given the degree of public interest which Britain's Victorian technology was attracting. In general the early technological collections were as random as many of the local folk life collections, providing little evidence that the museums had clear objectives. But as British industry, even in the 1930s, was still using much plant and premises that were at least 30 years old, if not older (for example, the textile industry), then the opportunity and incentive to view the situation more comprehensively did not immediately develop.

After the war interest in technological collections was revived and, for a short time, sought direction. During the course of a discussion on folk museums, held by the Royal Society of Arts in September 1949, Peate was asked by Wilfred Seaby, Keeper of the Department of Archaeology and Local History at the City Museum, Birmingham, how far he intended taking arts and crafts into the Welsh Folk Museum. Seaby was engaged in planning an industrial museum for Birmingham (opened in 1951). He put it to Peate that in an all-embracing folk museum, of the sort he espoused, the craft of coal-mining should be represented in some way. Peate's reply exposed the central flaw in his view of Welsh culture and history. He conceded the case for folk museums dealing with mining, and similarly with quarrying, boat building and industry. But in his view these could be only regional ventures. The Welsh Folk Museum, to his mind, had to be rural and traditional (Peate 1949).

This confinement of his view of the Welsh past which excluded the most significant of all economic and social changes to life in Wales during the nineteenth century, changes which did much to promote diversity and dissent in Wales, created restrictions for the Welsh Folk Museum and the part it could play in recording and explaining Welsh life. The reason for this may lie in exactly what it was Peate thought he was creating. As Stevens has suggested, St Fagans may have represented to him, however consciously, Llanbryn-mair, his rural, family home and his youth recalled (1986: 72).

But beyond the Welsh Folk Museum, in wider terms, his views also confined the potential of folk life or ethnological studies through museums, restricting the accepted field of interest to pre-industrial or agricultural societies. Whereas his approach to the whole culture, to the material and non-material aspects of ways of living, could most reasonably have extended to the urban and industrial experience, he failed to give a lead on this. In the late 1940s there was no-one else of his stature and influence who could have opened these doors and propose ethnological models from which the industrial museums could develop their work. As a result they became object-centred, rather than people-centred.

Public attitudes to Britain's 'industrial heritage', began to change significantly in the late 1950s and 1960s. Real public concern was created when a number of important and impressive industrial landmarks started to disappear through urban redevelopment and modernization. A turning point was reached when the doric portico at Euston Station was threatened. Sir John Betjeman took up its cause, only to see it removed in 1962 and replaced by a building of unsurpassable soullessness. In the same year the London Coal Exchange was destroyed. Two such losses, particularly because they were in London, the centre of effective political opinion and media attention, resulted in a wave of popular interest in the physical remnants of a once-thriving industrial country. Modern industrial archaeology was born and gave rise to the foundation of the Industrial Archaeology Society in 1973. This society became the springboard for much research, popular education and rescue activity.

As soon as the threatened loss was appreciated, its scale was found to be enormous. Industrial sites, buildings and machinery, for their entire existence of little interest other than to those who owned them and those who earnt their living through them, became the focus of attention. The remnants of Victorian industries were everywhere and their care was going to need cash, space and commitment. A survey of Victorian technology in Britain was conducted by Dr Norman A. F. Smith in 1968 and published in 1970: this helped to set an agenda for preservation. Museums had a part to play in this, although they did so alongside a host of civic, private and voluntary ventures.

In the 1960s numbers of museums were established or developed to take advantage of the situation and to respond to public concern. Perhaps not untypical was the National Museum of Wales. In the late 1960s planning began for a Welsh Industrial and Maritime Museum, to be situated in Cardiff. It was to be a museum of 'industrial archaeology' and plans were developed to fill the 3.5 acre site with a collection of technologically significant machinery. Conspiciously absent from the plans and the explained scheme was any accommodation or allowance for recording or explaining the ways of life that accompanied and enabled there to be a 'Welsh Industrial and Maritime Museum' (Standing Commission 1971: 45 –7). The object-centred approach adopted widely in Britain came to be exemplified at the Welsh Industrial and Maritime Museum, with its central power gallery and absence of reference to people who made, operated or experienced the effects of the material displayed. Hudson identified this approach, which is still very evident today, as springing from an antiquarian attitude, in which the important questions 'why ought we to preserve?', and 'for whom ought we to preserve?' are dangerously neglected (Hudson 1965: 38).

Perhaps the best known of the industrial museums developed in the late 1960s and 1970s is Ironbridge Gorge Museum. In 1959 Allied Ironfounders, who then owned the Coalbrookdale Ironworks, commemorated the 250th anniversary of Abraham Darby's coke-smelting process by opening to the public the Old Furnace where the experiments had been made and a Museum of Iron. The growth of interest in industrial archaeology in general and the site in particular, and the efforts of Dr G. F. Williams, Managing Director of the works, led to the Ironbridge Gorge as a whole being recognised as an area of outstanding historical importance. Not only had the place played a significant role in industrial history but it also was blessed with a large number of industrial remains largely still intact. In 1968 an independent charitable trust was established, with the co-operation of the local authorities and the Telford Development Corporation, to create the museum.

By 1971 the Trust had raised sufficient capital to appoint a Director, Neil Cossons (Cossons 1980). In its early days the Trust and its museum were very much to embrace the interests of the industrial archaeological movement. The Standing Commission applauded the museum for its plans to preserve monuments *in situ*, and to re-erect at Blist's Hill 'many large artifacts from the surrounding area'. These included two rare beam blowing engines from the Lilleshaw Ironworks.

The Standing Commission on Museums and Galleries was swift to see the scale of the problem for museums, and in 1970 established a working party to consider the preservation of technological material. The working party took a very wide brief. In its consideration of the preservation of objects, structures and archives, it reviewed the responsibilities of a number of different agencies. The report helped clarify a very confused area of activity, and its recommendations were as a result wide-ranging. Included in them was an important proposal, later acted upon, that there should be an annual grant-in-aid available from the government, to be administered by the Science Museum. This was to help museums purchase objects and archives, and assist with any transport costs incurred.

To guide the identification of the material that would be considered relevant for grant-in-aid, the Standing Commission drew up a list:

Industrial monuments in situ;
relics of industrial *social life;*
ships and relics of shipbuilding and merchant shipping industries;
art connected with industry;
archives, including photographs and sound and film archives.

The presence of 'relics of industrial social life' in this list was perhaps due to the presence of Frank Atkinson on the working party. Unlike, for example, those involved with the Welsh Industrial and Maritime Museum planned for Cardiff, Atkinson's view of industrial material, and indeed, the industrial past had a dimension that was not readily evident in the work of many of the new industrial museums. By 1971, when the report appeared, his ideas had been introduced to the broad church of museum curators, largely through a number of persuasive papers Atkinson had delivered at museum conferences (1967;1968)

At the time the Standing Commission's report was being prepared, Frank Atkinson was at a very crucial stage in the development of the North of England Open-Air Museum at Beamish in County Durham. The museum run by a joint committee of local authorities in the North-east, was being established at Beamish Hall and its grounds of 200 acres. Collection of material was well underway and approval had been given to a development plan. The museum, drawing on the open-air museum techniques of the Scandinavian folk museums, proposed to address the industrial and social history of the North-east.

Atkinson was at some variance with other industrial museums, and, as far as ideas in curatorial practice were concerned, years ahead of his time. The difference was that the museum was designed to represent the social background to its industrial and technological collections 'believing that such material should not be divorced from its human context'. Thus, the Standing Commission explained 'the museum will not place a colliery winding engine solely as an example of steam powered machinery, but will first re-erect the original building and then reinstate the machine in working order together with the screens, lamp shed and colliery trucks, whilst nearby will be rebuilt a small terrace of pitmen's cottages' (Standing Commission 1971: 31).

Here was the opening of doors that Peate had closed. Here also was the beginning of the enlargement of the history museum brief to be conscious of the cultural whole, the meeting, merger or juxtaposition of rural and industrial experiences; the databank that viewed the past not through the size, scale or diameter of objects, but through the nature of experiences in which objects had a part. But it was more than this. Atkinson's view was also a recognition that the object-centred approach spoke only to those with the vocabulary and experience to unlock its messages. To view the past through both social and industrial experience made it accessible to a much wider and more democratic audience. Indeed, it was the audience, the visitors, who were the future of museums.

Regional studies and social history

The late 1960s and the early 1970s marked a series of junctures for history museums in Britain. The first of these was the necessity, that could no longer be postponed, to examine the interrelationship between the areas of cultural studies adopted by folk life museums and those adopted by museums addressing industrialization and urban life, and the role that the collections being amassed by industrial archaeology curators could play.

The term 'folk life', about which a number of people had expressed concern, became increasingly disliked. This developed in spite of the fact that valid and relevant methodologies were emerging in its name, stressing the interrelationship of material studies with the study of sociology, custom, belief, linguistics and oral tradition (Jenkins 1969: 17). At a seminar held in York in 1966 to discuss 'folk parks', an early consensus of the delegates was their dislike for the word 'folk' (*Museums Journal* 1966: 220–2). There was much agreement on other issues, including the quality and orientation of the research needed to develop museums and the need to collect strictly relevant material. There emerged from two of the key speakers, Frank Atkinson and J. Geraint Jenkins (now of the Welsh Folk Museum), arguments to the effect that museums should seek to represent the cultural variety and characteristics of distinct regions. Indeed, the term and idea of 'regional studies' rather than folk life studies was emerging.

'Folk life studies' in museums became in a sense a victim of language, as much as proscribed views of the past. Peate had elected not to adopt the Scandinavian term 'regional ethnology' but instead preferred 'folk life'. This may have been an attempt not to 'over-intellectualize' the subject. But his rejection of a term under which the subject could develop and his confinement of folk life to the rural and traditional had by the late 1960s affected popular and professional attitudes to it. As Geraint Jenkins was to point out, the word 'folk' in itself seemed to breed a strange reaction, conjuring up 'a picture of woollen-stockinged, black-cloaked, brogue-shod women chasing fairies through glens and men with bells around their knees dancing merrily on the village green' (1972: 497). Yet, in spite of Jenkins's insistence that the word 'folk' 'signified the complete way of life in the community', the popular view prevailed. It is significant that during this time, the early 1970s, Swedish museums, from which many museums in Britain had taken the lead, were consciously replacing the term 'folk life' with 'cultural history' or 'ethnology', as were the university departments (Klein 1985).

The emergence of the idea of 'regional museums' had a liberating effect. It dispensed with a suffocating legacy and opened opportunities for broad-based and provocative studies. With this, the centre of much of the new drive for museums shifted to England, particularly to the Midlands and the North. In theory, the approach and subject-matter of regional museums made it essential to cross over discipline boundaries: geography, geology, archaeology, local, social history and sociology were each in their part necessary if a region was in any sense to be understood, recorded and explained through the medium of the museum. Moreover, the idea of regional studies through museums permitted rural and industrial life to be studied and recorded, in their historical and cultural contexts, either interlocking or at points of change. Further, it permitted a much more open chronological span in both collections and exhibitions.

'Regionalism' reached a high spot with the formation, by Geraint Jenkins and Peter Brears, of the Group for Regional Studies in Museums, in 1974. The group aimed to be a forum for not only the 'museological aspects of their subject' but also for stimulating the 'academic side of the work', the first time that such a group had been formed in Britain (Group for Regional Studies in Museums 1975: 2). Subgroups were established to further this aim at regional level. Motivation for the group sprang from a consciousness of the need to strengthen standards of recording and curatorial methodology. The promotion of an understanding of regional studies was a predominant part of the group's early intentions, as was a keen interest in the communication of regional studies to the public.

But it would be unrealistic to see these developments as, in any sense, a mass movement or a uniform trend. Many curators continued to run museums with an approach not far removed from the late-nineteenth century concern for 'bygones'. Similarly, many industrial and technology collections made little note of the human contexts from which their collections were derived. However, sufficient inroads were made both in terms of ideas and methodology to see this 'regional' approach as important.

It was at its best in the work of the Oxfordshire County Museum Service, particularly from 1974 when a new collecting and research policy came into effect. The policy helped the curators to identify gaps in the county museums' collections, from folk lore to car manufacture. One of the means adopted to fill those gaps was to establish joint working groups, pool experience and expertise, and study reasonably comprehensively subjects absent or only loosely represented in the museums' collections. The identified subjects (which included brewing, woodcrafts, pottery and brickmaking) were studied using evidence from museum documentation, site records, fieldwork, objects, oral testimony, and primary and secondary sources. The first project was on workers' housing. Later projects led to exhibitions which toured the county. Each was supported by both a learned article and a more popular publication. In this way the museums enriched their collections and archives, lifted standards of curatorship and successfully extended understanding of the subjects they researched. Too seldom in museum work are cross-disciplinary teams of curators used to advance research and collecting. In the Oxfordshire case, archaeologists and historians worked side by side. The potential exists for other, perhaps wider ranging initiatives.

But beyond the expansive trends in the ideas about the nature and direction of museum work, there were in many respects far more fundamental trends affecting and moulding the form museums took from the 1960s onwards. Museums from this point were at another juncture and were having to respond to profound economic and social shifts.

The massive decline both in heavy and manufacturing industries in Britain began to accelerate in the late 1960s. This continued to yield to museums vast quantities of obsolete machinery and, in some instances, sites and premises. Many museums were able to take advantage of this and by the late 1970s it was being said that one museum was being established every two weeks somewhere in Britain: it was roughly estimated that Britain must have something like 2000 museums. The sites of Britain's industrial, and in some instances rural, past were being taken over by museums and fostered either by local authorities or by a relatively new form of museum body: an independent charitable trust. Such museums were able to appeal to local goodwill and concern over the loss of such sites, and, with both financial and moral support, establish themselves.

Significantly, these opportunities also coincided with the reorganization of local government, when many authorities, either before or after the 1974 restructuring, sought to assert their identity or consolidate their resources. This they did in part through establishing or developing museums, or by supporting independent ventures locally.

In a survey of museums in Britain, published by the Museums Association in 1987, it was revealed that three-quarters of the museums in Britain were founded after 1951, with nearly half of these since 1971. Since 1950 and especially since 1971, 56 per cent of the new museums have been in the non-public sector and, of these, 64 per cent have been founded by voluntary associations or private individuals. The survey also reveals that since 1961 museums in the private sector have been predominantly within the fields of industrial archaeology, social history (particularly rural, social history) and technology and transport. Three-quarters of the site museums in Britain have been founded since 1971 (Prince Higgins-McLoughlin 1987: 26).

Social trends and social history

The growth of museums, however, needs to be explained not just in terms of the opportunities which presented themselves through redundant material and sites. From the 1960s onwards there have been significant changes in leisure and recreation patterns which, in themselves, have boosted museums and placed them within the service industry. In the 1960s the adoption of the five-day week by many industries and in services such as banking created a longer, continuous week-end, beginning on a Friday afternoon. There has also been a gradual lengthening of paid holiday entitlement and a lowering of the age at which retirement is taken. The proportion of households owning one (or more) cars increased from 31 per cent in 1961 to 58 per cent in 1980, with a swift rise from 31 per cent to 51 per cent between 1961 and 1969 (quoted in Patmore 1983: 11, 34).

These changes created a 'market' for a burgeoning leisure industry, in which museums, especially the independent ventures, sought a place. Frank Atkinson has been quoted as saying in 1968, 'nostalgia is going to be bigger and bigger business in the next few years' (Hudson 1987: 126). By the end of the 1970s local authorities and independent museums were discussing freely 'making money from museums', 'value of museums to the economy', 'marketing' and 'enterprise' (for example, Collison 1978; Emery-Wallis 1979; Lickorish 1979; Montagu 1979). A distinct branch of service activities grew—the 'heritage industry'—devoted to leisure, encompassing stately homes, theme parks, heritage sites and museums. A notable sector of the heritage industry has been and is astutely managed, not necessarily by trained curators, and has become highly successful, indirectly questioning the relevance of traditional curatorial skills.

For many of the history museums, old and new, effective marketing and commercial planning became essential, as they found themselves in a new and highly competitive market-place. The museum's relationship with the public became critical for survival during this period and remains so today. In the early 1970s it began to matter more than ever if the labelling was poor, the exhibitions dreary, the lighting dreadful, the car parks, shops, cafes and toilets non-existent. It also began to matter whether a museum was in touch with the public it sought to serve, testing their reactions to museum developments, and their range of needs.

From the late 1960s onwards there was tremendous growth in local history groups and societies, oral history workshops and local ventures. These vary considerably in their outlook and purpose. The local history group in a sleepy Home Counties commuter village is not necessarily responding to the influences that motivate an oral history group in the Rhondda.

W. G. Hoskins's published works on English local history (for example, 1955; 1967) popularized and made accessible the English, pre-industrial historic landscape. These books had quite a profound influence, especially in the Midlands and the South of England. These, coupled with works by Alec Clifton-Taylor (1965) and R. W. Brunskill (1970;1981) on vernacular architecture, generated a popular interest in rural and urban landscape.

Many local history and amenity societies in England developed in the 1960s and 1970s in response to a concern about the changes, mostly for the worse, to both the natural and built environments. This was particularly so in the self-conscious and more prosperous towns of the Midlands and the South. The Civic Amenities Act, 1967, which created the concept of the conservation area, the Town and Country Amenities Act, 1974 and the activities that coincided with the European Architecture Year, 1975 were very much fostered by this public interest and concern. The history societies that evolved were perhaps an expression of the way in which the past of the locality was becoming increasingly important to certain sectors of the population. Many museums responded to these trends. They tapped into, and in many cases sustained, this interest through local history exhibitions which, in particular, explored pre-industrial landscapes and vernacular architecture.

However, a different orientation was adopted by others, responding to a very different set of stimuli and needs. When Britain's industrial base began to be dismantled, particularly from the late 1960s, it was not just premises and machinery that were being put out of use. Whole ways of life, and all that went into individual self-esteem and community life which in many areas had developed over several generations, were also being systematically disengaged and discarded. For some areas of the country, such as the eastern valleys of Wales, there had been decades of periodic boom and slump, which culminated in the 1960s and 1970s with total economic collapse. Study of the past became a means of re-establishing self-esteem through greater self-knowledge.

In the late 1960s the combination of the emergence of the History Workshop at Ruskin College, Oxford, the feminist movement and the Workers' Educational Association (WEA), created and fostered an atmosphere in which workers, particularly women, and all those interested at local level, could reclaim their own history. The recognition of the value of oral testimony, which George Ewart Evans (1971; 1976) and Paul Thompson (1988) had helped to promote, and the employment of Marxist analysis gave the work of these groups, a sharp edge. A vigorous, questioning, probing movement developed, casting aside a great deal of humbug and received opinion in an effort to recover the histories that rightly belonged to those that had created them—ordinary working people.

Some museums were sensitive to this movement and to the circumstances that established and motivated it. For example, Bill Silvester, discussing the philosophy which informed the museum developments in the 1970s at the Abbeydale Industrial Hamlet in Sheffield and which underpinned the plans for an industrial museum at Kelham Island, wrote:

> The idea was to provide a museum for workers and their children, to restore that pride in heritage—so often denied or stolen by others—a museum where yesterday's efforts are recorded with the same dignity as were those of a pyramid sun king from ancient times; a museum where technology acknowledges its debt to working men and women—and not just the 'big names' but the unknown people of the workshops, factories and backrooms. Nor was the museum to pay nostalgic respect to hand-made goods and discard all machine-made articles as modern rubbish. Today's craftsmen and women work on machines; they don't go to museums to be told that machine-made goods are not worth preserving. (Silvester 1981: 164)

People's history, feminism and the techniques of oral history invigorated the study of the past. Indirectly, it also began to stimulate and sensitize some museum activity. For many curators, political and social awareness brought with it a recognition that the kind of 'cultural harmony' and 'cultural heritage' that many museums had sought to present and affirm had not only denied people their history but had also sanitized it of the dissent and diversity that were part and parcel of both the rural and urban social scene. So, a significant proportion of curators, in the main a new generation, moved into the 1980s under the banner of 'social history', with an eagerness to enlarge and further democratize the brief for history in the museum.

But with them were many traditionalist, antiquarian, industrial archaeological and romantic folk life curators, as well as heritage managers, who saw no reason to expand or revise their views or methods. Present, too, were those still committed to the ideas of 'regionalism'. Each in their turn crafted and shaped museums to their ideas of the past; their perceptions of the potential and limitations of the medium of the museum; and their view of visitor needs. In this, museums in the 1980s were to be just as much a creation of their own times and the curators' view of their task as they were 50 or even 100 years before.

Part two. *History curation:*
theories and methods

6. *History in History Museums*

The term 'history', especially qualified as 'social history', has become dominant in museums only relatively recently and is applied very broadly. In general, history is understood to be an open and highly controversial intellectual field, one in which borrowing from other disciplines can take place and is well practised. The use of the term 'history' varies. Sometimes it is used to refer to what happened in the past and at others to refer to the representation of the past in the work of historians. As there are many different views of social order, and about what creates and sustains change and continuity, so there are many different views about, and versions of, history. Similarly, in museum terms, amongst curators there are many different views of what it is about the past, or about the history of people, places or objects, that is being recorded and represented through the medium of the museum.

Whether curators are actually engaged in historical studies is open to question: 'history' in museums may, in fact, be nothing more than a catch-all term, a title of convenience rather than a deliberate affirmation of intellectual intent. Hence, professional self-definition has been a consistent problem. In a review of the achievements of the Social History Curators Group, Stuart Davies at the end of his Chair year 1984-5, reflected:

> The archaeologists are held together by dirt; the fine art curators are held together by taste, and the decorative art curators are held together by class.... The difficulty with the so-called social historians is that few of them are actually social historians... There are local historians, antiquarians, British ethnographers, industrial archaeologists, post-mediaeval archaeologists and all shades in between. [Davies 1985c: 155]

Affiliations and riders

The number of affiliations and orientations to history curatorship practice in Britain is quite dazzling and not a little confusing. Beyond the picture of fragmentation offered by Davies, history museum curators have worked, and continue to operate, under a number of different guises and influences. Thus, the terms bygones, antiquities, ethnology, regional ethnology, anthropology, social anthropology, evolutionary anthropology, regional

53

studies, folk life, folk lore, material culture, popular culture, history, social history, industrial archaeology and history, and more recently multiculturalism have had some currency within 'history' practice in museums this century.

This may be taken to indicate that there has been healthy diversity of approach, even a conscious discovery of new approaches and ideas about the past through the medium of the museum. Under the blanket term for the field or discipline which is 'history', this is, in principle, almost inevitable. After all, history has been described by John Tosh as a hybrid discipline 'which owes its endless fascination and its complexity to the fact that it straddles the humanities and the social sciences' (Tosh 1984: 24). It would follow, then, that the study of the past must evolve and change, and, hence, can appear under many different names with a variety of purposes and theoretical foundations.

Overlying the problems of defining what 'history' is or might be in the museum are three important riders that must be applied in some measure to all curatorial activity. The first is the question of relevance to the public, in that history curators are engaged to provide a service to the public through the medium of the museum. It follows, therefore, that the work produced and the collections amassed should be socially relevant. 'Relevance' may be, as the historian John Tosh has pointed out, 'not a matter of falsifying or diluting the past but rather rescuing from oblivion aspects of that past which speak to us directly'. Quite clearly practical purposes can be entertained without sacrificing scholarship. However, in the museum the reverse should also apply, curatorial scholarship has to have practical purposes. The measure of this can be read as a determining factor in the quality of museums.

Secondly, the representation and interpretation of elements of the recent human past must be pursued through the diverse media that distinguish a museum as a public institution. The museum's primary sources are predominantly physical, visual and oral evidence. There are now many means by which the past can be understood and rendered accessible and through which images are created and records kept. However, none can or does provide images, information or ideas about the past in the ways available to a museum. The museum's record and re-presentation of the past through material evidence of the social environment provide the curator with a specific and well-defined brief. The cultural life of an area and its diversity, both in terms of material and non-material expression, should be ideally the key concern. Thus, history curators are engaged in a very specific form of historiographic process.

Thirdly, the records and 'histories' produced should be accessible to a wide audience, both now and in the future. This means serving a very diverse range of interests and frames of reference. The museum's audience will be united in that emotionally and intellectually they find themselves with some form of social need for the past, however developed or varied this need may be. The central positioning of this within the museum's policy and plans creates the 'public museum'. Yet fulfilling it has become another matter. However, if museums are recording and interpreting the lives of people in the past, then it follows that the people in the present have something to contribute, upon which both empathy and understanding can be built. The human element of observer and observed is constant. Exclude in part or in total that human element and museums move into an increasingly incomprehensible realm where objects are complexly codified not according to their contemporary uses or relationships, but according to different and more obscure patterns of meaning, at the convenience of the curator.

These three riders would appear to prompt the opening-up of historical studies in museums to a broad range of inquiry. In an effort to address closely and faithfully the characteristics, experiences and cultural expressions of an area and its inhabitants, the museum needs to stray further and further away from what is commonly understood by the term 'history'. Indeed, the term itself may be unsatisfactory for the definition of the museum's discipline. This is because much that is undertaken by museums involves not diachronic studies, tracing changes over time, but primarily synchronic ones, where the texture and meaning of a specific moment or period is sought from the surviving material and social evidence of the people who experienced it. Indeed, what museums tend to be engaged in are regionally based cultural studies through which the interplay of social, political and physical environments are explored within an historical dimension.

History in the museum: current discussions

The evidence of coherent development in ideas about what history in the museum could, or should, be comes through occasional papers, published at irregular intervals. It is not necessarily a subject, as important as it is, that has occupied a central position within curatorial discussion. Instead, ideas of the curator's responsibility to record and represent the past are to be found more often implicitly expressed in direct curatorial activities, such as exhibition, rather than explicitly through debate and challenge within the profession itself.

The views that have directly emerged in the last 20 years have provided some guide to the range of perspectives to be found within the body of history curatorship. An analysis of the shifts in the range of interests in museums has been provided by Stuart Davies. He has argued that the influences on history in museums should be seen as a series of replacements. He writes: 'the influence of Geraint Jenkins was perhaps replaced by W. G. Hoskins and then by Raphael Samuel and other acolytes of the history workshop approach' (1985b: 158). Such a throw-away analysis does not necessarily bear examination.

Only one of the three cited is a practising curator, Geraint Jenkins, whose influences like many regional ethnologists working in Scotland, Wales and Ireland, spring from historical geography and the Scandinavian schools of ethnology or cultural history curatorship. Attention to the whole fabric of society and its position within the local, physical environment has characterized this way of thinking. The influence of Geraint Jenkins and his colleagues remains strong, not least because the literature they produced has a central place in the current considerations of curatorship practice. However, what Jenkins describes and argues is not necessarily 'history' curatorship, charting the cause and effects of change over time.

The influence of W. G. Hoskins on history at local level has been quite profound. By drawing attention to the evidence which the physical and built environment holds, particularly of pre-industrial England, Hoskins opened up history 'on the ground' to a very wide constituency both of amateur and professional historians. The influence of W. G. Hoskins on museums results from the very positive climate of local studies that his work created and the fact that for a decade or more post-graduate museum studies students specializing in history took a course on pre-industrial historical topography at the Department of English Local History that Hoskins founded at the University of Leicester. In the late 1960s and 1970s much of the new history curatorship in England adopted perspectives that were born of the Hoskins school.

The influence of the History Workshop has opened new fields of inquiry and has brought a depth of analysis to the production of histories. Most important of all it has unlocked the study of the past from its university preserves, enabling it to be engaged in not just by the intellectually privileged, but by all those with energy and a critical sense of inquiry, hence the vitality of history outside formal education.

The influence of this on museum practice is difficult to gauge in that although the term 'social history' in the last 15 years has come to replace 'folk life' and 'regional studies' in reference to museum work and representation, it does not necessarily follow that the 'social history' in museums has undergone the rigorous degree of analysis and peer-group criticism that has characterized much that has taken place under the influence of History Workshop. Granted, museums have now moved into consideration of the industrial histories of Britain and are using oral testimony more than before, but it is likely this would have happened anyway. In effect, much current history practice in museums has been in the shadow of History Workshop. The extent to which history in the museum as it is now practised has been directly influenced by it, in terms of methodology or criticism, is very much open to question.

Davies's contention appears to exclude a range of influences that are being brought to bear, particularly the work in material culture studies and artefact analysis that has emerged from the USA and Canada in the last 20 years or so. Nor does Davies point to wider intellectual trends that are pertinent to history museum practice (see, for example, Schlereth 1980), but have been ignored or not entered into with any seriousness, such as developments in cultural studies, Marxist critique or structuralism (for example, Pearce 1986; 1986a; 1986b; 1987).

If, however, Davies's overall contention holds good, that there have been successive replacements in the prime influences on the curatorship, then this exposes the vulnerability of curatorial practice to fashion and fad. The

Figure 4.   Subject specialization has produced very narrow views of objects in museums. This is especially true of transport museums.

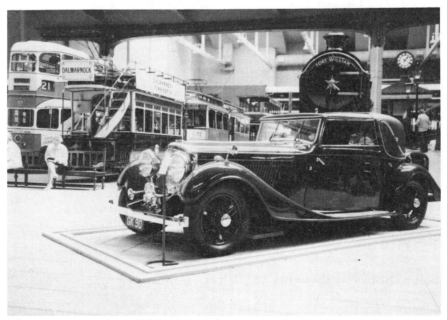

Figure 5.   In such exhibitions, questions about the context of an object and its social meanings are rarely raised.

multiplicity or self-definitions, terms and approaches may not necessarily be evidence of healthy diversity of approach but indicative of a state of intellectual chaos, where history curatorship staggers about in search of a viable name, common purpose and approach. The absence of in-service training in history curatorship theory and method has perpetuated the situation, failing to build on the worth and experiences of some of the best aspects of history in museums today.

This situation is compounded by the fact that there is not a body of British literature as such that reviews or criticizes the nature of history in museums or the practice of history curatorship. There is no comparative literature to that currently emerging from Nordiska Museet in Stockholm, or the material culture and folklore specialists in the USA and Canada. Therefore, there is a dependence on overseas material and on random, though often extremely useful, case studies of museum activities in Britain. This apparent 'ad hocery' in Britain obscures the fact that some thought has gone into aspects of the nature of history in museums, and that curatorship need not be, as some people might believe, a purely practical activity, with no place for theory or possibility for intellectual development.

The stage that history curatorship has reached in its own debate on the nature of history in museums may, in part at least, be born out of the fact that in the last 20 years or so, history curatorship has become in many senses a prisoner of its own self-justification and language. This has a historic dimension. When curatorship devoted to the recording and interpreting of a more-recent human past finally emerged as a specialist area in museums after the war, the broader perspectives of regional ethnology and cultural studies were the points of theoretical reference. In this the influence of the Scandinavian schools of ethnology, in particular the work of Sigurd Erixon, and of historical geography in Ireland, Scotland and Wales was strong. But this failed to develop in England, although it became established elsewhere in Britain, and, with the lack of any strong academic influence coming from universities, regional ethnology became, to some extent, intellectually isolated. This was especially evident when, in the late 1960s and 1970s, there was an enormous growth in the number of museums in England. These were established to deal with 'The Past'. As a result, for one reason or another, 'history' became the common currency in museum practice. Particularly in England, the skills of the geographer, sociologist or cultural anthropologists were to varying degrees set aside in an effort to operate under the 'history' banner. A new generation of curators emerged, self-styled as 'social historians'; they consolidated the immediate language of 'history' in the museum.

Some curatorial thoughts on history in museums

Curators themselves have substantially shaped the form and content of 'history' in museums. Although their views have appeared more often as statements rather than as part of a developing dialogue, they have, nevertheless, brought some influence to bear on, or at least disclosed, current concerns or attitudes. The only textbook, as such, on history practice within museums in Britain is a small but thought-provoking booklet by J. W. Y. Higgs, then curator of the Museum of English Rural Life, published by the Museums Association in 1963. In it Higgs identifies the museum's concern as being the cultural and geographical area in which it is situated. Higgs struggled with a definition of the museum's subject, folk life (at the time the dominant term), and the folk museum. He had to concede that 'the real truth is that the scope of folk museums is so wide that no one term really covers the subject, for such museums must inevitably deal with ethnology, ethnography, archaeology, anthropology and sociology not to mention history' (1963).

In this, Higgs may have been tapping into the essence of museum practice and its central dilemma. It needs to make reference to a broad span of ideas and lines of inquiry, but to do this it must be well-informed and flexible. However, possibly in recognition that museums were expanding without reference to these ideas and the necessary flexibility of approach, Higgs was forced to excuse the problem by arguing that 'the terminology is measurably less important that the work of the museum'. In sum, he believed that the folk museum should endeavour to show 'man's activities in relation to the environment in which he lives' (1963: 4). The terminology was, and is, too important to be excused and has been a matter to which some curators have returned.

Alexander Fenton, Research Director, National Museums of Scotland, writing in similar vein in 1965, argued that the historical museum should try to show that local history is not static, that it is and has been in a state of flux subject to all kinds of internal and external influences and stimuli which bring about changes. The study of material culture and dialect for Fenton reveals relationships between tools and their users and the tools themselves and the terrain; questions of geography, social organizations and economic status have to be raised. He sees complexes of material culture as resembling dialects, which vary not because of separation or isolation, but because each is in a fashion a reflex of the culture pattern of the community that uses it (Fenton 1985).

Geraint Jenkins, Curator of the Welsh Folk Museum, also ascribed to a view of museums as being a means of recording and interpreting the broad cultural context. He succinctly summarized his view of the essential task of the history museum and hence its territory:

> The mere collection and study of material objects, the mere recording of a building or workshop is not enough, for in ethnological research one has to go further and discover the social organization, the economic traditions, language, lore customs, and the whole culture associated with those objects . . . collection is not an end in itself but merely the means of reaching those people to whom those material objects had the meaning of everyday things. It is our duty to concern ourselves not only with the objects produced by the inhabitants of a region, not only with their homes, their fields and workshops, but with the whole tradition, the life that gave existence to those material things. [Jenkins 1974: 7]

This theme of the museum's concern with the social, cultural and material environment has been taken up by others. For example, in 1984 Roy Brigden, Curator of the Museum of English Rural Life, stressed that the distinguishing feature of the social history museum is its concern for context—historical, geographical and cultural (Brigden 1984: 170). Rosemary Allen, Keeper of Social History at the North of England Open-Air Museum, Beamish, saw a similar commitment for the museum although in terms of its responsibility to reveal the relationship in society between needs, resources and traditions. She argues that the main purpose of the curator is to record and interpret the way of life and tradition of a region, whether rural or urban through its material and non-material culture (Allen 1984: 179).

These views, which appear to hold in common ideas of cultural studies through social relationships, now have their detractors. Stuart Davies, Director of Kirklees Museum Service, has rejected such ideas, at least in terms of the twentieth-century, when he argued that 'the social and economic legislation of the late nineteenth and early twentieth centuries all but eradicated the influence of the local'. He goes on to suggest that the influence of general social and economic movements on the locality is much greater than most local exhibitions... would allow (Davies 1985b: 29).

This view appears to suggest a degree of uniformity and standardization of experience that perhaps would be as hard to find by social historians as would an organic relationship between people and their natural environment by purist folk life specialists. However, it is a view indicative of the direct influence of the traditions of British historical scholarship being brought to bear on curatorial practice, particularly as it appears to ignore the dimensions which social studies can contribute to curatorial work.

In a Britain which can still produce a hill farmer in the Scottish Highlands, a little Mester in Sheffield, a line operative in a cigarette factory in Glasgow, a Rastafarian band in Birmingham or a shop assistant in Harrods, it seems difficult to assume that the influence of the local has been all but eradicated by larger social and economic movements: their life-styles and experiences would appear to suggest otherwise. In the 1980s the locality may take on a very different meaning than say 100 years ago, and may be perceived as a broader area both geographically and culturally, but it is hard to see it not still existing. Perhaps in its most poignant it is revealed in the North–South divide: which in itself glosses over other, deeper, local divisions and experiences.

But Davies's arguments may also be indicative of the changing nature of curatorial practice that might be resisting the connection between recording and interpreting, as Iowerth Peate had it, 'the people who matter' and the tons of objects that now constitute museum collections. The evidence of the past as expressed through the collections amassed in many museums does not always bear the scrutiny that a historian would apply. Not only is the meaning of much of this material lost or obscured by poor documentation, it is also obscured if the questions put to it fall too closely within traditional history practice.

In 1987 Jenkins showed an impatience with current curatorial practice that had failed to move on and that eulogized and had become obsessed with the small and incidental while ignoring larger and more-significant cultural and historic trends. He observed how in many museums

> artefacts from sugar cutters to box mangles and from mortising chisels to candlesticks are held up to view as if they were Monet paintings without reference whatsoever to their historical, social or cultural background. There must be progress, there must be more professionalism not only in interpretation and research but also in marketing [of the museum] or we shall be plagued for ever with collections of bygones held up to view by a visiting public that demands more. These people and certainly our nations deserve better. [Jenkins 1987: 17]

Jenkins touched the nerve here. The manifestations of poor and irrelevant history practice in museums are found in strange and unbalanced collections, formed with little notion of the cultural past or present of the region. They are also found in meaningless moribund displays betokening 'social life' or 'domestic' with a rag-bag of odds and ends, and bits and pieces. He could have gone on and cited museums where more space is given to labelling than to visual images, or where objects have become little more than advertisements for publications on sale in the bookshop. The criticism is even more pertinent when held against museum practice that provides images which inform, challenge and even move the viewer: this we know can be done and reveals history museums operating near their best.

The museum has the potential and the capacity for touching the quick of local, human experience and for offering stunning and challenging insights into a personal and very human past. That museums often do not succeed in this regard may be due to a failure firstly to grasp ideas that have been offered by curators themselves, and secondly to be aware of the ongoing debates on the nature of history, its relationships with anthropology and sociology particularly through community studies. These are fruitful areas for the theory of history in the museums.

In sum, history curatorship and 'history' in museums is largely unquantifiable. It is not known how many history museums and history curators there are. Their principal frames of reference can only be assumed or deduced from the varied and, at times, contradictory practice of curatorship. If there is some form of intellectual basis to the work, say a notion of a 'social and material past', it is largely unexplored other than indirectly through curatorial activity. This does not, however, deny the potential of the museum or the contribution to be made to our understanding of the past through history curatorship. This is vividly indicated by a number of museums where highly professional curators provide a record and interpretation of the past which is purposeful, astutely directed and usually highly individualistic. But the absence of a firm and challenging intellectual foundation to history museum practice has to be noted.

7. *Theoretical Frameworks*

History museum practice may be united in its concern with the past, the historical dimension to its study, but divided over the nature of that past and how it should be seen and approached. Although a strong body of opinion holds that people are the essential subject of the museum, the positioning of those people within the museum's view of the past and the ways in which they relate to the objects gathered as evidence in their name is not so certain or well established. Some thought needs to be applied to the nature of history in the museum and how knowledge of the past can be put together there.

The purpose of theory is to strengthen museum practice by giving it a foundation from which such practice can develop. Curatorial activity should have some basis from which it launches its approach to social history. If it exists in a vacuum, it is likely to be a weak fabrication, based on convenience rather than conviction and depth of thought. A theoretical foundation for history museum practice may be found in the ongoing debate between historians and anthropologists. This debate has particular relevance for museums because it has been in part dealing with social signification and communication through the very means that are the museum's central concern: objects, custom and practice, and expression through language and music. It is given further definition in the ideas that inform community studies.

Social being or social becoming

In many respects the conventions and traditions of historical studies, particularly those expressed through narrative history, have their limitations within museum practice. For museums to operate under the 'history' banner is to align, however loosely, with the traditions of British historical scholarship. Kevin Thomas, in a highly influential paper on history and anthropology, described the traditions of such scholarship as 'resting upon a rigorous command of the primary sources, a distaste for theory and speculation, and a proper aversion to the superficiality which a nodding acquaintance with other disciplines frequently brings in its train' (Thomas 1963: 3). This must strike a chord of recognition, especially for those curators who resist the idea that there could, or indeed should, be ideas about history in the museum and museum practice.

The 'history' tag can impose a much too narrow, even inappropriate, range of interests upon the museum. That which constitutes the raw material of evidence in the museum is found to be singularly uncooperative and unilluminating if the historian's broad interests and inquiries about the cause and effect of change and continuity are brought to bear. The questions are not the right ones and as a result puzzling discord is found. This may be because the traditional historian looks through documentary evidence for movement, action and words. But material and sometimes non-material evidence in museums often remains still, inactive and silent to such questioning. Although objects may yield information through their fabric, form and construction, they are more co-operative as springboards for questions than as sole sources that can provide comprehensive answers.

Further dislocations can occur, born out of the misapplication of history models. For example, within the dominant narrative traditions of history, relatively narrow fields of inquiry have been engaged in, where a central theme, idea or incident has predominated. Research and interpretation provide images of people who have assumed a shape, usually one-dimensional, according to the historian's ideas and the definition of the area for study. They act, speak and perform with a degree of free will that is likely to be more at the convenience of the narrative rather than necessarily a product or reflection of the cultural setting or period of study (Philipp 1983). Thus, people are viewed as 'historical figures', operating solely within the historian's range of interest and not owning to any other network, connection or relationship.

Arguably, this is a recurrent problem within history curatorship, where the material amassed is treated as sole sources and exclusive documents, employed in linear story-telling to the convenience of a pre-set narrative. Its use is liable to push around, even obscure, the people and situations whence the material came. Thus, machines, modes of transport and costume-clad mannikins are held up for public view as conclusive statements, admitting no social and cultural meaning or connections. This often crude over-simplification of messages, through exhibition and publication, denies or avoids a much more complex although illuminating reading of people as both creatures and creators of their own societies. In this respect, museum collections are the remnants of a vital, operative part of individual lives which responded to the larger cultural norms and values.

The museum databank of objects and a range of other visual material and sound records needs to be understood from a different standpoint, as much more than the raw materials of the historian's craft, but as part, a remainder and reminder, of cultural expression and social signification where material can have multiple layers of meaning. Objects, customs and oral transmissions are the instruments of a complex and highly coded social language. To begin to grasp this means that the museum historian must come to terms with elements of human experiences and relationships which may be interactive, shifting and complicated, but the appreciation of which reveals a texture and humanity so frequently denied in the narrative traditions.

The historian E. P. Thompson, in his rejection of the narrative's conventional ambiguity and crude reductionism, has argued that 'history is made up of episodes and if we cannot get inside them, we cannot get inside history at all ' (1965: 338). But to get inside such episodes requires an ability to reach inside and understand the experiences, behaviour and attitudes of people in the past. This is a crucial and challenging process demanding new questions and methods of inquiry. June Philipp has pointed out: 'to discover the experience of people in the past, what they made of it, and with what effect, expressive behaviour or social action must be painstakingly attended, its forms uncovered and its meaning construed' (1983: 350).

With these needs identified, some historians have acknowledged the value of anthropology with its emphasis on 'social relations and treating culture as a vehicle or medium for social interaction rather than an end in itself' (Lewis 1985: 19). Thomas suggests that for such historians 'the attraction of anthropology, whether 'functional', 'structural' or 'cultural', is that it does constitute . . . an attempt to explain things in terms of each other rather than treating them separately, like patients in a hospital' (1963: 7). Essentially, it helps pose new questions and, in turn, creates new problems that have to be solved. If, as Thomas has reminded us, the justification for historical study must ultimately be that it enhances our self-consciousness, enabling us to see ourselves in perspective and move towards the greater freedom that comes from self-knowledge, then the people in the past need to be seen as more than shadow puppets moving over the historian's stage. The historian needs to be acutely conscious of people, the traces of whose lives are the substance of museum collections and, hence, the devices of any historical study the museum undertakes.

Therefore, in the museum context, the ability to reach inside contexts, to follow through historical episodes is crucial if the very material which is the *raison d'être* of the museum form is to be understood and interpreted. Although curators have stressed the need to see objects in their physical contexts, this displaces and even perhaps obscures a prior need, to see a wider cultural context and the human action within it. The way that people act is seen by June Philipp as being generated within a social and cultural context 'whose forms—relations, roles, rules, values, norms and symbols—shape its logic and project its meaning' (1983: 350). Through these means human actions are, in Philipp's view, either constrained, regulated or classified, or, alternatively, enabled. Philipp goes on to make observations on the reflexive process of social life wherein forms, expectations and messages are received and assessed by participants. In this, the use of objects and the communication of ideas and experiences through oral transmission and through custom is an important, if not central, part of the reading.

The emphasis therefore shifts from the telling of the past through the narrative. For the historian and the museum this prompts adjustments: the event giving way to action, story to episode, the diachronic to synchronic, sequence to structure and relationships. Shared or common experiences through which the processes of expression, expectation and communication operated and continue to operate become the central concern in the effort to read past action and to get inside an episode. But to make any sense of the past, the cultural context has to be reconstructed.

Philipp insists that looking through culture is a different exercise from looking at culture (1983: 351). From such an approach, complexity of experience and a multiplicity of meanings can be construed and ordered which, in turn, will reveal forms of institutional relationships and webs of structured meaning. Hence their inter-connectedness may be sorted out or suggested. But this takes careful collection of data and the willingness to strip away received interpretations, and the re-casting of events, in the effort to find or construe a form of lived reality.

This moves the potential of history in the museum away from the historian's traditional practice of the narrative to methods which borrow ideas and concepts from a range of other disciplines and fields. Although there is now ample precedent, this is very dangerous ground as such borrowings bring with them their own heresies and detractors, and it is here that the claim of superficiality could be made. Similarly, such electicism runs the risk of being dismissed as opportunism or sheer amateurism. However, history museum practice is continually weakened without strong, relevant ideas to support it. Most important of all, the museum has the potential to aid the recovery of a past made up of a massive stage cast of individual players. The museum has to find ways of fulfilling this potential.

Essentially what has to take place in history practice in museums is the locating of new questions. If history can be seen, as E. P. Thompson argues, as the study of 'meaning in context', then museums are well placed to reveal such meaning, dealing as they do with the material through which meaning was conveyed; the possession and juxtaposition of objects and space, and social expression through various forms of oral transmission and custom. These forms were part of what Thompson has described as the 'symbolism which derives from the ulterior cognitive system of the community'. The past considered in this way offers the opportunity for highly textured, multi-faceted insights into the lives people have led and their experiences. The past considered alternatively as a linear process risks moving over people, their experiences and relationships in an effort to reach the tidy piece of text that conveniently and finally says, or implies, 'The End'.

Thompson urges an examination of the questions asked of the evidence available to us, and the examination of customary culture, not so much through the process and logic of change as through the recovery of past states of consciousness and the texturing of social and domestic relationships, 'questions which are more concerned with being than becoming'. The museum would seem a not unreasonable site for such discoveries.

But to do this there is also a need to be conscious of the act of historical production and the forces and influences brought to bear upon it; history is written in our own contemporary images. The much quoted, even over-quoted, first line of L. P. Hartley's novel *The Go-Between* (1953) is particularly relevant here. 'The past is a foreign country, they do things differently there'. The reference to the 'foreign country' should remind us that the cultural norms, rules, values and experiences are not our own and that we risk making grave or misplaced adjustments to the past if the histories construed avoid this recognition. The second part, 'they do things differently there', implies the casting of the historian almost as colonial explorer-cum-missionary, searching for the 'otherness' of people in the past, but in so doing taking with them on their travels all their ideological and cultural baggage and the effects of modern living. The historian can be sensitive, careful and questioning, but never a totally impartial or innocent observer: the cultural baggage is always there.

Taking bearings

Some form of framework for museum activity needs to be established within which museums can address questions concerned with 'social being'. One of the ways this can be approached is to consider how the museum sees and views the area in which it is based.

Most museums have terms of reference which give them a defined geographical area of coverage, for example, the Museum of 'Lincolnshire' Life, 'Somerset' Rural Life Museum, the 'Welsh' Folk Museum. Alternatively, they may be concerned with a workplace or activity such a Quarry Bank 'Mill' Styal and 'Big Pit', Blaenafon. Occasionally, national, and even international, coverage may be implied: the 'Imperial' War Museum, the 'National' Museum of Labour History.

Within these geographic or locational frameworks, there are various ways in which museums can seek access to the past. One means currently developing is through the concept of the community. Museums of community history are growing in number. They aim specifically to get close to the kinds of experiences and ways of being that belong to people of the museum's area. Community museums also tend to have a firm commitment to involving local people in a partnership with the museum, so that the past becomes something real because its discovery is a co-operative venture.

One such example is Springburn Museum in Glasgow, opened in May 1986. Under the curatorship of Mark O'Neill, the museum has been developed not to romanticize the past but to express 'the ideal of the community which was once a living reality in Springburn'. The museum can be seen as a monument to 'the resilience and courage of people who, often in conditions of extreme hardship had the creativity to organize a wide range of formal and informal organizations of mutual support'. But the Springburn Museum is not seen as an escape from the need to face the present and the future, but a place where history can be uncovered and used to give perspective to current events and concerns. With this end in view, the museum is committed to both retrospective and contemporary recording. Its exhibition in 1988 on the young people of Springburn, which explored the contemporary concerns and culture of local people in their teens, was a case in point. O'Neill has two beliefs underlying his approach. The first is that the 'real demand is to express people's tenacity in preserving human values in hostile environments and their determination to bring those values with them into the future'. The second is that 'the response of museums to this demand is not a matter of resources, but of will and imagination' (O'Neill 1987).

The notion of 'community' is a useful means of identifying common interest and concerns: their manifestations, contradictions and changes. It can be used in all history museums as, regardless of degrees of wealth or location, the social nature of our existence creates bonds through common interests. Whereas not all societies are communities, all communities are societies, with distinct cultural norms and values. They provide the fine and sometimes definitive textures to our means of social being. Through community studies, ways of organizing, interpreting and comparing data can be developed. This approach has both resonance and currency as the popular, social expectation and experience of 'community' is very strongly held.

However, it should be kept in mind that the real nature of 'the community' has been seriously questioned. For example, Alan MacFarlane has argued that

> the belief in such communities is one of the most powerful of myths in industrial society, shaping not only policy and government, with the movement towards 'community centres', 'community welfare' and 'community care', but also affecting thought and research. Expecting to find communities, the prophecy fulfilled itself and communities were found. [1977a: 632]

A similar observation was made at the Museums' Association Conference in 1987, when Martyn Heighton was prepared to describe the word 'community' as a catch-all to give credence to protect group and government action alike (1987: 61).

So, given that there is a body of opinion that would see the word 'community' as a title of convenience, how has, and is, the 'community' generally seen? Ronald Frankenberg defined the community as a body of people having overriding 'economic interests which are the same or complementary'. In his view the community

> work together, also pray and play together. Their common interest in things gives them a common interest in each other. They quarrel with each other but are never indifferent to each other. They form a group of people who meet face to face, although this may mean they end up back to back. [1969: 238]

As a form it may be defined in a variety of other ways: working (or not working), praying or playing together may each in themselves be some basis for community. These activities provide circumstances through and by which people come together, find and consolidate the interests they have in common. It follows that as people may easily find themselves belonging to more than one set of 'community interests'—at work and at leisure as well as place of residence or worship—the 'community' cannot be a total and exclusive unit. Instead, it is fluid and in constant change, if only because people grow older and their needs and attitudes change. Inevitably, the size, scale and characteristics of communities will vary enormously and, by virtue of their origins, be distinctly individual. In this, a loose grouping of individuals may be defined by themselves, or by others, as a community because there is something which they appear to hold in common. This may be a place, goods or things, or even a sentiment or sense of belonging.

This poses major theoretical problems as the lack of consistency, especially in complex societies, renders 'communities' an imprecise term. Communities may not be directly comparative: the characteristics are frequently idiosyncratic, even contradictory. All may be defined simply in the eye and mind of the beholder or participant and will almost inevitably be multi-layered. Indeed, the idea of the community may be more sustainable than the community itself. Even so, the notion of the community is a useful one, creating a point of cohesion for people otherwise divided and isolated, or undergoing social stress or dislocation. If people need history to establish their sense of belonging, they also need some notion of community which is both geographic and social, to locate further their past and their present. The notion of community may then be extended consciously or otherwise to a cultural reference, to the social norms and values that distinguish people and their 'communities', one from the other.

In any given geographical area, a museum may be addressing a range of community interests, both explicit and implied. This gives a museum a means through which it can explore and recover past experiences, looking at coherence as well as division and change. The curator may be observing or dealing with a number of dominant communities or alternatively 'ideas of communities'. Inevitably, these may overlap, change and, at times, redefine themselves. In form they may vary from the very close-knit (often in itself a product of adversity such as wartime, industrial action or shortages), to the loose-knit (such as the leafier suburbs), where individual interests in the community are not so demanding. Given that the idea of homogeneous communities that work, pray and play together is too rigid and simplified a notion through which to view past actions, it might be more useful to view 'communities' through what MacFarlane has called the 'activity-specific' sense (1977b: 13), by looking at communities as they have emerged either through work, domestic settings or social contact.

The emphasis is, therefore, on those aspects and manifestations that are thought to bind people together and the means through which communities signify or expose their cultural characteristics and joint experiences. This runs the risk of continually dealing in those experiences or aspects of the past that were largely consensual. Indeed, emphasis on those characteristics that divide or differentiate communities one from another is rarely entertained within the museum, even though this is a vivid indicator of social definition: for example, the juxtaposition of the clothes of the rich and the poor is rarely made in the costume museum. This is not to say that it cannot be done, as the Museum of Oxford illustrated when it explored living standards in the 1880s by the comparison of working-class housing and consumption, in the Jericho area of Oxford, with that of the rising middle classes in the north of the city.

Looking more closely

To accept an approach within the community studies framework, requires that museums also address the parts individuals play within the notional or real community. When an individual acts according to a part, a role is being played. Roles can be ascribed by birth or social position, attached through some form of social purpose or achieved through qualification and effort. The prerequisite of playing a role is that there are other people playing complementary or supplementary roles. Role performances must have a relevant audience with which to interact: thus, the mother–child roles, which in the child's mid-life appear to reverse to child–mother roles. Every individual has more than one role to play: thus, mother, sister, child, lover, friend, customer, client, employer or colleague may be played by one person within a life-span. When these multiple roles lead to conflict, some system of prioritization has to be employed. But it would be unreasonable to compartmentalize these roles too strictly as performed by one individual as they may overlap.

Each role is played with its own separate means of signification and expressions of role-relationships. Thus, the use of objects and space, customary practice and communication through speech, story and music can be part of a complex pattern of personal and cultural expression appropriate to the norms and values of a role and role-relationships. These operate according to the patterns and accepted systems that apply within the cultural norms of the wider 'community'. Frankenberg has suggested that there are five categories of roles: kinship and ethnic, economic, political, ritual or religious, and recreational. Their study can reveal inequality of role-relationship, a factor which may be closely associated with social class, status, ethnic origin and sex.

The structure of the community and the roles played by people within it are reinforced and at times developed by the networks that exist within and through it. Networks do not have boundary, unit or co-ordinating organization, but instead consist of a web of friendship and acquaintances that the individual builds up through life. Such networks can enhance and bolster social roles, for example 'the old-boy network'. Feminist history has revealed the importance of the women's networks that developed in local working-class neighbourhoods. These acted in support of women and their families, especially through the difficulties of work, child-rearing and poverty (for example, Ross 1983).

The community-role-network models have a use in that they offer a means of looking at the place in which the museum is located and the various social layers and connections the curator encounters. The notion of community helps the museum locate the common-interest social groups within its area and the broad spans of cultural patterns to which these gave rise. This prevents generalizations such as the 'working class', and forces a closer look at the individual nature of the social bonds created locally through the forms and varieties of work, housing, religious observance and leisure that existed at any point in time. The idea of role helps the museum to appreciate means of being and behaviour that existed within local community/groups, and the multiplicity of roles that any individual plays. The notion of network gives museums a means of tracing the connections; the ways in which people related to and supported one another. Such a model is relevant to museum work because the signification of community, role and network exists precisely through the material that is the museum's prime interest: through objects and other forms of social expression. Within this framework, it is possible for the museum to identify key areas for study, recording and acquisition of material. These can consistently hold the museum to the distinct social characteristics of the locality and help expose both its variety and stages of change.

But for sociologists the imprecise concept of the community has rendered 'community studies' highly questionable. In 1971 Bell and Newby identified 94 different definitions of 'community' and concluded that 'all of the definitions deal with people. Beyond this common basis there is no agreement' (1971: 21). In its stead, models based on the concept of local social systems have been developed (see, in particular, Stacey 1969). These have particularly been advocated, in the light of the dubious nature of 'communities', to explore instead local social structures and processes. This is a fruitful area for curators in as much as it tests the assumptions about a locality, forcing them to examine wide generalizations and conclusions arising from more-vague concepts.

But where to begin? Many museums begin with dominant modes of production and question how these shaped the forms of community and cultural patterns within the museum's area. This approach tends to be concerned with dominant hegemonies, but can be expanded to consider forms of resistance which give rise to subcultures through which deviation and dissent were conveyed. Other approaches can stem from systems of belief, the ways in which people define themselves through their religious observance and, in turn, determine their views of themselves and the world (Goa 1979).

Curators will find that from any approach to the study of the past there are many questions to be raised. Indeed, any production of history is ultimately about both questions and the questioner. These will vary according to who you are, when you are and where you are. The questions left unasked by the museum shatter our ears with their silences. Ten objects in a glass case with a label saying 'domestic life' or 'Victorian things' does nothing to recover the past. However, questions that lead to their exploration as signification of domestic roles, social domination, advanced levels of skills, or late nineteenth-century mass production and consumerism might provide something of value.

These broad theoretical frameworks offer means through which museums can connect more fully and, indeed, more purposefully with the past and present they are intended to record and interpret. They offer not just guidelines, reminders and food for thought but a continual challenge to museum practice to live up to its social responsibilities and fulfil its potential. This is vital in as much as museums must have some form of theoretical starting point in order 'to make sense of reality' (Szabó 1986: 10). There is limited point in collecting information and repackaging it for the public through the forms of exhibition and publication without some preliminary hypothesis about the connections between researched data.

The ideas outlined above are particularly appropriate in that museums are situated in a very privileged position and can easily avail themselves of opportunities to pursue recording and collecting work in fulfillment of the spirit in which these ideas were constructed. This is so because of the local and regional location of museums and their positions—real and potential—within popular consciousness. This gives them direct access not just to individuals and public archives but also to the many mechanisms which facilitate or give life and purpose to 'social being': from workplaces, co-operatives and unions to employers' organizations, self-help groups, parish concils, Gingerbread Groups, Tenants' Associations, old people's homes, hockey clubs, Round Table, political organizations, folk clubs, schools, community centres and religious organizations. Omitted from such a random list are the individual and the outsider, who can be just as valid a point of contact for the curator as formal and informal groups. Sensitively and astutely working through and with local people and evidence of their past enables the museum to centre itself as active social recorder and participant, engaging in both contemporary and retrospective work.

But the extent to which any museum is prepared to become involved in this way will depend upon a number of factors. Not least of these will be how the role and responsibility of the museum is perceived. Whichever approach is adopted will be ultimately revealed in the sum of the collections and data the museum builds. This is the central and most fundamental of all museum activities, as the information a museum gathers forms the bedrock of all its subsequent activities, whether these are defined and determined in the short term according to immediate exhibition needs, or in the long term, through the building of a social archive.

The gathering of information not only creates the identity of the museum but also to a large extent it shapes and determines the images of the past and the present which the museum conveys and hands on to future generations. Unlike any other agency in the history field, the museum acts as both an archive or databank and as an interpreter and arranger of its material. In this, it is continually determining how the past should be seen, as much by what it chooses to acquire and the depth of information recorded, as by what it chooses to leave out. The museum is an archive; the curator is its editor.

8. *Methodological Foundations*

In Swedish museums the word *dokumentation* (documentation) is used to refer to the broad range of activities, research, fieldwork, recording, acquisition and cataloguing associated with creating museum archives and collections. In Britain 'documentation' is used almost exclusively for those procedures involved in cataloguing museum material and there is no blanket or collective term for this central area of museum activity. However, the application of the Swedish sense of the word prompts museums to provide well-rounded and thoughtful studies of 'social being' and everyday existence.

Indeed, to cast the museum in the expansive role of documenter, rather than the narrow role of collector, is to presuppose a broader range of record and acquisition. In this, the curator is concerned with the depth of knowledge and, hence, qualitative rather than quantitative archives and collections. The critical nature of this fundamental area of curation is obvious. Information gathered during such processes creates the bedrock of all subsequent museum activities. From it, exhibitions will be formed and educational activities developed. It will provide primary sources for researchers and the basis from which publications will emerge. Further, it will be a reference archive used to answer enquiries. Collectively, this information will form a long-term archive for public use and a record of human existence.

The evidence gathered and acquired by museums takes many forms. The principal and traditional interest has been material evidence, that is three-dimensional objects. These range dramatically in size, shape and substance: from a pigeon loft to a commemorative teacup; from a fiddle-drill to a CND badge; from a power loom to a pay-packet. In general terms, the distinguishing feature of all museums, in fact their determining characteristic, has been this emphasis on the object. Museums directly concerned with the recent human past are consistent with this, but the scope has had to be much wider. The social and cultural emphasis has necessitated, even demanded, that equal weight be given to all forms of evidence. Film, photography, oral testimony, dialect and language studies, music, song and story, are as important to history museums as objects.

The skills involved with the curatorial processes of research and acquisition are wide-ranging and by no means confined to being academic. The degree of discernment and ability required to gather, collate, order, evaluate, analyse and synthesize evidence is considerable. This is because history curatorial practice is a very public and, hence, influential area of historical production. It can form public understanding of the past. Facts have to be correct; interpretation has to be reasoned with due regard to available evidence. Therefore, academic skills are essential. But in museum work they have to be strongly supported by a range of social skills. The curator must be able to communicate, inquire, observe, record and, most important of all, listen.

The gathering of material and its quality very much depends on the abilities of the curator. It is presupposed that the curator has a special talent for the work and an ability to draw on the required academic and social skills. It can be, essentially, a very personal field, especially where research by interview and participant observation is concerned. If these social encounters are omitted, avoided or handled badly, then subsequent records in the museum will be mechanical and lacking in the vital human contribution to the study. The equipment and resources available, from cameras and tape recorders to acquisition budget, will be of little relevance if the curator's thoughts, feelings and judgement are not brought to bear or are in some way inadequate (Szabó 1986: 10).

The mechanisms through which theory is put into practice include the strategies adopted in the formation of collections; the choice of fields of study and areas of interest; and the means by which these are tested and checked for relevance.

Strategies in collection and documentation

Museums adopt a number of strategies to fulfil and perpetuate their collecting role. In many respects these are founded on what might be termed museum tradition: accepted procedures and areas of interest. For many museums this process operates, in general terms, on two levels: first, in what is commonly known as 'passive acquisition', the acceptance of material, usually objects or photographs, as offered to museums at will from members of the public. This material remains largely passive until researched. Many museums are highly dependent on such gifts and most have 'collecting policy' statements which define their interests and strengthen their hand when wishing to acquire material or refuse unwanted offers.

The museum's relationship with the public in this regard is an important one. In the public's mind, the museum is quite simply that which is on display, and therefore when material is offered it is usually of like kind. Museums that strike the public's imagination and affiliation tend to receive a significant number of offers of material. Of these, although much will be useful, there may be a proportion that falls outside the museum's area of interest or that duplicates material already held. However erratic, this well-established point of contact holds out real potential in the building of collections. In particular, it provides opportunities not only to extend the information a museum holds but also to enlarge its network of contacts. A wealth of information can be derived through passive acquisition: behind most of the objects offered is a host of ordinary, everyday, personal connections, and occasionally some extraordinary stories, too.

The role of the museum in this is to determine whether the material offered, and what it represents and relates, has significant meaning in terms of the social and cultural past of the area. This is more complex than it seems. It is not difficult to make sets of arguments for the relevance for any object, by virtue of age and locality. But assessing the degree of relevance calls for considerable judgement. Thus, a high degree of discernment is called for; in theory the museum's resources should be accommodating only essentially primary material rather than hosting tons of 'maybes'. Lack of discrimination in the collection of material can radically affect museums by filling scarce storage space and, hence, inhibiting the opportunities for more appropriate collections being formed as and when the occasion allows. Conversely, lack of discernment and hesitation can lead to lost opportunities and ultimately the absence of relevant material.

The second level of the process of gathering material operates through directed research and active fieldwork, where a museum targets specific areas of interest and uses a combination of methods to build an in-depth profile or study of a subject. In this, the gathering of material and non-material evidence will be interdependent. This process of careful study aims to create collections and data in the museum which are well rounded and thought out, and militate against the effects of random collecting through passive acquisition. Unfortunately, for some curators, the word 'research' has come to have an elitist air, symptomatic of an activity that keeps curators away from genuine inquiry and prevents contact with the public. But the fact remains that those museums that are positively engaged in research or 'advanced bothering' about the accuracy, depth, relevance and quality of their collections are building archives of significance.

Directed research and documentation and active acquisition can take many forms. It can be a thorough recording and collecting process concentrated on activities, individuals or episodes through which an integrated archive is built. This would consist of fieldnotes, photographs and film, recorded interviews, and collected objects, ephemera and other forms of expression, such as music. It can also be, quite simply, an immediate response to an evolving situation, such as recording the closure of a key local workplace; temporary social phenomena, such as passing adolescent fads; of a current event, for example, a protest rally of a pop concert. At its most fundamental, directed documentation can be a photographic survey, which can take relatively little time and yet provide a vital source of information and a vivid record.

The balance between passive collecting and active documentation work influences the quality of any museum's collections. Neither method can be relied on absolutely. Passive collecting brings the museum in touch with people willing to help the museum; people who have memories, experiences and ideas that are often of value to it. Active documentation sees the museum directly fulfilling its responsibilities as a social recorder. The fundamental difference between the two is that the passive is always at random, a chance affair. Active documentation is a positive and creative approach, an insurance policy against the museum becoming a warehouse for unconnected debris.

Curators have become increasingly aware of the need to attend to contemporary life as well as more traditional historic interests. Contemporary collecting and documentation has become an absorbing issue since the 1970s, when Swedish curators devised a means of creating thorough and well-balanced records of contemporary life in Sweden (Rosander 1980). Their influential work has precipitated a great deal of discussion in museum circles all over the world, and not a little misunderstanding and underestimation of the quality and depth of the contemporary documentation work that the SAMDOK scheme co-ordinates and encourages.

Curators have been particularly concerned about the amount of attention that should be given to contemporary documentation work. To a degree, this concern about balance of activities is a red herring in that all recording and collecting in museums is 'contemporary'. Museums create their archives and their collection through the present day: there is no avoidance of this. Hence, decisions made on grounds of relevance and quality of material are decisions profoundly influenced by contemporary attitudes and values. The material and memories that are available for retrospective studies are available only through the multiple accidents of social and political conditions to date. This needs to be taken into account and appreciated.

More pertinent, perhaps, is the proportion of a museum's resources and time which should be spent in what can only be described as rescue missions, that is gathering information about incidents or practices that remain, perhaps only just, within living memory, as opposed to contemporary issues and trends. Collecting and recording as an urgent response to changing situations has been a dominant characteristic of curatorial work. For example, much museum activity in the 1950s and 1960s was involved with recording the last remnants of generations of craft people and agricultural workers whose ways of life were more or less gone for ever. Similarly, folk stories, music and traditions were recorded in the awareness that they would either soon disappear or be changed into new forms.

Currently, curators are finding that researching local experiences of work before 1914 and of the first World War is more and more difficult to carry out as survivors are few. Faced with the choice between spending time on recording people in their seventies and eighties about episodes of importance to the museum, and recording much younger people and more recent incidents, the curator would be wise to select the former. Sometimes, factors outside the control of the museum dictate the timing and depth of the work undertaken. Taken as a whole, the value of some of this rescue activity needs to be carefully assessed in the light of the extent and depth of established archives and collections, changing social and cultural patterns, and museum resources.

Without doubt, there is a need for balance between retrospective work and contemporary documentation. The Swedes aim to devote 20 per cent of their active research and acquisition activities to documenting contemporary issues and phenomena, with the remaining 80 per cent being devoted to the 'documentation of the first seven decades of the 20th Century' (Nyström and Cedrenius 1982: 13). The virtue of contemporary documentation is that it permits thorough recording of experiences and events, undiluted and unaffected by the loss that occurs in memory and material over the years. It also serves as a constant reminder of the complexity of life which, as much today as in the past, profoundly complicates our view. Furthermore, it acts as a guard against creating consensual and uniform images.

Overall, it is the subject which should first be assessed for relevance: its date of occurrence is critical, but only one of a number of contributing factors in the decision whether to document a subject. This is an area of choice for museums. The last 70 years, up to and including the present day, are the museum's most fruitful period of inquiry. The length of living memory very much determines this. However, the history museum's period of concern, in the main but not exclusively, begins with the birth of consumption and consumerism—the mid-eighteenth century. It should be able to offer a broad and consistent archive stretching from that time to present day. Some history museums will be dealing with even earlier periods: merging their interests with those of the archaeologists for the medieval period and with those of decorative art specialists for the sixteenth and seventeenth centuries. Determining where to concentrate a museum's energies is by no means straightforward.

Selecting fields of study

There is no fool-proof system by which a museum may be guided to concentrate on certain episodes or practices rather than others. Choices have to be made, and these can and should be made by the museum only from its reading of its region or subject. The broad theoretical frameworks described in the previous chapter can help to locate the areas of the past to which the museum might direct its attention. In practice, some museums have concentrated on survivals, others on certain industries and crafts or on completing 'sets' of established collections. In contrast, many museums have been prepared to be guided instead by a detailed knowledge and appreciation of changing social characteristics and cultural expression.

The options are numerous, even infinite, but have to be assessed, if a viable programme of research, recording and acquisition is to be implemented. An extremely useful 'check-list' or source of inspiration is available in G. P. Murdock *et al., Outline of Cultural Materials* (1982). This was developed at Yale University and is an attempt to classify systematically essential sectors within all human life and environments. It is a comprehensive subject classification system pertaining to all aspects of human behaviour and related phenomena.

Discussion of the past and present, based on *Outline*, requires that objects and other material are understood within the larger cultural whole and not as ends in themselves. Thus, it operates well within the theoretical framework discussed in Chapter 7. *Outline* was devised as a classification system that would allow cross-cultural referencing within a range of anthropological and cultural studies research. But it can work as a thesaurus, expanding the range of questions a curator can apply and the perspectives that can be adopted in the interpretation of material. *Outline* also encourages both historic and multicultural perspectives. Its viability within museum practice is such that it is the standard classification system used by cultural history museums in Sweden.

Other forms of information may provide guidance. Museums have often used official publications in their research. Royal Commission papers and Blue Books are particularly useful and well proven. In the selection of fields of study, especially in terms of contemporary documentation, the Central Statistical and the Census Offices both publish research that is useful to museums. *Social Trends* and *Regional Trends*, produced annually by the Central Statistical Office, are invaluable and should be on every history museum's bookshelf. They are useful tools in determining the nature of social change and how this evidences itself.

Testing the relevance and worth of selected fields of study will inevitably involve professional and sometimes subjective judgements. These will involve weighing values and it has to be appreciated that, in these choices, no museum can be value-free or unbiased. Avoiding perspectives, or decisions, is just as significant a political act as having a logical well-thought-out approach with which inevitably someone may disagree. It is far more important that museums have reasons why they are developing their activities in certain ways, than allow themselves to drift.

As part of the process of evolving means of contemporary documentation, SAMDOK in Sweden went back to first principles of museum work. They questioned how museums determined areas in which they would document. They arrived at a set of four criteria which, individually or collectively, have to be present if a project was going to be pursued by a museum. These are as relevant yardsticks for retrospective studies as they are for contemporary ones.

The first criterion is the *socio-economic*. Documentation work which aims to explore people's livelihoods and, hence, their life-styles would be appropriate here. Such work would involve looking at the correlations between work, income, quality of life and the cultural norms and values within an industry or geographical area.

The second criterion is the *human*. This relates to those projects that record the daily lives of ordinary people. The documentation of homes in Sweden by five museums co-operating in the Homes Pool of SAMDOK would qualify under both these criteria (Stavenow-Hidemark 1985). In this work the museums carried out extensive documentation of domestic environments through recording a number of representative households throughout Sweden.

The third is *historical*, and relates to the kinds of recording and collecting which are dictated by the history of the museums and the content of established collections. There are circumstances where the need for long series of material and data necessitates the continuation of studies and collection over a long period. For example, the People's Palace Museum has documented the Women's Suffrage Movement in Glasgow and continues to build on this with research and material on later and current women's movements and feminist issues.

The fourth criterion used by SAMDOK is one they have called *genesis*. It advises that each country should document aspects of its culture that have a wider, international significance. In Britain perhaps this would involve museums in recording, for example, the efforts of the relief agencies, especially Band-Aid in 1985, to raise funds for famine relief in Ethiopia and Somalia, to the issue of acid-rain and the presence in Britain of American Air Force bases, and associated protests.

These four criteria represent very wide notions, but are sufficient to keep museum activity purposefully directed. With these in mind, a museum should be able to establish broad policy for its research and collecting activities. This should be much more than a 'collecting policy', which in current practice appears to work more effectively as a defence against unwarranted collecting. Instead, it should be a wide-ranging plan of action, seeing the museum positively through a period of at the most five years' duration, with annual reviews and reassessment of policy built-in. A good example of this is the collecting and research policy created by Oxfordshire County Museum at Woodstock in 1974. This analysed established collections against existing information, and from this projected future research and collecting requirements. It has been a sufficiently strong and detailed document to act as a medium-term basis for museum activity in the county.

Defining fields of study

Once a museum has determined for both the long and short term where energies will be concentrated, then some definition has to be given at a practical level to the extent and depth of coverage and the various methods to be adopted. For each project or broad subject area four theoretical elements have to be viewed and considered: the context (or milieu), the field (or topic), time (or period) and area (or geographical space). These can be applied within the community-network-role model to provide focus and specific record of distinguishing cultural phenomena.

'Context' and 'field' are two alternative models which are very useful in recording what Göran Rosander has referred to as 'the stock of culture'. 'Field' can be used as a generic term for the specific areas of interest or topics adopted by the museum, which might range from processes to events, activities and experiences. A field might be defined as an aggregate or expression of the relationship of social and/or economic structures. In other words, the embodiment of experience and expression created by a complex web of political and socio-economic forces.

This might sound glibly defined in theory, but not clearly delineated in practice, although G. P. Murdock *et al.*'s *Outline* provides much guidance.

There is infinite choice here. Indeed, the fact that there is not a standardized project format renders the whole process of curatorship exciting and challenging. A museum may be attending to such 'fields' or 'topics' as children's games, aspects of religious observance, community health care, rites of passage, cider-making or car manufacture. These offer a 'vertical' division of cultural encounter and phenomenon, that is a strict and fairly rigid view of one element, usually in some depth. Thus, children's games might be explored in their various forms, but may not be researched with reference to family relationships and incomes, child health, schools or the commercial production and sales of toys.

In comparison, the 'context' model offers a 'horizontal' division that interacts with selected 'fields', preventing such work developing along too narrow a band of activity and relationships. Contexts can be defined as the specific 'planes' on which the environment, and the sets of relationships that construct and are experienced within those environment, are encountered. Very simply, there are four distinct contexts: home and personal; work; public; and commercial. Within each context a specific range of roles is played, which is socially and culturally recognized. Roles and their relationships change according to the nature of the context. Similarly, the use, operation and view of the objects and expressions within these settings will vary.

With this in mind, it would not be sufficient to record a factory as a work context by collecting machinery or recording on film a particular process. Instead, the many dimensions and characteristics of the individual work environment, of which machinery or the process are an integral but not exclusive part, would have to be questioned and considered. The work environment is thus seen as both physical and social, with many devices that indicate and declare the nature of experiences and relationships which will be both social and economic. These characteristics and phenomena in themselves are bound up with issues of personality, power and processes. In recording the work context, the museum would have to look at the experience of working in that factory, the various meanings of that work, the signification of this and how it changes according to staff positions within the factory, and indeed, its industry as a whole. Thus, there is a movement in the recording process to looking beyond the machinery to the people, their created and imposed environments (from clothing to tea-rooms), and their opinions, testimony and memories.

The main difficulty with the 'context' model is that it is so simplified it frequently cannot supply viable boundaries to limit the study or provide a strictly comparative field. For example, the home is an environment in which many people, mainly women, work and would view as a work context. Cleaners, community nurses, child-minders as well as mothers work in the 'home'. The sea and the harbour may be the working context of the fisherman or artist, but the public context of the holiday-maker or day-tripper. Conversely, the countryside may be the public context of the walker, but part of a working one for the farm labourer. The shop or the restaurant may be part of the commercial context of the shopper or diner, but the work context of the shop assistant or waitress, as well as the home context for the owner's family, if they live 'over the shop'.

Problems are associated with both the field and context models where they exist in isolation. If, however, they can be used so that they intersect, the horizontal of the 'context' model with the vertical of the 'field' model, then balance of inquiry can result. This intersection allows the overlaying of questions from each, in an effort to deepen research, and, hence, uncover layers of meaning, which if used separately the models might not allow. This brings the record closer to being about 'social being' and 'episode'. A field or subject such as feeding infants can be explored in the contexts of the home (patterns of feeding, objects, rituals and means), commercial contexts (promotion and sales, provision of facilities for infants), public contexts (official attitudes and provisions) and works contexts (manufacture of baby food, work environment, materials, provision of childcare for workers).

But further definition may be required. The time element has to be accommodated. Any research will take place within some boundaries of a specific time or period. Thus, the factory discussed above has to be seen in the context of the moment in which it is being viewed with all the social, economic and political pressures that are then brought to bear. Research in any study must admit to wider influences and effects than the immediately obvious. Appreciating the influence of time and period is a very vital part of the interpretative and recording process. For example, a study of the livelihood of small farms between the wars in an upland area, where, before 1914, mixed farming and, hence, degrees of self-sufficiency were to be found, would have to take into account the effects and after-effects of the first World War and the implications of the formation of the Marketing Boards in the early 1930s. Without this, changes in farming practices and lives of those who worked on the land could not be properly understood.

The final element is geographic. Because the majority of museums are run by local authorities, they tend to have research and collecting territories defined by political and administrative boundaries. However, the social and cultural expression and experience which is the museum's interest do not necessarily obligingly conform to these. Therefore, local government boundaries have to be seen as fairly arbitrary or artificial impositions.

Delineation is created by local and regional topography, distribution of resources, routes of communication and climate. The natural environment, now much interfered with, is the fundamental basis from which the museum needs to operate. Overlaying this will be areas designated by economic ties and interests, as well as cultural and social groupings. Traditions, marital connections and work have rarely been tidily confined to a uniform area. Inevitably, the areas a museum has to deal with change over time, through evolving social or economic circumstances. This renders them very confusing and they can only be defined through careful study. But as important as this process of definition is, it runs the risk of over-simplification: where the local and regional is not questioned in the light of larger national and international trends. These too have to be understood.

The intersection of the elements of field, context, time and area provides a viable point of discovery, and offers a means of defining a project in such a way that the records made have some coherence and meaning. Beyond this, much depends upon the skills available, the type of fieldwork employed and the range of recording methods used.

9. *Fieldwork, Recording and Sources*

Such general texts as are available on curatorial research methods implicitly, but more often explicitly, cast the curator in the role of 'expert' (for example, Greenaway 1984). This is a partial and dangerous falsehood. The curator may be an expert in museum theory and practice, may have a broad and sometimes deep knowledge of sources, and may be very experienced in a range of museum-applicable techniques, including artefact analysis. But the experts are the ordinary people who make history and who create and shape it.

Realizing that in research and fieldwork the curator works not as much as the expert as with the experts and their various forms of evidence, creates a positive and co-operative work attitude rather than a superior and possessive one. This is particularly relevant as curators are now working alongside libraries, reminiscence centres, pensioners' groups, schools and oral history societies that purposefully stimulate an atmosphere in which self-expression through the recovery of individual and group memory is encouraged and assisted. Historians can no longer 'own' their field.

This was especially evident in the exhibition 'Exploring Living Memory', held annually in London until 1987. The exhibition brought together over 100 societies and organizations from all over the city concerned with recording and cherishing, warts and all, the memories of ordinary people. The individual elements of the exhibition spoke with a frankness and directness that comes from a deep personal appreciation of the experiences being represented through words, pictures, sound and objects. The exhibition was, therefore, a reminder and a lesson to museums: if they claim to being about 'social history', then they can do no other but work for, with and on behalf of, the experts.

This offers the curator a number of possibilities for the way in which fieldwork is conducted. The curator can carry out and control the museum's own research and fieldwork activities: this is the principal approach encountered in museum work. Alternatively, recording can be carried out in partnership with others, such as the caring agencies, oral history groups and community centres. Or, it can be handed over to people who, once having established a framework and being loaned or advised on appropriate equipment, can create their own self-portraits for permanent record. The latter has been successfully tried in Sweden, where museums have been able to co-operate with evening classes, workplaces and the unions in an effort to stimulate original research projects (Fägerborg 1981).

Once completed and celebrated, these have been subsequently housed in the museum's archive.

Whichever approach is adopted, one thing is certain, curators cannot extend their understanding of the past of their area or enlarge the museum's collections from behind the security of the museum's office door. It requires the active and imaginative use and recovery of a range of sources and information. This means fieldwork, positive social contact and investigation of all available sources. This presupposes that the curator has put aside or accommodated the supposition which Szabó described as 'antiquated'; that an object is collected first and researched later. The basis of this chapter is the idea that the museum has the capacity and duty to be a documenter of social and cultural expression and change, using material and non-material forms as its central evidence.

An examination of sources and methods of curatorial research and fieldwork effectively means a volume in itself. It is possible within the space of one chapter to draw attention to some of the more useful literature available, in the hope that the reader will be prepared to pursue the texts further.

The primary and secondary sources available to museums are discussed helpfully in a range of literature directed at the local and social history fields at both professional and amateur level. Similarly, a variety of survey and analysis methods is outlined in a number of publications serving sociology, anthropology, geography and history. There is a certain amount of self-generated museum studies literature, too. Its most productive elements are case studies which bring together ideas about sources and their use and explore them in the contexts of museum practice. From these rather diverse sources, there is much to be learnt of benefit to curatorial practice.

Supporting literature and its place

The fundamental basis of a curator's understanding of any region must be an appreciaton of its geography, geomorphological structure and early settlement patterns. History curators in county and city museum services will find themselves working alongside geology curators and archaeologists. The forms of co-operation that can develop from this can be mutually beneficial and productive. In the absence of this support, there are standard texts available from which guidance can be taken. L. Dudley Stamp, *Britain's Structure and Scenery* (1959) is still a classic. It very usefully describes and explains the physical characteristics of Britain. This work should be used in conjunction with texts which discuss the archaeology and historical geography of Britain. Helpful overviews can be found in R. A. Dodgshon and R. A. Butlin (eds), *An Historical Geography of England and Wales* (1978) and G. Whittington and I. D. Whyte (eds), *An Historical Geography of Scotland* (1983).

Such preliminary reading provides the curator with a broad historical framework from and within which local and regional studies can be developed. Inevitably, this will involve much original research which will include observation and fieldwork, and the use of maps and aerial photographs. The reading of the human environment in England has been much encouraged and substantially influenced by the work of W. G. Hoskins. His books, including *The Making of the English Landscape* (1970) and *Local History in England* (1972), provide guidance and food for thought. In Scotland two books cover similar ground: M. L. Parry and T. R. Slater (eds), *The Making of the Scottish Countryside* (1980) and T. H. Adams, *The Making of Urban Scotland* (1978). To this reading should be added publications by architectural historians, in particular R. W. Brunskill, *Illustrated Handbook of Vernacular Architecture* (1971); and by historians and archaeologists who draw on architectural evidence, for example, Colin Platt, *The Parish Churches of Medieval England* (1981). To extend further and explore some of the issues and subjects of interest arising from such fieldwork and reading, use should be made of primary source materials, in particular maps.

There is now an extensive literature dealing with the documentary sources available to local and social historians. Several texts very usefully explain not just what sources are available but also how they might be used and the problems to be expected. *Historical Sources in Geography* (1979), by Michael Morgan, deals with sources and illustrates the forms of analysis that can be employed in their use. Alan Macfarlane's book, *Reconstructing Historical Communities* (1977), provides an excellent description of the range of archive data available, and how it can be analysed: the examples used to illuminate and explore the points made are vivid and easily engage the reader's interest. Further, there is a helpful discussion of the quality and uses of the data. These texts make reference to probate inventories, and Morgan deals with trade directories, both of which are sources in frequent use by curators. Beyond these, there is a great deal on local history studies. One of the more interesting is by Alan Rogers, *Approaches to Local History* (1977). This explores alternative ways of examining a 'local past' by discussing both the sources and the historical contexts from which they sprang. For curators working in England it is a very supportive handbook.

Overall, local historical literature suffers in part from a number of omissions. Much of it has been based on English records and conditions and, therefore, is of limited use in other parts of Britain. Moreover, it often falls short of discussing the source material for industrial and post-industrial periods. In particular, the local histories of labour, women and racial minorities are frequently excluded from the texts. Advice on possible sources for these have to be found elsewhere. Fortunately, there is emerging a small but growing body of literature to fill these gaps. Deidre Beddoe, *Discovering Women's History: A Practical Manual* (1983) is a very good case in point.

Beyond the general texts, local publications on the use of archive material now exist and make a valuable contribution to our understanding of the possibilities of such material. These are often produced by local studies librarians or archivists and aim to equip readers with the tools of historical enquiry. For example, as part of Birmingham's centenary celebrations (1989), to stimulate local history especially in the light of a competition held that year, a publication was produced called *Five Ways into Birmingham's Past*. This was written by Andrew Blizzard and Patrick Baird of the Local Studies Department of Birmingham Central Library and was sponsored by the BBC. It provides a lively and very helpful introduction to local history. In a similar vein, although not part of a major event, *Settlement History for Geographers* by Mary Aris and Glynn Jones, published by Gwynedd Archives Service in 1983, is a very useful guide, full of good ideas, sound advice and well-chosen illustrations.

The historical contexts and the episodes that give rise to the material which now forms the bulk of museum collections can be found discussed in a good number of papers and books within the social and economic history field. Three particular texts stand out in this regard and are essential reading for curators. They are Neil McKendrick *et al.*, *The Birth of a Consumer Society: The Commercialization of Eighteenth-Century England* (1983); W. Hamish Fraser, *The Coming of the Mass Market 1850–1914* (1981); and Kenneth Hudson, *The Archaeology of the Consumer Society* (1983). Each in different ways considers the social and economic forces that give rise to consumption and consumerism within specific periods. Most museum collections are the residue of changing patterns of consumption and, in part, some testimony to their effects.

Recording methods are discussed and well supported in available literature. Surveying techniques, illustration and photography are outlined in *The Techniques of Industrial Archaeology* (1974) by

Figure 6.   Stockholm City Museum working with members of a trade union at their factory, which makes surgical instruments. Recording in progress.

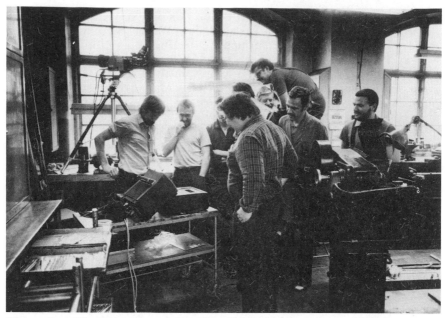

Figure 7.   Discussing the results. The video being made here was used as part of
an exhibition co-produced by the museum and the union.

J. P. M. Pannell, edited by J. Kenneth Major. This book was written at the
height of the industrial archaeology boom and, therefore, has its
limitations, especially as far as social recording is concerned. This can be
overcome if it is used very carefully and alongside the *Making History*
handbooks published by the Television History Centre. There are four in
the series: *The Factory* (1983), by Ruth Richardson *et al.; Women* (1983),
also by Ruth Richardson *et al.; The School* (1984), by Stephen Humphries
et al.; and *The Hospital* (1985), by Greg Lanning and Jeanette Mitchell *et
al.* The *Making History* series gives clear and positive direction to anyone
interested in instigating a research project in these specific fields. In each
volume advice is given about ideas worth pursuing and relevant
techniques, especially the use of tape-recording, photography and video.
The ideas here can be extended to other subjects and issues.

The possibilities of oral testimony and the techniques involved with its
recovery is exhaustively dealt with in a mass of literature on oral
historiography. Three particular books stand head-and-shoulders above
the rest. George Ewart Evans, perhaps more than any historian of his
generation, opened up the potential and necessity of oral records. His many
books incorporate his own patient listening to the tales and testimony of
the people of his adopted East Anglia. One book in particular, *Where
Beards Wag All: The Relevance of the Oral Tradition* (1970), was a
landmark. The publication of this coincided with work being undertaken
by Paul Thompson at the University of Essex, which, in time, led to his
influential book, *The Voice of the Past* (1978, revised 1988) and to the

formation of the Oral History Society. To the accumulated wisdom of Evans and Thompson must be added that of Anthony Seldon and Joanna Pappworth. Their book, *By Word of Mouth: Elite Oral History* (1983), although primarily pitched at 'the practice of interviewing the leaders . . . rather than the led', gives both pertinent advice and astute criticism of oral testimony as a source. The chapter by Margaret Brooks of the Imperial War Museum on the establishment and running of an oral archive is a bonus for museum readers.

The use of objects as evidence is an area receiving a growing amount of attention. Curatorship is exceptionally well served by *Material Culture Studies in America* (1982). This anthology, which was selected, arranged and introduced by Thomas J. Schlereth, provides a challenging range of ideas and approaches. It is an invaluable sourcebook and, hence, required reading for all museum professionals in the human history field. Similarly, a stimulating summary of the principal ways in which objects can be interpreted is provided by Dr Susan Pearce in a series of articles called 'Thinking about Things' in the *Museum Journal* (1986a; 1986b; 1986c; 1987).

Curators have themselves contributed to the literature available and there are notable papers. Attention can be drawn to the work of Anne Buck, especially her paper, 'Dress as Social Record', which appeared in *Folk Life*, 14 (1976). Another useful article is by R. Batchelor, 'Not Looking at Kettles', *Museums Professional Group*, 23 (1986), in which he explored a kettle for its idea or invention, its materials, its making or manufacture, its marketing, its form, its use, and ultimately the information about the kettle most useful to the museum.

But beyond a number of such excellent papers, there are contributions from non-curatorial sources. Of note is *Objects of Desire: Design and Society 1750–1980* (1986) by Adrian Forty. This is a set of essays which seek to explore the connection of the object to the mind and the pocket, as opposed to the eye. In both approach and analysis it has much to offer the curator and curatorial practice. Forty's centering of the object as evidence of social and economic phenomena and conditions provides a methodology that can be applied within the museum.

Turning theory into practice

There is a fairly lengthy history of the use of fieldwork, recording and surveying techniques in museums. In Sweden a range of fieldwork methods, including questionnaires, was being used in the 1870s and 1880s in studies of dialect and popular tradition. The cultural history fieldwork section of Nordiska Museet has been in existence since the founding of the museum in 1873. The first questionnaire survey took place in 1905. This work was sporadic until 1928, when it became a regular method for the fieldwork section (Airey 1980). The Institute of Folklore Research was founded in 1914 at Uppsala University and was swift to build on and develop the methods established at Nordiska Museet (Cheape 1978). The

Irish Folklore Commission (O'Suilleabhain 1942) and later the School of Scottish Studies at the University of Edinburgh adoped the classification systems and recording methods used at the University of Uppsala in Sweden.

An integrated approach to recording which drew on this experience was instigated on the Isle of Man. In 1948, with the assistance of the Irish Folklore Commission, the Manx Folk Life Survey began. A full-time collector, Leslie Quirk, trained by Sean O'Haughey, one of the Irish Commission's fieldworkers, was assisted by a group of volunteers. They used a range of methods, which included recording dialect, testimony and song on an Ediphone recording machine, and the collection of photographs. Some of the people involved in the survey were supplied blank exercise books 'to record in written form the memories of a lifetime's experience' (Harrison 1986: 200). The survey has continued steadily to the present day and is a remarkable record of the life of ordinary people on the island.

Person-centred recording has been much used in Scandinavia. Until the advent of oral history societies and projects in great numbers from the 1970s, it had only occasionally been used in Britain. However, the most suitable parallel to the Scandinavian recording work comes not from a museum but from an organization called Mass Observation. This was an anthropological study of life in Britain initiated by Charles Madge, who, with Tom Harrison, built a remarkable archive of life in Britain between 1937 and 1949 (Calder and Sheridan 1984). Efforts have been made to update and extend this work, however, it has had only limited impact on the ways in which museums conduct their recording.

The questionnaire has been employed in several museums to recover information or to conduct a preliminary survey before more detailed work is undertaken. Less well used are the essay competitions and biographical writing that have been successfully encouraged elsewhere. Essay competitions have been undertaken by libraries, for example, those run by Leicestershire libraries. There has been some development in the number of classes in biographical writing, which aim to encourage people to commit their own ideas about the past to paper. Many of these have been established by the WEA (Workers' Educational Association), extra-mural classes and by reminiscence centres.

In 1974 Geraint Jenkins's paper 'The Collection of Ethnological Material' was published in the *Museums Journal*. This helped to demonstrate how research methods can be co-ordinated and integrated with the processes of collecting material. In this he highlighted how curators could work from 'research files' in which all material relating to a particular craft or industry could be brought together. One of the examples he gave was a research file on the tanning industry, which might contain: an exhaustive bibliography, along with note and summaries from the literature listed; transcripts or copies of manuscript material; transcripts of tape-recordings relating to tanning; lists of tanneries that operated or continue to operate in England and Wales; a list of place-names associated with leather production; catalogues of tanning equipment and lists of material in established collections; photographs from various sources; and trade catalogues of tanning and leather tools (Jenkins 1974: 8). This example, of course, can be revised and amended according to the subject in hand. The simple approach of co-ordinated research filing that Jenkins advocated helps the curator to build multi-faceted bodies of information about a research topic.

But inspiration for recording and collecting, more often than not, has come not through exploration of theory, as valuable as this may often be, but through the observaton of practice. The work of the People's Palace in Glasgow has been a continual source of such inspiration. In all its work there has been a sharp edge of purpose and astute response to a city in a state of convulsive change. The recording methods have been skilfully adapted to capture sympathetically and vividly the essence of a people and a place (see for example, King 1986; 1987; 1988). In particular, the use of documentary photography and commissioned artwork, and the deliberate and selective collection of material has enabled the People's Palace Museum to get very close in its recording to the feeling of a moment or the experience of a specific episode.

The People's Palace is the fifth best-attended museums in the whole of Scotland and has a popular and very public image, with somewhere in the region of 310 000 visitors a year. It is housed in a sturdy, red-brick Victorian building, which was designed to provide leisure and educational facilities

Figure 8.   The People's Palace Museum in Glasgow. Opened in 1898, fosters a sharp view of the City's past and present. It collects and records widely, centring its activities on issues and topics of key relevance to the people of Glasgow.

Figure 9.   Desk of Marxist revolutionary and great protagonist of adult
education, John Maclean. Socialist politics are a central strand of
Glasgow's past and present. The People's Palace Museum has
collected and recorded much from the organised and unorganised
labour movements.

for the working-class people in the East End of Glasgow. It opened in 1898 and from the beginning material relating to Glasgow's history was gathered there. In 1940 the Art Gallery at Kelvingrove deposited what local collections they had, and the People's Palace Museum thus became the official repository and treasure-house of 'things past'. The collections now on display deal with key aspects of Glasgow's past and present. The themes include the history of the tobacco trade, social and domestic life in Glasgow, politics and religion, trade unions, the suffragettes and women's movements. The museum also displays material illustrating the rise of socialism, temperance and drunkenness, the history of photography, life in the two World Wars, the peace movements, and entertainments, including music hall, cinema and boxing.

The People's Palace fosters a critical and sharp view of the past, treating it with the respect and affection it deserves, without stooping to mawkish sentimentality. To achieve this there has been a willingness to deal with the subjects and issues which are central to Glasgow. This has meant much movement away from tried and traditional museum subjects, and the continual breaking of new ground in terms of method and material gathered.

This is perhaps most apparent in the recording of events and experiences in Glasgow's recent past, and the collection of contemporary material. The work here is underpinned by an appreciation that the 1980s are proving to be times of acute social crisis in Glasgow, as the city loses its industrial base and, therefore, the reason for its existence. It is now being 'redefined' as a 'first-class tourist and conference centre' and to this end Glasgow has been designated 'European city of Culture 1990'. This is regardless of the fact that vast areas of the city remain untouched by the sort of 'culture' referred to, and anyway have their own distinct forms of cultural expression. Therefore, as with much of the museum's retrospective work, the approach has been not through objects but through the issues directly affecting people in Glasgow.

In a paper delivered in 1985 Elspeth King outlined the range of activities in which the People's Palace was engaged, particularly those which charted 'the embourgeoisement of the inner city', through recording some of the principal processes which are giving rise to physical and political change in Glasgow, such as the housing developments and the growth of wine bars and bistros. Other work included recording and collecting material illustrating Glasgow's response to the Ethiopian Famine Appeal of 1985; the local support for 'Ally's Tartan Army' in the World Cup Finals in 1978; the 'Glasgow's Miles Better' and 'Glasgow 2000 Campaigns'—the former to boost Glasgow's image, the latter to make a Glasgow a non-smoking city by 2000 in spite of the threats that posed to the tobacco industry workers in the city; responses to, and alternative views of, such campaigns; the Peace Campaigns of the 1970s and 1980s; unemployment and the 1983 People's March for Jobs; and local industrial action, including the city's various efforts to support the miners through the 1984-5 Miners' Strike.

In recent years a number of in-depth recording projects have been undertaken by museums. These have often concluded with an exhibition or a publication, and sometimes both. These indicate how research, fieldwork and recording in museums have developed and are now capable of dealing in detail with a range of subjects and issues. Essentially, they reveal curatorial practice as being capable of penetrating and illuminating social studies, dealing either with past or recent experiences. They also indicate the degree to which the museum can play a strong and central role in creating and maintaining records of their area.

Three projects are worth citing. The first is a project undertaken in 1984–5 by Peter Jenkinson and Karen Hull for Birmingham City Museum. This was funded by the Inner City Partnership Programme and was part of a large project, 'Change in the Inner City'. The theme adopted by researchers was aspects of eating in Birmingham between 1939 and 1985. This was selected as it was felt that changes in food distribution, demand and consumption reflected the changing social patterns in the city. The research involved the use of archives and photographic collections, interviews, photography and fieldwork. The results were published in *A Taste of Change* (1985; see also Jenkinson 1988).

A wider chronological span was adopted in a project undertaken by a three-person Manpower Services Commission team (Steve Dodsworth, Catherine Evans and Julie Barnett) in Cardiff for the Welsh Industrial and Maritime Museum. This was to create a photo-historical survey of Cardiff's docklands to 1983. What emerged was an intimate portrait of a distinct part of the city, Butetown, that, by its physical separation and its relations with the sea, had developed to be an inward-looking community. The city itself had largely ignored Butetown, whose local reference gave the book its name: *Below the Bridge*. Using original research, photography, interviews and an essay competition in which local schools took part, the project team created a lasting record. The importance of this work is likely to be thrown into sharper focus as Cardiff Docklands is prepared for 'redevelopment'.

The third project is a survey of the garment industry undertaken by Gareth Griffiths and Phil Philo at Gunnersbury Park Museum in London in 1986. This led to an exhibition and publication called *A Stitch in Time: Clothing in West London 1880s–1980s*. The project involved the use of a similar range of sources and methods to those described above, but was distinctive for its use of colour photography. Taking as a starting point existing collections, the museum set up a comparative study of the clothing industry in the Gunnersbury Park area over the 100-year period, bringing the survey up to present day. To do this the project had to question the social and cultural changes that have influenced the industry. It, therefore, became not only a description of industrial change but an exploration of how the area had been transformed in that 100-year period, although in many respects it remained the same.

These three projects are instructive on many levels and are cited here to draw the reader's attention to them and to the methods that were used in their research. Largely absent from these was an integrated programme of collection of objects and ephemera. Given the amount of research involved with the work, it would have been feasible to conclude the projects with the acquisition of materials as well as the research records. This has been very much the basis of operating methods of curators engaged in contemporary documentation in Sweden.

In 1985 Nordiska Museet and SAMDOK published the first of a series of the work of the 'pools' or committees of curators working together on contemporary documentation. The publication, edited by Elisabet Stavenow-Hidemark, is called *Home Thoughts from Abroad: An Evaluation of the SAMDOK Homes Pool*. The Homes Pool is the area of SAMDOK's work which is farthest advanced of the eleven pools. The publication is a summary of, and reflection on, their work to date, and an assessment of possible future directions. The research projects detailed have involved curators working very closely with five families in various parts of Sweden. Careful profiles have been built of their lives, their domestic settings and their use of their homes. This has involved a comprehensive recording process, including the listing of family acquisitions over a one-year period and interviewing different members of the families. The projects have been concluded with research reports and the acquisition of material for museum collections. *Home Thoughts from Abroad* is an insight into the painstaking and purposeful techniques of contemporary documentation in Sweden today.

Riders and reasons

From the foregoing it is clear that curators can, and do, use a wide variety of sources and methods in their recording. The question arises, why is it important? If some museums can happily exist without undertaking any original work, simply naming and exhibiting objects and any other donated material as they feel fit within the safety of museum premises, why put all this stress on fieldwork and recording?

There are many answers to this, not the least being the social role of the museum and the professional integrity of the curator. The most eloquent case for patient, questioning curatorship is set out in George McDaniel's book *Hearth and Home: Preserving a People's Culture*, publishing in 1982. If the reader selects only one text to follow through from those recommended here, it should be this. It is a book about a research project on a tenant house from Mitchellville, Maryland, USA, which was acquired by the Smithsonian Institution, Washington in 1969. But the book is about much more than this. It is about curatorial practice, which, even in a national institution, can fail to ask questions. It is about how a museum can possess an object, subvert and reform it to suit the convenience of the museum rather than historical accuracy. It is a book about omission and exclusion of black people from national histories and how important it is for museums to record and recover the black experience. It is also a book which indirectly challenges curators to face up to their own cultural baggage and their reservations about conducting fieldwork.

The tenant house had been rescued from the bulldozer when the land on which it stood was being developed for a shopping centre. Moved to the

National Museum of American History in Washington (part of the Smithsonian), it was reassembled in the Hall of Everyday Life. Some modifications were made to get it into the hall. One side of the house was lodged flush against a wall, and several feet were removed from the top of the structure to fit it into the space available. Thus located, the house was furnished as the museum thought best and opened to the public. But concern about the lack of information on the house grew amongst some of the curatorial staff and led, ten years later, to George McDaniel being hired to conduct research on it for the museum.

His book relates how he traced and contacted people who knew or who had lived in the house, and how they were concerned to 'get down the history of that house and get it straight'. He also records their reactions when he brought them to see the house reassembled in the museum, where they found it 'backwards', the back of the house exhibited as the front, and the original front out of view against the wall. McDaniel was able to extend his research of this particular house and to consider its form and the lives people led in it within the known contexts of the history and material culture of Afro-Americans in the Southern states. In this he was able to draw strands that led back through the slave years to African origins.

The intellectual basis for his research was that the people who lived in the house did not live in 'shacks', were not stereotypes or mere ciphers but people we could know in remarkable detail by examining what they left behind. He writes 'material culture is more than lifeless artefacts. The study of objects should lead back to the people who used them' (1982: 16). But even given the depth and importance of his work at its conclusion, it could not influence change at the museum. Except for sessions organized at the museum by McDaniel, the museum, at least in the 1980s, was reported as lacking the funds to implement changes. As important as the initiative of the museum was to present the poor in its collections, as it stands the tenant house is a symbol of the tokenism that all museums, to some extent, engage in, curating collections through convenience rather than through conviction and solid evidence.

Also McDaniel's book is a frank exploration of his feelings and the experiences of conducting this and earlier research. He recalls his first interview and his self-consciousness at the prospect of interviewing a black tenant farmer and photographing his house. He reflects:

> Over the years I have interviewed scores of people in North Carolina, Maryland, Virginia and Washington D.C. Though I have met with a few hostile receptions, the overwhelming majority of people have been cooperative because they have been concerned about recording the history they knew. Some may have had reservations because I was white, from Georgia, too conservative, too radical, a stranger; but more important, it appears, was the fact that I was there and sincere. Better me than nobody. They opened up their store of knowledge and led me to old-time houses and people they knew in their communities. [1982: 12]

History curatorship can avail itself of a wide range of sources and recording techniques. But the products of such work will be only as good as the questions asked, the initiatives taken and the judgements brought to bear. It follows that whatever recording is undertaken by museums it will, in some way, be inadequate or open to criticism within its own time or in the future. This is inevitable, but there is little to be gained by hanging back on research because the curator believes he or she to be too white, too black, too male, too female, too conservative, too liberal, too young or too old for the work. It matters much more that someone bothers at all and that what is carried out is done well. In the long run, whatever research and recording are undertaken by curators shoud be full of life and full of questions. Most of all it should be full of the testimony of the 'experts' and the meaning that only they can bestow.

10. Selection, Acquisition and Care of Material

The deliberate acquisition of material for history museum collections can never be totally unselective. Decisions will be made against a number of different criteria before an object, a document, photograph or audio-tape is formally added to a collection. But a growing proportion of museums is compelled to modify the selection of material according to urgent and pragmatic reasoning. Purchase price, size, condition and cost of long-term care are weighed in the balance, sometimes even overriding fundamental considerations of historic or cultural worth. Because of this, a significant number of museums in the real world may well be dealing in balance-sheet collecting policies, rather than ones developed from social and professional considerations.

Faced with pressure on resources and space, museums are required, perhaps more than ever before, to give careful thought to what and why they are collecting. Gathering material together because it is old, available and free is not a firm basis for building collections of social worth. It led Neils Jannasch, former director of the Atlantic Museum, Nova Scotia, to write:

> Imagine what the world, especially the western world, would look like today if past generations had been as keen on collecting and preserving as we have been during the last twenty years. Perhaps one fifth of our countries would by now be covered with museums, historic buildings, villages and towns, industries and historic harbours full of ships. . .there is such a thing as trying to preserve too much [quoted in Jenkins 1987: 9]

It follows that the acquisition of material needs to be informed, highly selective and part of a clear understanding of the museum's task. This calls for many things: a constant vigilance so that important material and key social changes are not missed; a well-defined research programme which identifies and prioritizes subjects to be studied and material to be sought; a willingness to look for alternatives in the recording of material and social data: and a preparedness to react quickly and to go outside the tried and tested in museum practice.

Criteria in selection

The issue of contemporary documentation has thrown into high relief the need to be clear about why any piece of material evidence is brought into the museum's care. This is an area where, once again, Swedish curators, through SAMDOK, provided a theoretical framework within which more selective acquisition could take place. The criteria they cited, although drawn up for fieldwork conducted to record our own times, needs but little adaptation to be used for historic material.

SAMDOK laid down six criteria that might be applied, individually or collectively, when selecting material for acquisition (Rosander 1980). They represent a process of measured assessment: as no museum can collect everything, it should be in a position where it can critically evaluate the material to hand and the options available. What is at issue is the degree of relevance and the museum's ability to recognize this and prioritize choices. While it was recognized that more than one of these criteria may apply if considering material in context, it was expected that curators would use these and rationalize their choices against them.

The first is the *frequency criterion*, and is the test of the recurrence of material within the subject being studied. Frequency of occurrence, experience or form will provide the basis for further analysis. It can lead to questions about the reasons for recurrence; the factors that create change and deviation from established patterns; and cultural variation. The use of a flat iron was a frequent and recurrent feature of a large number of homes and commercial laundries at the turn of the century. The length of period in which they were in common use; the differences between those used domestically and those used commercially; the degree to which the meaning of that object varied between different regions, households and users can be partly construed by frequency of occurrence. In turn this could lead to more-informed decisions about what to collect and what to display as being representative of the experiences of laundering clothes: a highly skilled and labour-intensive operation.

The criterion of *form* is an essential one for curators. Within this falls a wide range of material that in its physical characteristics, either through design, material or even redeployment, reveals something about the relationship of the people who created or used it in their immediate environment. The evidence any object carries in itself is of central interest to museum practice. However, some objects are more obvious information-bearers than others. Indeed, many are purposefully designed to be self-proclaiming: the Imperial Crown and the constable's tipstaff are examples. It is, thus, in the capacity as interpreter of the object's form that the curator acts, especially where the decoding of the object's immediate messages presents difficulty.

SAMDOK identified another criterion as *step-ladder*. This relates to those objects that incorporate some technical or cultural innovation that had, or have, consequences both for manufacturers and users. It relates to those objects, the presence, or in some instances the absence, of which precipitates change or development. As with step-ladders, one step leads to another above it, but comes from another below it. This criterion allows for the collection of material in type-series: a preoccupation of several generations of curators. In this a complete set of objects is sought: the earliest breast-plough or field-stick to the most up-to-date, fully automated ploughing machine that John Deere can provide.

The essential rider here is that the step-ladder criterion has to apply as much, if not more, to the changes and developments experienced by the user and consumer as in manufacture. For example, it would allow for the acquisition of material reflective of major advances in computers, disposable nappies and food processors if there is a demonstrable reason that these created significant changes for people using them. On a broader plane, material that is indicative of major social changes might also be considered here. SAMDOK refers to the logarithm of time, suggesting, for example, that in 500 years time the notion of the car could be represented by just one vehicle. In this extreme example, one object is used to summarize a major phase in an evolving process, in this instance travel and transportation.

The fourth criterion is that of *domain*, the physical closeness of a group of objects to the user and to each other. Thus, through a study the curator will see groups of objects that, together, make sense or represent in some way the subject of study. For example, in the study of an office the clutter of the desk (which may include personal touches such as family photographs and plants as well as equipment and work papers), the contents of drawers (which again, may include more personal details such as sanitary towels and lunch boxes) and the immediate environment, including work and safety notices, posters and jokes cut from newspapers, create the 'domain' which in this case reveals the workplace as both an official and personal environment. The individual objects on their own do not create such powerful images. Objects as 'sets' have to be considered here.

The *appeal criterion* is relevant when a museum is presented with the opportunity to acquire material which has an affective, ritual or fetish value. Thus, Martina Navratilova's tennis racquet, the wooden bottle currently being used each year in Hallaton, Leicestershire at the annual Hare Pie Scramble and Bottle Kicking, or the good luck charm that sits on the examination desk may each qualify under this criterion. In this the material may have a set of connections and meanings that can be conveyed only by adequate documentation and recording. Knowing that this particular racquet belonged to a Wimbledon champion, or that the bottle is part of a set ritual with known characteristics and associations, or that a charm on an examination desk has perceived good luck associations confirms the object's appeal, even in a sense creates it.

The last criterion is perhaps the one that museums use most frequently, the *representivity criterion*. This applies when things or parts of things can be used or seen as a symbol or illustration of an idea, a process, a phenomenon or structure, especially in an educational sense. The River Don Engine now at Kelham Island Museum was built and used to roll armour plating for battleships. It is not possible to show a First World War battleship, but a piece of armour plating would illustrate well the purpose of the engine; why it had to be so big and powerful and the scale of operation in constructing such a vessel.

This device has to be employed where the original object or setting is manifestly too big, too frail, too complex or too expensive to be available to the museum. In these sets of circumstances other ways have to be found: key pieces of objects; alternative and more portable material associated with the whole; other forms of visual representation and sound recordings may have to be gathered. With this in mind, it may not be possible to collect a commercial sailing vessel, 'the most dangerous form of transport ever devised', but if it is pertinent to the study, then other material can be gathered to represent it and the way of life of which it was part. This may involve a range of visual evidence and fragments of memory and material. Collectively, these may be more expressive of an existence which was 'cruel, hard and where nothing came easily', but where a curious and close sense of belonging developed (Jenkins 1987: 12).

Direct and alternative forms of acquisition

Museums acquire objects either through gift or purchase. Some are made available through unsolicited offers from the public; others through fieldwork, auctions and appeal. The objects acquired are normally ones that have been in use and, therefore, can be accounted for by the user. This offers a number of choices for museums in terms of how used material moves into the collection. Active acquisition that seeks to acquire objects as part of a recording process requires a responsive attitude both to the study in question and to the opportunity it presents. In this there cannot be a set range of procedures, as each situation will be different. There is, however, a broad choice of options.

Objects can sometimes be acquired at the point of redundancy, when fashions or technology dictate change. Alternatively, they may be recorded in use and acquired at a later date, when the point of redundancy is reached. For example, a study of young people's attitudes and fashions can be undertaken by collecting regularly from a selected group of adolescents the clothes they have grown out of or away from. This can be done in a thorough manner by recording their views, the cost of the garments and accessories, their use and the reasons for superseding them with other fashions. Over a period of a few years a detailed study can be built.

The speed with which any object is made redundant and, theoretically, becomes available can be very rapid indeed. It can also be full of illusions about change. The material from a union meeting, pop concert, industrialists' conference or protest rally will be rendered obsolete even before the event is fully concluded. In contrast, a vital piece of agricultural machinery, a uniform or a means of travel will have a much longer life-span. Moreover, they may be superseded in subtle and overlapping ways, long before they become totally redundant. This can easily lull the museum into a false sense of security about objects, memories, buildings or images. The rough jolt comes when it is realised that the point has already come when such material is already scarce or even no longer available.

Objects which become redundant can often be acquired free or at low cost. Indeed, it is possible to trace past patterns of museum acquisition against cycles of redundancy in certain goods and practices. But using the point of redundancy requires skill on behalf of the curator. Many objects quickly move from having no sentimental or market value to having a swiftly increasing scarcity and, hence, financial value. When a major cycle of redundancy is over, for example, craft trades, pre-war agricultural practices, certain skilled industries, it becomes much more difficult for curators to get access to relevant material, and different approaches to acquisition have to be adopted.

There are many occasions when objects need to be acquired and recorded at the peak of their use. The costume and textile section of Nordiska Museet acquired a set of punk clothes by identifying a good example on the Stockholm streets and then approaching their owner. A new set of clothes was offered in exchange. The museum now has a fully recorded and authenticated example of clothing representing a distinct subculture of modern Stockholm society.

Where objects cannot be acquired at the point of redundancy or through exchanges, alternatives have to be sought. These might include considering material which is not used but which is representative of material that is. Thus, from a study of, say, a home, from which crockery or furniture may not be made immediately available, duplicate samples from the manufacturer or other sources might be sought. The documentation of these would have to be cross-referenced to the content of the study (see, for example, Stavenhow-Hidemark 1985).

Museums ease the passage of material into the collections in many different ways. One of the most frequent is to negotiate for the loan of material. This practice is becoming increasingly common, especially as people become more aware of their heirlooms and their financial values. But, perhaps more critically, much which is of interest to history museums is now of commercial interest to the antique trade. Ordinary, everyday things now have considerable value. Museum acquisition budgets, always inadequate, have not been enlarged to deal with this changed market situation and represent only a very small fraction of those available to curators of art collections. That art acquisition funds are themselves pitifully inadequate for the development of modern art collections is some measure of the near-impossible position in which history museums find themselves when considering purchase.

Although loans are not an ideal solution, they do offer the museum an opportunity to create a record of an object, through photographs of the object and oral testimony. This is particularly well recognized by new museums, such as Slough Museum in Berkshire which finds itself having to build collections from scratch. A co-operative loan arrangement can help to develop the public's confidence in the museum as a community archive, a place of common interest and may, in some circumstances, lead to the donation of material at a later date.

The pressures of finance, space and availability of objects creates real dilemmas for museums. All too frequently it is simply not possible to acquire key objects. Theoretically, this weakens the museum because, as a result, it must inevitably fall short of the ideals of being a community archive. However, there are in practice alternatives worthy of exploration that can militate against absences and that in themselves create more useful and informative collections.

The most obvious example of this is, of course, the use of photography and film to record an object. This is partially to separate the use of film and photography as a regular and integral part of the museum's recording function from their use simply to provide a full and detailed image of objects. Photography has been widely used in the cataloguing of objects, and museums are confident in its use. Clear, sharp black-and-white photographs, showing a proper scale are required here.

Besides photography, a museum can acquire catalogues, technical data, scale drawings, sales and advertising material to represent and explore an object not available to it. In the case of a rural life museum, it may not be possible to collect a combine harvester. But it would be possible to take photographs of the one currently most used on local farms, and acquire copies of its manual, advertising literature and other ephemera. If it was part of a wider study, then film and audio records would also be made.

Beyond these means there are other alternatives not often used by museums. Models used to be quite popular, but their frailty and sometimes absurd images have rendered them unfashionable. Occasionally, they are engaging and invaluable. For example, Sheffield City Museums has had on loan a detailed working model of Mosborough Fair, made by a local man from memory. It encapsulates something about the spirit of the fair and its meaning locally.

History museums have tended to avoid the commissioning or purchase of paintings and sculptures due to the expressed interest of art departments in museums. As Elspeth King has observed, anything with a frame around it is construed as being not relevant (1986). In fact, as the collections at the People's Palace illustrate, visual images in art can be powerful and evocative of a moment or movement in ways that other material might not achieve. For example, the People's Palace holds a series of paintings by a Glasgow lorry driver, Andrew Hay, who taught himself to paint as a response to the National Union of Miners strike in 1984-5. His paintings express his depth of feeling about the strike and his own union's lack of support for it. King comments, ' . . . they are interesting documents of their time rather than great works of art. While they will never be regarded like Hockneys or Bellanys, neither Hockney nor Bellany were out there painting the miners' strike' (1986: 7). The use of visual imagery has been taken a stage further in the Ukraine, where holograms of material are prepared and used in exhibition areas (Yavtushenko and Markov 1982). The most celebrated, though isolated instance of this in Britain is the hologram of the York Anglo-Saxon helmet on display at the Jorvik Viking Centre.

Finally, in the absence of an important object, a museum might have to consider acquiring a sample piece of its material; a section of its total to represent the whole; or a surrogate or replacement object. This is

Figure 10.   One of a series of paintings by Glasgow lorry driver Andrew Hay who
taught himself to paint in response to the miners' strike 1984/5.
by People's Palace Museum, Glasgow.

particularly so where the materials from which the object is made are
unstable, for example nitrate cine-film and certain of the early artificial
materials and fabrics.

Care

The creation of collections brings with it the responsibility to provide
adequate record and care for all material gathered. This is enshrined in the
Code of Professional Conduct and is, in effect, the first tenet of the curator's
faith (Thompson *et al* 1984: 530–40). Even so, this is not without
controversy. Attention has been drawn to the poor conditions in which a
significant proportion of museum collections, of all disciplines, is kept and
the startling lack of adequate collection documentation.

A detailed survey undertaken by the Scottish Museums Council reveals a
very disturbing picture of the standard of collection care in Scotland. The
findings cover all museum disciplines and not just history. Only half of the
museums surveyed had a conservation plan, had undergone a conservation
assessment in the five-year period before the survey, and had an emergency
or disaster plan. Few museums had programmes of environmental
monitoring and less than half included conservation guidelines in their
loans policy. One-fifth of the museums surveyed had inventories of their
collections and 41 per cent had inventories of less than half of their

collections. Nine out of ten museums continue to add to their collections, even though three-quarters of museums have no opportunity to expand their storage facilities. Of the total gross expenditure on Scottish museums only 4 per cent is spent on conservation (Ramer 1989).

The Scottish Museums Council's survey will focus attention on the problem and promote the development of strategies through which museums can meet their responsibilities. The extent of poor collection management throughout Britain has yet to be fully assessed, although it is likely that when the Museums and Galleries Commission's Register of museums is compiled (1988–92) some indication of the scale of the problem nationwide may be evident. However, there is every reason to suppose that the extent of the problem revealed in Scotland will be found elsewhere. The degree to which the problem would have been much worse without the quality of museum council support and training in collection management can only be a matter of speculation.

Collection management is not a visible area of museum activity. Unlike exhibition, publication and education work, it is the least likely of the museum functions to attract sponsorship. It is also a time-consuming, labour-intensive and highly skilled activity, to degrees which opinion-formers and decision-makers on museums seldom grasp. It is also the area of museum work most likely to suffer if pressure is put on the museum to concentrate on other activities. Professional collection care needs the best of management skills. It requires a detailed understanding of techniques and standards. But it also needs excellent organizational and planning skills, so that collection management is an integral part of museum affairs and a constant strand in activities. Without this it can easily become a low priority and consequently suffer from neglect.

History curators find themselves with many difficulties in the management of collections. These often stem from the very diverse physical nature of the objects collected. A museum store may contain objects which are constructed of organic and inorganic materials. There will be complex objects made from a variety of materials, each with its own environmental requirements, and simple objects made from basic substances. Some objects will be huge, needing specialist lifting equipment; others will be tiny, perhaps only fragments of evidence. Costume and leather objects have presented particular problems and, hence, have attracted a good deal of attention. Their care is discussed fully in a number of publications (see in particular, Leene 1972; Waterer 1972; Finch and Putnam 1977; Glover 1984). In contrast, the standards of curatorial care for wooden, iron and plastic material, although covered in archaeological and conservation journals, have not been as cogently discussed. Only recently has a group of papers emerged which help lay down a framework for action, and even these are seen by conservators as being out of date (Turner and Yates 1984). Preventive conservation is a rapidly developing field, where changes in thinking and techniques are infrequently brought together and published as they were in October 1984 in the seminar held by the Area Museum Council for the South East of England, *Taken into Care*. However, collection management will be dealt with in some detail in the forthcoming *Social History Curators' Manual* and this is likely to prove of considerable support to history curators. There are three particular issues worth touching on here: responsibility for care; open or visual storage; and restoration.

Responsibility for the care and documentation of museum collections usually rests with trained curatorial staff; with specialist conservation staff carrying out urgent work on important material. In terms of collection management alone the curator is fulfilling many roles: researcher, fieldworker, collector, documenter, storehand and removal firm. At some point it has to be questioned whether these are the appropriate uses for skilled curatorial staff.

Changes are already taking place in the ways in which museum collections are managed. Both the Victoria and Albert Museum and the Science Museum have moved towards the separation of research from collection management. The Welsh Folk Museum operated under a similar scheme until the early 1980s, when it reverted to a more traditional pattern of curatorial control. The earlier scheme gave documentation and conservation distinct roles in the organisation, in theory to enable the curatorial staff (at that time called academic staff) to concentrate mainly on research, fieldwork, interpretation and writing. In the revised organisation, the functions of conservation and documentation remain, but are currently more integrated with curatorial processes.

The division of curatorial duties and the creation of collection management sections or departments are not new developments. In North America, the specific post of 'Registrar' has emerged: a professional museum person who specializes in museum collection management. This area of professional work has reached the point where registrars have formed themselves into a distinct professional group, with their own code of conduct (Rose 1985).

The development of specialist care of collections is not without its detractors. Two schools of thought exist. One believes that museum activity can be strengthened, promoted and better developed if there is a clear division of labour, especially where specialists can co-operate and work in teams. In this view, curators are liberated from what is sometimes referred to as 'house-keeping' to spend their time more productively on understanding and enlarging collections in ways that can more satisfactorily benefit the public. Further, collections receive better care as they are managed by information and conservation experts who can devote all their time and effort to their preservation and organization.

The alternative view is that collections should be in the charge of curatorial staff with broad-based functions and that collection management would be eased if adequate numbers of technicians and junior staff were available to carry out this work under supervision. It is believed that the separation of curatorship from the care of collections ultimately leads to the dilution of skills and weakens appreciation of the objects in the museum's care. In this view, the scholarship is inevitably eroded if curators do not have regular intimate contact with collections.

This is a controversy that will be with curators for some time. But as

museums increasingly find themselves needing to change quite dramatically, to prove their worth and to maintain adequate levels of funding, it is
inevitable that new ways of looking at the functions of curatorship will
develop. Greater diversification in museum work and further divisions of
labour are an inevitable development. In turn, management methods
hitherto neglected by museum directors, such as corporate planning,
performance review, task-forcing and communication strategy, will
become essential tools in bringing a very diverse workforce together in ways
that prohibit rigid demarcation of ideas and opportunities.

Public access to collections has not proved so openly controversial,
although there are different ideas about the extent to which people should
have access for research or other purposes. The possibilities of developing
'open' or 'visible' storage is one which has begun to occupy museums. The
arguments for and against the idea have been clearly laid down (Johnson
and Hogan 1980). These rest largely on the extent to which it is thought a
collection can be made available for the public's benefit in ways which do
no physical harm to the material and provide adequate information, yet at
the same time release curatorial staff from the need personally to supervise
researchers. There is also some concern about the effect on public opinion
of revealing the extent and condition of reserve collections. Open storage is
substantially more than putting all the collection on view or revealing
masses of stored materials through viewer 'port-holes' in the galleries.
Being 'visible' does not necessarily render a collection accessible:
information adds the essential element.

For some museums, in particular the Museum of Anthropology,
University of British Columbia, Vancouver, the visible storage of reserve
collections, made available with appropriate documentation, is a means by
which visitors can make their own choices about what to see and
researchers can make their own way through the collections without
supervision (Ames 1977; 1985). There are some benefits in terms of
collection security: the collections can be more readily checked against the
catalogue. But this has to be weighed against potential physical damage to
objects through exposure to higher light levels and environmental changes
than occur in stores. Because of this, vulnerable collections, such as
costume collections, cannot readily be made available in open storage.
Alternatives may be found. For example, Warwick Museum, in response to
the heavy use of their costume collection by history, fashion and design
students, devised a very detailed record card which, supported by excellent
technical drawings and photographs, provided the information students
generally required. This went some way to prevent over-handling of the
costume collection.

In the management of collections, curators have to make decisions about
the extent of care given to any object. They often have to make decisions
about whether an object should receive conservation or restoration. These
are entirely different processes, with sometimes radical consequences for
the appearance and meaning of the object. Conservation involves arresting
an object's decay and stabilizing it as far as is possible. This means allowing
its appearance to remain as it is at point of acquisition. Restoration

involves direct and purposeful interference in the fabric and form of an object; in a sense recreating it. There are considerable ethical issues involved here, and each object has to be treated on its merits, in terms of both fabric and form.

Some objects need to be put in working order either because they are to be used and demonstrated in the museum or because their long-term interests are served by this care. This is particularly true of some forms of machinery and vehicles, where lubrication to moving parts prevents deep corrosion and ultimate collapse. Other objects are restored because they are to be used in educational work and can expect to be handled a great deal. But some museums restore collections for other reasons, including a local curatorial preference for objects to look as though they were new and had just arrived from the manufacturer. In some agricultural museums tools and equipment appear as though they had never seen a farm. The mass restoration of objects to the extent that they are painted in bright shiny colours to suit the curator's taste with no research on original colours and appearance, cannot be countenanced. It is unfortunate that it is still found in some professionally run museums.

11. *Objects as Evidence*

A very basic definition of a museum would be 'a keeping place for objects'. The museum as an institution exists because it is believed that objects have meaning and convey not just informaton but knowledge, and that certain objects do this in such a way as to make their retention in museums desirable for the public good. Curators make judgements about the meaning of an object in the decision to acquire or reject it. When that object is put on exhibition its meaning, plus further interpretation derived from comparison and additional research, is what should be conveyed to the visiting public. But how do objects 'mean' and how does the curator begin to understand the material world? There are many different ways in which curators can interpret objects and oral evidence (see Pearce 1986a; 1986b; 1986c; 1987). One obvious approach is to consider the material a museum acquires as part of a complex system of social language.

For any society to function some form of communication has to be developed so that ideas can be shared, information exchanged and feelings made known. The more complex the society; the more complex the communication processes. The study of societies, either now or in the past, requires an examination of the communication processes, as they reveal patterns of social relationship and layers of meaning that are central to the functioning of any society.

Meaning and the material world

The social languages used by most societies have three component parts: non-verbal communication (gestures and movement, body language, physical etiquette); verbal communication (speech, tones and structures of human sounds, and written communication) and signs and symbols (especially the use of objects and space). These do not exist in isolation but are used in integrated forms and patterns to indicate with reasonable precision a state of mind or the form of an idea.

These languages are something that people learn from birth and provide the cultural frameworks within which we operate. They articulate cultural norms and values and provide opportunity for their continual refinement. They are, therefore, subject to change: the ways people communicated in Leicester in 1689, 1789, 1889, and 1989 are very different indeed. Fragments of those languages are left behind in street names, buildings, certain kinds of local industries, popular memory, story and song, and a number of objects in private hands and the Leicestershire Museums collection. The museum in this instance, as in others, can choose to not only find meaning in these languages but also fill in the gaps and the silences.

Non-verbal communication can provide as vivid a cultural language as speech. Forms acceptable in one society or group may not be acceptable or interpreted in the same way elsewhere. For example, to point at a person may be a useful way of indicating someone with whom the pointer wishes to talk. But in some groups it is rude, even highly offensive, to point. The abrupt, tense stabbing movements of aggression are visibly different from the glowing, relaxed, gentle moods of shared enjoyment. These things do not need words. The blowing of a kiss or a raspberry, a hug of a child and the embrace of one's enemy, the grasp of a hand in friendship or in arm-wrestling are gestures with very different social meaning. The violence of the Luddites in 1811–13, like that on the streets of Toxteth, Liverpool and St Paul's, Bristol in 1981, can be read as part of language, too, as symptoms of the effects of social change, perhaps more simply as the 'voice of the unheard'.

Verbal communication permits precision of language. We talk and write in ways that define our roles as well as extend our messages, using words in forms that give meaning to the listener or reader. So the language used to a parent will be different from that used to a colleague, employer, friend or client. Similarly, written languages vary. Children's books are often written to be read aloud, using words that are within the child's vocabulary or which can be progressively added to it. A quality daily newspaper is written for immediate and silent consumption in a language which is thought to be used by a major cross-section of its readers.

The spoken word is similarly used in a variety of forms to convey specific meaning. Remembrance can be filled with words in dialect form used to convey their contemporary meaning and may be delivered with weight of emotion and technical detail. In comparison, an eye-witness account will not bring the same form of self-esteem to the bearer nor be filled with wide-ranging information, but may in itself have a tone and a pace not applied to other forms of verbal communication.

Poems, the lyrics of songs and the content of stories are means of dealing with a range of social experiences, feelings and issues: love and loss in modern pop songs; a record of feelings and events in the songs and poems of the women in support groups in the 1984–5 Miners Strike; and the mythologizing stories told about AIDS or road accidents. Such verbal forms of language as these are both a means of communication and a way of dealing with life. But our reception of these forms of communication will vary. True communication is an impossibility: the transference of information from one person to another cannot take place exactly. This is simply because we read and hear what we are permitted, able or are willing to understand.

The third form of communication is through objects and the use of space. Objects are derived both from the natural world or are created through artificial processes. They add subleties and vividness to non-verbal communication, allowing messages to be connected and amplified. For example, punk culture in the late 1970s was violently anti-establishment. It developed into a subculture with its own norms and values. Rejection of mainstream society was indicated in music, language and dress which in form embodied the reverse of contemporary norms: instead of coiffured hair, brilliantly coloured, severe and dramatic hair shapes, including the mohican; instead of subtle make-up aiming to improve natural attributes, self-mutilation with common objects such as safety-pins, tatoos and the use of black and other strong colours in facial make-up.

Dress is an obvious form of social language used by everyone. It defines the roles we are playing, our self-perception and mood and the functions we are carrying out. Domestic dwellings, public architecture, choice of car, sophistication of office equipment or assembly-line tools are similarly significant. They are our ideas about ourselves given physical form and differ from those held by others, both within Britain and without. The rate at which we change objects; the range we own and how they are distributed; the form they take and their effective use; the meaning they offer to different people in different situations; and their perceived level of sophistication add complexity to our understanding of material when it eventually reaches the museum.

Study of the systems of language and communication around us reveals social language as extraordinarily complex. As Raymond Williams has pointed out: 'once we start thinking about the nature and processes of language, or of what we now call non-verbal communication, or of the making of signs and symbols, we find that we are faced with some of the most difficult as well as the most central questions about ourselves' (Williams 1981: 16). It is some of these questions that museums should be answering.

By collecting fragments of the signs and symbols that are part of any social system of communication, the museum should aim to encapsulate the physical and oral evidence of being and behaving. The material so gathered needs to be studied as indicators of social language. This is an area explored by Adrian Forty in his book *Objects of Desire* (1986). Dealing exclusively with manufactured goods, he sets out a central argument which he then explores through case studies. His central point is that

> the design of manufactured goods is determined not by some internal genetic structure but by the people and the industries that make them and the relationship of these people and industries to the society in which the products are to be sold. [1986: 8]

As an example, he suggests that 'to look at the range of goods in the catalogues of nineteenth century manufacturers, department stores and mail order houses is to look at a representation of society. Through the design of knives, watches, clothes and furniture to suit every rank and station in life, one can read the shape of society as manufacturers saw it, and as their customers learned to see it' (1986: 93). In this instance, objects have to be considered as being designed for intended social purpose, as existing as part of the language sets of different income groups and social classes.

The quantity of material as well as the speed of change is dictated, to a large extent, by consumption and consumerism. Societies which are relatively wealthy will have a high turnover in manufactured goods, ephemeral objects and means of creative expression. Societies that are poor and under-resourced are more likely to cling to established ways and materials, and recycle rather than throw away. In such societies tradition and established skills are likely to have a central and, hence, long-term presence. The comparison of Delhi with Dallas illustrates this point.

The consumer revolution in Britain began in earnest in the eighteenth century, riding on the back of the Industrial Revolution. Neil McKendrick graphically described this process and how objects which for centuries had been the privileged possessions of the rich came, within the space of a few generations, 'to be within the reach of a larger part of society than ever before'. He continues:

> What men and women had once hoped to inherit from their parents, they now bought for themselves. What were once bought at the dictate of need, were now bought at the dictate of fashion. What were once bought for life, might now be bought several times over. What were once available on high days and holidays through the agency of markets, fairs and itinerant pedlars were increasingly made available every day but Sunday ... As a result 'luxuries' became to be seen as mere 'decencies', and 'decencies' came to be seen as 'necessities'. Even 'necessities' underwent a dramatic metamorphosis in style, variety and availability. [McKendrick *et al.* 1983: 1]

Many objects typical of those made to satisfy this new consumer demand exist in museums in decorative art, costume, social and industrial history collections, where much of their social significance is lost because of this division of care.

The beginnings of the consumer revolution, described by McKendrick, gave way to even greater demand and profound changes signified by the possession of goods and space. Indeed, the consumer revolution is still with us, although in a much revised form. It feeds as much on the market economics of supply and demand as on the compulsion brought through changing social languages in which objects are a strongly signifying part. For example, Renault advertised its small car of the Renault 5 with images appealing to the young high earner and a slogan which read 'The Renault 5. What's yours called?'. The mechanical characteristics and reliability of the vehicle were not part of its advertised image.

Objects as evidence

The history museum explores the more-recent human past through a much wider and, hence, arguably more-complex web of evidence than other museum-based disciplines. Unlike art and archaeology, it is not confined to the artefact as the principal source of information. Because of this the museum can look not only at the messages the object itself conveys in its material and manufactured form but also at the meaning and interrelationships of this within contemporary social codes. Two particular sets of examples serve here (Kavanagh 1988b).

A blanket is a heavy-duty piece of woollen cloth which may have some form of pattern at its border or over its length. It can be considered for its weave, its fabric and its design. But blankets are used in many ways and like other objects have taken on different meanings according to use. In the mining valleys of South Wales, until relatively recently, women carried their babies in blankets carefully pulled around their own bodies, the 'Welsh way'. There were many reasons for this, including long-term, grinding poverty that placed both overcoats and prams outside the budgets of many families. The warmth and security of the child had to be combined with the warmth of the mother: they therefore bound themselves together in this way.

In Glasgow at the end of the last century blankets became something akin to a unit of currency. Some of the poor families in the East End of the city pawned their blankets each morning to release sufficient funds to buy fruit and vegetables to hawk on the street that day, with the hope of raising enough money to buy food for the family and get the blankets out of pawn that night.

In rural Lincolnshire a sheep farmer retained a blanket brought to him by the man who each year bought his fleeces. The blanket came from the factory which the buyer supplied. Subsequently, it was kept as a symbol of the chain of production in which the farm was part. More recently, between 1976 and 1981, blankets were used in the H-Block protests in Ulster and became a symbol of the prisoners' struggle to be treated as political detainees.

If a museum collection contained one blanket from each of these cases, they would be significantly more than samples of woven woollen cloth and would have to be explored as integral and signifying elements of the societies from which they were derived. Their meaning would be reached through the study of women, poverty, production and protest, but not necessarily through the blankets' dimensions and physical descriptions.

The study of objects in their context of use and in the wider patterns of social and cultural signification provides the essence of history museum practice. It is, however, a process which is profoundly complicated by the fact that the meaning of any object undergoes tremendous revision, from its creation to its ultimate destruction or loss, and even beyond. It can never convey one single message, uncorrected, unambiguous and unqualified. Different social perceptions, needs and changing attitudes will see to that.

For example, one museum observer commented that a stuffed tiger in a case was not a tiger: it was just a museum object. Here is one simple change of position in meaning: from live animal to dead museum object. However, the likelihood is that this is just one in a whole range of changes that have transformed such a tiger, given that in the case of so many 'museum objects' of this kind, it is a process that may well have been going on since the last decades of the nineteenth century.

In its natural environment the tiger has meant cub and sibling, perhaps it also meant mate and mother. Most probably it had been predator and hunter, an object of fear. Its ultimate demise may have transformed it into a prize, evidence of accomplishment, the gratification and confirmation of the perceived socially superior status of the big game hunter. For others involved in the event, it may have simply represented the means by which meagre incomes were supplemented through the service of a self-indulgent sport. The carcass as economic device would have been maintained as a trained taxidermist transformed it, fixed it in shape and altered its substance.

For the museum that acquired it, it may have been a prime acquisition, connecting the museum to the donor and thus indirectly to his class and class values. As time changes the tiger becomes evidence and symbol of imperialists at play, disrupting and wasting wildlife and natural resources. The quality of natural history programmes on television deflect the public gaze from the tiger, and it is transformed from evidence of the exotic wildlife of other lands to a kind of community cuddly toy, a source of popular affection, as is the case with the tiger at Kings Lynn Museum, the brown bear at Sheffield City Museum and the polar bear at Paisley Museum (Blackburn 1987). The chances are that, with the current pressure on museum space, the tiger may now be read quite differently by curators and may simply be a nuisance, a symbol of folly in acquisition. The tiger can change in meaning yet further, for example, it might become a convenient device in multicultural museum teaching. In sum, it is and has been much more than simply a tiger or a museum object and the way in which it can be read will continue to change up to and maybe beyond its ultimate destruction.

The curator has, therefore, to enter into a process of questioning: the evidence that the object (or story, song or testimony) presents internally, that is in itself, and externally from its contexts and relationships. The internal criticism will reveal its material, form, design, evidence of use and re-use and possibly dating. This is the classic reading of the museum object, and is derived from the limited and partially misplaced view that objects can speak for themselves. Museums have long collected material which is self-proclaiming, the trade union banner is a well-known case in point. But such questions may not be enough. Cross-referencing to external questioning may be required if the object is to be understood. External questioning will raise issues of provenance, authenticity, place and survival. It will also raise questions aimed at construing the object's meaning and significance, its cultural context and changes in relationships. In sum, the object is more successful as a springboard for inquiry rather than as a concluding statement.

Judgements and values

Inevitably, the process of questioning cannot be value-free. But the scope for originality will be as wide as the scope for bias and prejudicial views. Because of this museum practice will vary not just between individual curators but also between museums in different political systems and economies. This overlies all museum activity.

In an effort to systematize the selection of objects through the process of contemporary documentation, Swedish curators in the organization SAMDOK attempted to categorize the values which we attach to objects and which, in turn, affect our view of them. They achieved a framework through which the process of questioning described above could be refined and developed (Rosander 1980: 28–30). In this, curators have to be aware that the values they ascribe will not necessarily be those given by others. But this is a central curatorial activity, one where the professionalism, the extreme competence of curatorship is most required.

The SAMDOK Council argued that cultural material could be ascribed a number of more-specific values. The first set of these is concerned with symbolic values, of which there are several. They include affective value, that is connections with people or events that hold some popular or historic meaning: David Bowie's guitar, Queen Elizabeth I's glove and the chair used by Karl Marx in the British Library. Some objects may have fetish value, that is they are associated with dreams or fantasies derived from the dominant cultural structure, such as the adolescent's posters of pop stars or salacious stickers in the back windows of cars.

Ritual values may be associated with objects used ceremonially and symbolically in the performance of a cult or religious ceremony or in some form of acceptance of rite of passage, for example, the communion cup, the green boughs used by the Druids at the midsummer service at Stonehenge, or the tools used to 'bang-out' an engineer leaving his place of work for the last time. A further definition of the symbolic, comes in the representative values some objects hold. For example, a wedding ring stands as a symbol of marriage, a national flag as a symbol of nationhood, and a union banner for the comradeship of union membership. Finally, within this group SAMDOK identifies *pars pro toto* value, where a piece or section of an object has to symbolize the larger whole. This is instanced by the ways in which maritime museums can use figureheads and steering wheels to suggest or indicate complete vessels.

The remaining values in the SAMDOK list are more specific. The first of these is unique value: certain objects have intrinsic values of their own. An object may be the only one made, or it may be the only one left in existence: in either case it might be ascribed a unique value.

Other values identified by SAMDOK fall into similarly definable groups. The first of these make some reference to the object's position within technological and cultural development. Objects which provide a clear insight into historical processes or present conditions may be said to have a key value: for example an army recruitment poster from the autumn of 1914. Similar to this are component value, when an object provides a link to a larger thematic or geographical context, and reference value, when an object can be used to refer to cultural change. Both of these find illustrations in the development of modern communications: an example might be the Morris Minor, one of the vehicles that constituted mass car ownership after the war, with all that car implied for travel, work, leisure and status.

The final group is well known indeed. First, illustrative value: this is a judgement usually employed in educational contexts, in that an object has to be assessed in terms of its ability to illustrate an idea, or an experience or a person. Aesthetic values need little introduction, although they are rarely defined other than in terms of connoisseurship: an instinctive response to quality in art, based on a detailed knowledge of form and style. Some museums may identify objects for their prototype value in that they served as patterns for further technological developments. The final value encountered with increasing frequency is 'collector' value: there are distinct groups of material that become of value to collectors. This often affects the museum's ability to acquire or record such material, which may well include things which are not necessarily seen by some museums as having historic and cultural relevance and are, therefore, positioned within decorative art.

By laying bare such a structure of values, the SAMDOK Council was giving clarity to a crucial aspect of museum practice that until this point had operated largely by professional instinct. It is possible to see that many objects will fall into more than one group, or will be viewed differently according to the nature of the inquiry. Therefore, it is necessary to recognize that these categories are an attempt to help curators think more carefully about the objects they interpret and, from this, identify more closely the values they are attempting to ascribe to them. In many respects, this is a means of examining basic curatorial assumptions and value-judgments.

Part three.   History in the museums: exhibitions and the public

12. *History Museums and the Public*

Without the public the museum could not exist. The 'keeping place for objects' has always been justified in terms of the people it seeks to serve. This element of service has been with museums since the nineteenth century and has become part and parcel of the argument for their continued presence in contemporary society. Much curatorial work has rested on the assumption that museums are by definition 'good things', accessible to all and an instrument for the 'public good'. Such assumptions have rarely been challenged or tested, regardless of the fact that they are, in some cases, palpable falsehoods, delivered with a smug, purposeful ignorance of real social and cultural trends.

But this disregard for the interests of the public is already being undermined. Museums of all disciplines and constitutional forms are increasingly being forced into thorough analysis of their levels of presentation and service. This is not a symptom of a new awareness, the product of born-again social concern. Instead, it is evidence of the changing nature of museum funding. As both national and local government slowly begin to withdraw from absolute financial support of museums, other forms of funding have had to be sought.

The visitor is one such source of income, through the payment of entrance charges, purchases at the museum shop and involvement in special museum schemes such as sponsoring objects. Museums can no longer overlook the public. They must identify and meet visitor needs, and provide a quality of visit that, in turn, promotes attendance. The aim is not to increase the museum's social contact or extend its messages to new audiences, although with luck this may happen. The ultimate aim is to increase attendances in order to increase income and assure the future of the museum. New forms of analysis come into play, not based on effectiveness of the exhibitions or the social or educational benefits of museum visiting, but 'spend-per-head'. The economics of the market-place are now with museums and they are having an effect which decades of sophistry about the social good of museums have failed to provide.

But market-place philosophy, while bringing a more caring and generous attitude to visitor services, is also developing museums deliberately targeted at those groups with sufficient income to benefit the museum. Museums are, therefore, becoming tailored to the predetermined cultural patterns of a paying public which may not be a representative cross-section of British society. While a body of curatorial opinion fortunately still holds to the social value of museums and their potential within a plural society, their voices and positive examples of museum work are being drowned by other interests.

Museum visiting and visitors

Information about how and why people visit museums is fairly scarce. Although museums carry out museum visitor surveys, the form and analysis of such vary enormously and few are published. Several major surveys have been conducted, although these have their limitations and add only fragments to our understanding of museum visiting (for example, English Tourist Board 1982; Henley Centre 1985; Social Trends 1988). Important advances have been made in this field by Nick Merriman in his positioning of museum visiting within the scope of leisure activities and wider social phenomena (1988). Eilean Hooper-Greenhill has similarly assisted our understanding of patterns of visiting, relating them not only to leisure and social trends but also to the effectiveness and range of services provided by museums, and ultimately to the quality of curatorship (1988).

In general terms, it is thought that somewhere in the region of 47 per cent of the British public visits a museum or gallery at least once a year, and that most people visit at least once in a four-year period. Regular museum visitors are likely to be reasonably affluent, educated and mobile. Adult visitors are drawn from the 'middle-age group 35–59' and are generally well educated. Non-museum visitors tend to be in lower income brackets, with less formal education. They also tend to be without private transport and to be retired, unemployed or in part-time work (Merriman 1988).

These profiles and the majority of the statistical information about museum visiting tend to be generalized, applying to the very broad group of 'museums and galleries'. There has been very little analysis of visiting patterns according to the form or discipline of a museum. There has also been an absence of comparative studies of the audiences drawn to art galleries, natural history museums, technical museums and history museums. Even within the wide category 'history museum' there is the need to find out whether visiting patterns vary between open-air museums, community museums, site museums, national museums and local authority museums. There may be differences between the visiting public for agricultural and industrial museums, and also for specialist museums on, for example, costumes or a recognized historical figure.

It is thought that history museums attract a visiting public from a broader social band than other forms of museum. Research conducted by the Scottish Museums Council revealed that visits to history exhibitions were the most attractive option for people visiting museums: 44 per cent of respondents chose history exhibitions compared with 35 per cent special exhibitions and 25 per cent art exhibitions. It seems logical to advance the explanation that history museums are in their subject-matter and presentation far more accessible than art galleries, and that they have a strong nostalgic appeal. Therefore, they are more attractive and receive more visitors than other forms of museum. But Merriman's research revealed that whereas 91 per cent of the people in his survey sample believed it to be worth knowing about the past, only 7 per cent identified museums as an enjoyable way of finding out about it. This staggering revelation, while needing to be further explored through research and survey work, suggests museums have been failing in the ways they explain the past and the degrees to which they make it real and relevant.

Future developments have to be based on detailed assessments of the history museum and its relationship with the public. These should be very extensive, taking into account visitor needs and expectations in three areas: social, physical and intellectual.

Visitor needs

Perceptions of the visitor have varied enormously. On the one extreme is the view that 'too many visitors are bad for the fabric of our buildings, and our displays, and push up maintenance bills, too few visitors and we scent failure and we rush off to commission visitor surveys (Cumming 1985: 35). On the other hand, and of long standing, is the view that the value of museums is 'in direct proportion to the service they render the emotional and intellectual needs of the people ... It may be helpful to remember that one [the curator] is in a sense the host to a visiting guest' (Madison 1925: 19).

Visiting museums in the main tends to be a social activity. It is voluntary and takes place for most adult visitors outside work hours. That their decision to visit a museum is taken at all implies a level of expectation that there will be some reward, especially satisfaction, through stimulation of interest and quality of experience. For children and students, museum visiting may be part of formal education, either organized in the form of a group visit or a personal enquiry for project or research work. For many researchers, visiting museums may be neither strictly speaking a leisure activity nor part of formal education, but a specialist form of work. Researchers, therefore, tend to visit museums on their own, as may the casual visitor acting on impulse.

However, the majority of museum visitors are people who come within their own time and usually in groups, often family groups made up of more than one generation, and both sexes. It has to be construed from this that the basis of the visit is the experience of being together as a group and enhancing the bond of the group through shared encounters. The size of the group may vary; it could consist of two people (a couple of friends, parent and child or partners) or 20 (for example, from an organization or society). But the sharing of the time and the visit will remain the one constant feature.

For the visit to work, therefore, that preparedness for joint participation within the group, regardless of size, has to be anticipated by the museum. People will want to feel comfortable in their surroundings and capable of dealing with all the museum has to offer. Effectively, visitors need to feel valued, and museums leave visitors in little doubt as to the extent their presence is appreciated. These messages are evident in the courtesy extended, the welcome given and the ways in which needs are met. Dark entrance halls, a mass of prohibition notices, unsmiling, uniformed security staff, no gallery plans and incoherent displays are sufficient clues that visitors are not thought about, let alone welcome in the museum concerned.

Visitor needs have also to be acknowledged in terms of access. Recognition of the social nature of visiting has led museums to an awareness that the opening hours of museums are, to a degree, anti-social. Established patterns of securing and warding museums have maintained hours of opening to levels set in the early post-war years. Today, it is more fully appreciated that group visits take place when there is leisure time and that this takes a very different form now from that of 40 years ago. The office-hours openings of some museums are of little assistance to people who wish to visit together, if one or more member is in work or school. Full opening on Bank Holidays, Sundays and early evenings, especially in summer would be an important development. Staffing museums for extended opening will be just one element of the changes in work conditions and variety of employment opportunities likely to be experienced in the years ahead.

One of the most obvious signs that a museum cares about its visitors is the way in which it caters for physical needs. Success or failure of a museum visit can sometimes be determined by the ease with which the museum is located and whether the visitor can park a car. Trouble-free travel to a museum and a provided parking place ensure an excellent start to a visit. The need for public toilets has long been recognized and it has become obvious that cloakroom facilities, first-aid points and changing rooms for parents with babies are also required in museums aiming to provide a full public service. So, too, are museum-provided back-packs or push-chairs for toddlers and an adequate means of getting youngsters round the museum. Children constitute one-third of the visiting public and, whether on their own, with adults or part of a school group should encounter a supportive atmosphere in the museum. The quality of a group visit with children is often determined by the extent to which the museum understands and prepares for the children's needs and whether this is done in a spirit of joy and co-operation, or not.

Physical requirements vary enormously. Many people have limited mobility and find difficulties with stairs. The prospect of a visit to a museum which will inevitably involve a long period of walking and standing can be daunting. Alternative routes around museums, lifts and museum-provided wheelchairs are some of the solutions museums have found. Braille guides and labels and induction loops at audio-visual presentations should be standard provision. Such aids should be offered willingly and clearly, without people having to ask if they are available. Planning for people with physical difficulties should be present when exhibitions are constructed. Sightlines are very different when the visitor is sitting in a wheelchair. The view of an object is also very different when sight itself is partial or substantially absent.

All visitors, regardless of age and agility, require the opportunity to sit and relax at various stages of their visit. This may mean sitting to view something special or simply to rest the feet. 'Museum fatigue' happens in all museums and the best of them give visitors frequent opportunity to sit down. Refreshment is also important. Museum cafés offer history museums the opportunity to show off local foods and specialities. Even the smallest of museums, if without room for a refreshment area, can rise to a coffee pot and biscuits.

The needs of the visiting public in the event of an emergency have also to be considered. Fire and explosion can happen in museums as in any other public place and the museum must have established drills and procedures, based on specialist advice, so that galleries and museum spaces can be emptied quickly, with the minimum of panic. Museum developments need to be carefully scrutinized not only for the security of collections but also for the safety of the public. It is in these instances that museum and gallery staff should be identifiable and capable of taking control.

People learn about the past through many different activities: through hearing and listening, reading and watching, touching and talking, asking and thinking. The decision to visit a museum is in part at least a decision to learn. There is an expectation that the visit will be worth while; that there will be the challenge of new experiences. People are prepared to learn actively and to participate. How often is all this positive motivation lost by museums?

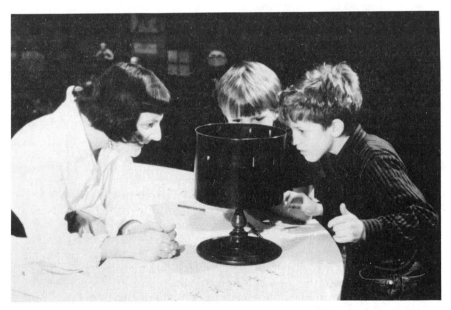

Figure 11   The great success of the Museum of the Moving Image (MOMI) in London can be ascribed, in part, to its willingness to engage at many different levels with its visitors.

Figure 12   The Animation Gallery at MOMI.

Poor exhibitions, on badly developed themes, seen elsewhere in other museums, are no aid to learning; nor are incoherently written labels that offer no new information or insight. These kill any potential curiosity the object or subject might invite. Equally pointless are erudite labels that satisfy no one but the curator who proudly produced them. It would seem that museums profoundly underestimate the intellectual capabilities of visitors. Curators cling to the tried and tested formats, even when it is obvious that these are banal and without substance. Efforts to break new ground in exhibitions can sometimes lead disastrously to exhibitions overwhelmed with text that nobody but its author will read and understand in full.

Adventurous exhibitions and displays are born of adventurous ideas and are not necessarily conditional on major financial investment. They work because unexpected and sometimes unexplored ideas are presented through objects and images untypical of the museum's usual range; or occasionally, where typical museum objects are displayed in untypical combinations. There is no evidence whatsoever that the public cannot enjoy and rise to new themes in exhibition displays. An over-dependence on established themes, especially the Romans, the Victorian kitchen and the Second World War, will do nothing to convince people that the history museum is capable of being a challenging, stimulating place.

Catering for the intellectual needs of the public will involve other initiatives. These include: labels and guides in a number of languages; good quality publications; educational programmes targeted at different age groups; special tours of the museum; joint projects; and outreach exhibitions and services to those people who cannot easily get to the museum, or for whom the museum is still not seen as a welcoming environment.

For a museum to meet visitor needs adequately, it must in the first instance develop a conscious approach through a well-defined communications policy. Visitor surveys and local research will play an important part in its development. But the most important foundation for such a policy will be a commonly held belief about the museum and its subject. This requires staff to work together, possibly drawing on outside advice and opinions, in an effort to define joint goals and rationalize these against likely visitor response. The museum is a complex institution with many functions, some of which are at odds with one another: for example, the security of collections and public access. The development of a

Figure 13   Actor-guides at MOMI draw people into the museum's subject, raising their awareness and their curiosity. Here an actor-guide presents a lantern show using a triunial lantern.

Figure 14   An actor-guide on MOMI's Hollywood sound stage working with visitors on a 1940s-style screen test.

communications policy is a way of finding a balance from which the growth of the museum can be promoted.

Whereas it is quite feasible for a museum to concentrate exclusively on either the quality and interpretation of its collections or on the manifestations of visitor care and comfort, it actually requires the careful and critical development of both of these areas in equal measure for the museum to communicate and operate effectively. Good car parking and well-lit cafeterias are no substitute for well-researched and stimulating exhibitions. Similarly, spirited displays and learned publications are limited compensation for no public conveniences and attitudes which clearly imply 'children are not welcome here'.

Interaction: the museum and the public

The predominant assumption is that the relationship between the museum and the visitor is one confined to the experience of passing through the museum's public space, observed but unaccompanied. With the exception of the formal display areas and certain educational activities, the visitor is a figure seen as being detached and separated from all other museum processes. Thus, with visitors tidied away in public spaces, the museum staff, in the private spaces beyond, get on with deciding what should be collected and displayed in their name.

It does not have to be like this, a fact which many museums well recognize. People are now encouraged to participate in, and respond to, many aspects of museum activities. One of the best-established manifestations of this is the practice of accepting volunteers to work on and with museum collections. In 1987 it was estimated that 40 per cent of the private sector museums, most of them operating within the field of recent human history, 'make use of volunteers for their top seven activities (guided tours, conservation, documentation, library work, curatorial work, sponsorship and fund raising and security and warding duties)' Prince and Higgins-McLoughlin 1987: 98). The phrase 'make use of' is indicative of a widespread attitude, where the volunteer is seen as an instrument of the museum, rather than someone both giving and receiving from the process of participation. The figure of 40 per cent applies to both the national and the local authority museums. Those national museums that 'use' volunteers do so for library work and documentation; the local authority museums add research to this list.

People 'volunteer' for museum work for many different reasons, including entry to the profession through accumulating experience of museum work and the pursuit of a personal interest (Mattingley 1984). They do not come to be 'used' but to give, to contribute to something in which they believe. Volunteers and untrained temporary workers have had a hugh impact on museums. They have enhanced museum practice by increasing the network of contacts and provided skills which supplement those held by the staff. Indeed, such is their importance in museum work that it is unlikely that much museum development in the last 20 years, especially in the private sector, could have been so rapid or so extensive, without this input.

In Sweden the position is very different. The use of free, unskilled labour in the public museum is discouraged by the unions, who want to maintain the strength, coherence and position of a highly professional museum workforce. Participation from the public takes other forms as a result. These include the stimulation and delegation of research and recording tasks in workplace, education and pensioners groups. Exhibition space and facilities are provided so that people can construct and present their own exhibitions within the museum. At Rikstutställningar, a state-run organization that creates and distributes exhibitions to museums and elsewhere, the involvement of the public is encouraged to the point where ideas for exhibition are eagerly accepted and followed through. In an average year they may receive anything up to 200 suggestions for possible exhibitions (Westerlund 1986). The public in this way becomes both a respondent and participant.

There are many examples of museum practice in Britain which values and encourages interaction with the public. Many of these are found at those museums which consciously plan to involve people in their activities. Story-tellers, remembrancers, musicians, crafts people, actors, film-makers and many others are taking part in ways that are mutually beneficial and constructively add to the quality and variety of the museum. Whether as part of performance, research, or education—paid or unpaid—they and the museums in which they operate are distinguished by an attitude centred not in 'use' but in purpose.

The museums in which such participation is found are frequently the ones where the visitors' needs are most thoughtfully cared for. They are likely also to be the museums which attract a much broader cross-section of the public and, as a result, are experiencing steadily increasing visitor figures. Quality pays, and so does care and co-operation.

13. History in Exhibitions

The museum makes public the histories it produces through the medium of exhibition. As with all other forms of history, exhibition is a construction, a representation and interpretation of a past moment, based on ideas derived from consideration of available sources. It is a version of the past and not the past itself. That is always beyond our reach and cannot be truly reconstructed. There are several reasons for this. Our cultural perspectives limit our appreciation of past languages and social codes. The availability of evidence is affected by time, decay and the foresight of others in the retention of vital clues.

But more than anything, the histories produced are invested with, even determined by, current concerns and ideas. As a result, museums are, in Dr Jeanne Cannizzo's words, 'symbolic structures which make visible our public myths: the stories we tell ourselves about ourselves are institutionalized and materialized in our museums' (1987: 22). This is not to negate the value of history in museums. But, as we cannot ever perfect the art of recovering the past, we must face the problems and find means to locate some form of balance. This means accepting that history is a field in which finite answers cannot be given. Neither can museums provide 'essential historic truths'. But what they can do is open up a dialogue about the past.

Museums are part of a set of official apparatus that people use to find information. Histories in museums have automatic credibility as a result. This equips museums with considerable power and influence on how the past should be remembered and understood. Where, for example, museum histories discriminate and omit, they further legitimize discrimination and omission. Where they commemorate and celebrate, they permit commemoration and celebration. Where they question and consider, they promote questioning and consideration.

History content

The choice of exhibition themes and display topics in museums warrants examination. How does a museum decide what will be displayed and what messages it wants to give? Space, available collections, perceived public interest will come high on the list of considerations. But what about ideas?

In some museums it is hard to find evidence that thought has been given to the displays and that practical matters, conditioned by notions of what a

Figure 15.   Messages museums offer about the past have to be questioned. Is this just an exercise in the naming of objects?

museum should look like, have predominated. This is epitomized in one of the county museums in Wales. Its entrance hall is graced with four bicycles (although no explanation of their use locally is given) and with a recent acquisitions case with the negligent sounding notice that the objects there are 'to be sorted'. A temporary exhibition gallery, which catches the eye through the large notice asking 'Are You Sitting Comfortably?', displays some recent oil paintings of local topography and an assemblage of objects on which sitting is possible. At the back is a case containing six manikins draped in clothing as incongruous as the High Sheriff's uniform worn at the coronation of King George V, doctorate cap and gown from the University of London worn by Professor William Rees, a 1920s crepe and lace cocktail dress and a black mourning dress. The labels are a naming exercise, if that. No connections are drawn between the items of costume. Interpretation of their meaning or relevance locally is not provided. The mourning dress label reads 'Black brocade dress with embroidery and black jet decoration 1880s'. No mention is made of local rites of passage, mourning rituals or Victorian ideas of death.

The main gallery is given over to three separate sections. A Victorian farm kitchen is one of them. It is full of excellent material which, again, is denied local interpretation. The viewer is assured that the objects are local and typical, but is given no reasons as to why this was so, or whether they had different meanings for men and women, rich and poor farmers, or local tradespeople. The agricultural section provides a rare moment of local information: that after the First World War, many new mechanical methods made hand tools redundant; that most men in the county worked on a farm; and that a livelihood was dependent on the good management of livestock and crops. Although sweeping statements, these are a degree more useful than the naming process in the temporary gallery. Agricultural tools and photographs of presumably local farm workers fill the display and another naming operation takes place. But, how was life on the land here different from other parts of Wales? Were there local ways of doing things or specific forms of social relations? Were some skills more valued than others, and if so why? How was labour hired and paid? Did women and children work on the land? What were the seasonal patterns of activity? What did these tools mean to the people who used them and how long were they in use? How has life on the land altered? How and why did it change? None of these questions are answered, because none of them seem to have been posed.

The third section is a reconstructed blacksmith's shop. The tools and equipment displayed came from one particular place and had been owned and used by a known blacksmith. Yet the material is interpreted generally. The photographs provided could be of any blacksmith. Why was this one special? What was his local role? Why did the museum feel this material sufficiently important to the social history of the area that they were prepared to devote part of the gallery to its display? A further social history gallery which might have been full of the answers to these questions is located on an upper floor. The sign said 'gallery closed'; no explanation was given.

This deadly approach to exhibition is repeated in museums throughout this country. The high standard in content of history museum exhibitions elsewhere makes them all the more obvious. They exist for a number of reasons. First, the academic and professional skills in history curatorship have always been underestimated. This has significantly affected the recruitment to museum posts. Secondly, lack of understanding of the necessary skills involved and the neglect of museum theory have lead to the mistaken assumption that successful interpretation involves no more than the simple juxtaposition of the best objects to hand. For some curators it has been taken as acceptable practice for the examinaton of the meaning of objects and images to stop once the naming process has been successfully concluded. Finally, they exist because, for some, they are a distilled version of how the past should be recalled. This is a past without conflict and inconsistency, a past where generalization of view is adequate because it does not disturb or disrupt received truths. The range of human feelings, alternative means of being and becoming, and the essential variety of life which exists regardless of the dominance of one industry or agricultural system are totally denied in such museums. In turn, they rob history museums of their true potential and perpetuate notions of museums as passive and peripheral institutions.

These bleak processes have been justified by some curators in terms of visitor figures. Validation of the museum's approach has been found in the number of feet that pass over the museum's mat. Evaluation of quality of experience or the effectiveness of the displays in these cases tends to be rudimentary, if it exists at all (Kavanagh 1987). But perhaps the most worrying argument for the status quo in museum exhibitions has been that people like what they are given in museums. This attitude has rarely been tested by the museums concerned. But it may, in part, explain why in Merriman's survey only 7 per cent believed that museums contribute to our understanding of the past (1988: 162). New ways of determining what it is about the past that museums must address have to be found.

Visitor preference for certain topics is being used by developers in the heritage industry to determine the coverage they will provide. The White Cliffs Experience, to be opened in Dover in December 1990, has taken detailed soundings of public perceptions of their ideas and the sort of things they would like to see there. Whereas such research is valuable in providing public input into schemes, there is still a risk that established ideas may prevail, as may the dominant preferences of the company or museum concerned.

In the absence of any wider view, many museums presuppose an innate conservatism on the part of the public. The comparison with museum developments in the USA is useful here. Michael Wallace in an article called 'The Politics of Public History' considers the powerful role American museums play in re-inforcing myths about the past. In so doing he nevertheless envisages the museum as an institution superbly situated to inform people of the continuities between past and present. But he draws attention to the ways in which public histories in American museums are produced for a 'market', as a commodity, which people do not have to buy if they do not want to. He writes:

> Consumers have their own conventions and assumptions and tend not to gravitate to presentations that don't re-enforce these. For producers who aim to *change* their audiences' minds on some matter, the prior necessity of attracting them as customers can act as a drag on innovation. But more often than not, I suspect, audience conservatism is simply taken for granted. The cry that something 'won't sell' is often used as an excuse by those who want a program killed on other grounds. [But] conventional wisdoms are fluid things; audiences change with the times, and when challenged, often respond favourably. Witness the triumph of *Roots* in a culture once seemingly mired in the pieties of *Gone With the Wind*. [Wallace 1987: 43]

In an effort either to justify established, entrenched attitudes or to locate a commercial position, museums appear to have radically underestimated the public's interest in and ability to cope with challenging and alternative views of the past and present. Moreover, they have ignored the capacity of people to use their minds and imagination.

So museum histories need to shake themselves free of the bondage of established practice and look more closely at the past. Museum histories need to be exposed to questions of historical epistemology: how curators know what they know about the past and how they communicate that knowledge through the techniques of exhibition. This requires questions about histories in general and dominant myths in particular. Just as

Schlereth was forced to remind us 'that for generations, American history was something which happened primarily to prosperous white males in the middle years of life' (1981: 261), so we must remind ourselves of the dominance of similar ideas in Britain. With this recognition, we can develop programmes that admit alternative orders and perspectives, and reflect the past in all its contradictions of consensus and conflict.

Forms of interpretation and exhibition

One starting point is the consideration of the histories produced in museums in terms of their historiographic form. This requires comparison of history exhibitions with styles found in the writing of history, where there are three principal traditions: narrative, descriptive and analytical. The narrative tradition comes closest to story-telling. It is the historian's most basic way of relating a sequence of events. Chronological patterns and strict areas of theme are maintained. The reader is led through time, with little opportunity or encouragement to consider causation, effects or complex issues of context. Narrative at its best is a form of explanation of events and characters. Descriptive writing concentrates on presenting a visual image or impression of a person, idea or event. It is generally composed of statements of fact and interpretation, dealing with a restricted moment in time. Analytical history is the most common form and the most difficult to write. It seeks to lay bare the true nature of an event or episode not just through an appreciation of the causes and results. The discovery of the way people thought, felt and were motivated is central to this form of history-writing. In style, analytical writing may involve both narrative and description, but is distinctive for its questioning of all sources and received truths.

Analysing exhibitions against these three traditions presents difficulties; they just do not relate that easily. However, it is possible to suggest exhibition forms that roughly fit each category. The Royal Naval Museum in Portsmouth takes the visitor through a narrative of the Navy's history. The narrative, given in panels of graphics and illustrations, is punctuated with objects. Collectively, these lead the visitor through an essentially progressive history of the British Navy. Most museums that attempt to 'recreate' a period or a process are dealing in the main in a descriptive style of history-making. The open-air museums, with their reconstructed houses, furnished and fitted to pinpoint one moment in time, are essentially descriptive. Their concern is to describe how things were, leaving the visitor to draw conclusions about how things have changed. Why things have changed enters the realms of analysis and this is often absent.

The analytical is far harder to identify in museum exhibitions, but it can be found. The current exhibition at Nordiska Museet in Stockholm, called '*Modell Sverige*', attempts to explain how and why Sweden has changed over the last 130 years, from being a largely self-sufficient peasant society into one of the Western world's most advanced social democratic states. Through the use of comparisons and carefully selected symbols, the exhibition looks at changes in the nature of work, social and domestic environments, power and energy, and the roles of women. Through the use of film, it also considers wider issues, such as Sweden on the world's stage.

This willingness to pose questions was also evident in the same museum's exhibition which explored the nature of long-distance travel. This was staged in 1982. Instead of holding up a sequence of gleaming vehicles in chronological order for the public's admiration, as kinds of grown-up Dinky toys, the museum presented an exhibition that considered not only how people travelled long distances but also who such people were. The underlying point was that from the earliest coaches to modern jet aeroplane long-distance travel has been the prerogative of the more wealthy. To present such thought-provoking exhibitions, in forms which excite the imagination and promote natural curiosity, and to do so in ways that make the reading of labels not essential to the communication of the exhibition's argument, demonstrates something of a museum's capacity to analyse, as well as describe and narrate.

History in museums tends to be offered in a descriptive form because the principal medium (objects) appears to allow few alternatives. How can cultural and social change be discussed through material which is so fixed in its form? How can life, which is essentially active and changing, be explained by things which are essentially lifeless, and therefore constant? The answer to this lies in the ways in which we understand objects as evidence; the ways in which meanings ascribed to them change; and the museum's ability to juxtapose images and objects. This is far more than an issue of exhibition techniques. It relates to all the fundamental processes of fieldwork, acquisition, documentation and collections care. Ultimately, the museum's message directly corresponds to the degree to which history is grasped by curators.

Göran Carlsson and Per-Uno Ågren in their excellent book, *Utställningsspråk* (1982), provide us with a means of categorizing forms of exhibition. These can be understood on one level as springing from traditions of exhibiton-making, but can also be viewed as indicating the depth of understanding about the past which a museum brings to the public through the sum of all curatorial work, expressed in the form of exhibitions. Carlsson and Ågren have five categories of what they call 'exhibition language'.

The first is mass, where a complete collection, or an extremely broad selection of objects, is shown together, usually unlabelled. Often associated with local, possibly amateur-run museums, this form of exhibition is, in fact, sometimes encountered in the most polished of museums. In this form, objects tumble over each other in a chaos through which visitors must pick and chose their own paths, making assumptions and guesses as they go. Used as a visual break, with objects that have established meaning, this can sometimes be an interesting way of looking at things. But more often than not, the mass approach is a disorganized jumble. It is the farthest a museum can move away from explaining the past.

The second form is a label exhibition. This is where objects are ordered in seriated ranks with basic labels identifying the name, donor, provenance and classification number of each. This is a classical approach to exhibition. Avoiding anything that might approach context or comment, such exhibitions provide little but a visual catalogue. Where nothing more than a type series is required, the label exhibition can suffice.

The exhibition form takes a massive leap forward with the thematic, which deals with strictly defined topics. This is a very familiar form of exhibition in Britain. It applies where material is brought together under broad headings, sometimes derived from the museum's classification system. Exhibitions headed 'domestic life', 'law and order', 'dairying', 'local trades' or 'toys' can be loosely categorized as thematic. With limited extension of the selected theme through the use of photographs and some general explanatory labels, such exhibitions tend not to move beyond the technical or descriptive.

The fourth form identified by Carlsson and Ågren is the narrative. This is where the exhibition form has been developed to communicate a point of view or to narrate an experience. Usually employing fieldwork, the results of active collecting and the actual words of local people, the narrative form relies on the use of very diverse media. At a further and more advanced level, this evolves into the final category: total or comprehensive exhibition. This form is distinguished by the use of many different exhibition styles and techniques to allow active exploration of the museum's subject. Objects, illustrations, photographs, texts, light, colour, movement, texture, smell, noise, video, reconstructions and models are joined together in ways that

Figure 16. The agricultural gallery at Västerbotten museum, Umeå is an example of the 'total' approach to exhibition. This section compares men's and women's work through the seasons. Photographs, models and objects are used.

Figure 17.   Key themes are addressed. These include the dilemma that many families faced over whether it was worth keeping a cow through the hard winters, and the choice of equipment for tilling the land.

allow many different access points to the exhibitions theme. Moreover, the element of choice is built in so that people can elect to learn more and can select what they are particularly interested in. Communication is extended and maximized through the use of drama and educational programmes within the exhibition area, and through the use of publications, both learned and popular.

This 'total' approach is increasingly found in museums. The most recent and perhaps best-developed example in Britain is at the Museum of the Moving Image (MOMI) in London. Although well aware of the ease with which affective learning can take place, dealing as it does with the media which has become central to twentieth-century life, at no point does MOMI appear to lose an opportunity for cognitive learning. It leads the visitor from the familiar to the unfamiliar; from established knowledge to new understanding. And it does this by providing a 'total' approach, which has pace, choice and opportunity. The 'total' approach is not confined to well-funded or new museums. It can be seen used in many science museums and provincial museums, such as Västerbottens Museum, in Northern Sweden.

Such a complex form of exhibition is only possible and, indeed, viable where there is a considerable depth of understanding and a solid range of collections and documentation on which to draw. In the case of Västerbottens Museum, throughout the re-display of the museum, completed in 1982, museum staff were able to call on the experience of much fieldwork, in particular an excellent film archive and collections built up painstakingly over many years. The exhibitions there, as with other examples of the total approach, are derived from professional, long-term curatorship. It is this which gives them their social credibility and intellectual worth. Add to this an infectious regard for people (past and present), the willingness to communicate to visitors of all ages and sizes, and the originality of mind that can break away from established traditions of what a museum exhibition should look like, and we start seeing exhibitions of the calibre of those at MOMI and Västerbottens Museum.

Considering the five forms of exhibition language suggested by Carlsson and Ågren, it can be proposed that the more adventurous and challenging an exhibition form becomes, the greater the need to have a grasp of the complexities of history and the range of evidence being offered. Without this, the complexities of the 'total' approach collapse. Instead of offering a choice of tantalizing routes into an interesting subject, the material falls about in a 'mass'. The circle turns and the museum is back at the most rudimentary and confusing of exhibition forms.

Social perceptions of objects

Exhibitions operate in a social sphere where there is more than one participant. Theoretically, an exhibition is a silent partnership of curator and visitors exploring and questioning; thinking and looking. The curator will bring to the experience not just the role of guardian of the goods but also of interpreter, editor and exhibition-maker. The visitors will also bring roles: critics and learners, experts and participants, sceptics and converts. The age range, social background and motivation of visitors will vary enormously. Practically, museum visitors are not one audience but many, with diverse needs and expectations. Dr Paulette McManus argues that differing audiences remind us that museum communication 'cannot be thought of as being made to an individual, or even differing sorts of individual—a sort of dry transmission from head to head. They are made up of distinctive groups of people and the behaviour of these groups affects the individuals within them (McManus 1988: 43).

McManus's research has indicated that the social nature of a museum visit, the anticipation of satisfaction, the combinations in the groups that visit independently affect the manner in which people take information from the museum. They also strongly influence the ways in which people work within their groups to make meanings clear to each other. So the museum is the provider of an informal learning situation, where visitors exercise a good degree of free choice. They select that in which they are willing to be interested. Where this occurs, it will spring from a self-motivation to know and learn more. The museum can substantially help or hinder these processes through its attitudes to visitors and its readiness to provide stimulating and involving exhibitions. Part of this process is dependent on an awareness of the ways in which people relate to objects on exhibition.

It is thought that the social reading of objects imposes an overlay of the histories, myths and stories we weave about our past. People relate more

Figure 18. The central exhibition area can be used for drama, teaching or group work. Otherwise, it contains a reader at which visitors can refer to slides of buildings and objects relevant to the exhibition's theme. To the right is a seating area where visitors can watch a selection of videos on agriculture in Västerbottens.

immediately to things about which they have some knowledge. Those things which pass beyond our immediate experience and needs, or exist outside our understanding of the past, become very difficult to comprehend. In discussing 'a sense of another world', the work of American history museums in 'recreating' and interpreting the past, James Deetz (1987) draws attention to the difficulties of explaining the extent of cultural change over time. Drawing from his own work at the Plimoth Plantation Massachusetts, Deetz discusses how simple it is for modern visitors to take one seemingly familiar object, like a wooden trencher, and make automatic assumptions about its use and significance based on their experiences of a modern dinner plate. The trencher would seem to be evidence of continuity, but, in fact, it is a symbol of discontinuity. Research shows that a trencher was used corporately, with more than one person eating from it. It was indicative of a way of sharing living and burial space, attitudes and responsibilities. This way of life altered in the more prosperous and consumption-orientated eighteenth century. Without interpretation that message of difference would be lost. What in effect the museum is describing is a very different world, where people saw life, held beliefs and did things in ways very different from today.

Figure 19. Each of the exhibition areas at Västerbottens Museum has an area where visitors can make a selection of videos on aspects of the exhibition's theme. These draw on the museum's extensive film archive.

Similarly, many objects in British museums pass beyond popular comprehension because of the visitors' inevitable lack of foreknowledge and the absence of interpretation. A case in point is at Bishops House Museum in Sheffield, where an important collection of seventeenth-century furniture and furnishings from South Yorkshire and North Derbyshire is being made. On display in the parlour is a wassail-bowl made of *lignum vitae*. It is large, glossy and beautifully turned. Wassailing, the ceremonial drinking of toasts from one large cup or bowl, took place in the festive season, and was an affirmation of social cohesion. It is one of many social customs, the meaning of which has been lost, as has understanding of the corporate nature of seventeenth-century yeoman life of which the bowl was a signifying part. Lost, too, is the appreciation that *lignum vitae* was thought to have medicinal properties which were helpful in the curing of venereal diseases. Also unspoken is the fact that the skills to make such a large and beautifully shaped vessel in Sheffield were helped considerably by the early production of high-quality steel tools in the town and surrounding areas. The bowl is a complex statement about relatively prosperous, socially cohesive, industrially adventurous but unpleasantly unhealthy life in seventeenth-century Sheffield.

In contrast, objects which are very familiar to us may be obscured not so much by our ignorance as by our selection of preferred views. This is well

Figure 20.   Seventeenth-century wassail bowl from South Yorkshire at Bishops
House Museum, Sheffield.

illustrated by research undertaken by Edward L. Hawes in Springfield,
Illinois (Hawes 1986). Hawes sought to test his hypothesis that there are
certain objects or ranges of objects that gain symbolic content when placed
in a museum. He took as his example the history of European settlement of
the American Mid-West in the nineteenth century. Hawes selected a group
of material that included axes, open-hearth cooking pots, rifles, wool-
cards, spinning wheels, looms and prairie ploughs. He asked volunteers to
handle and consider the objects and to then give their own interpretation of
these things through the construction of story-lines.

   The tests revealed that certain objects, particularly the pot and the axe,
repeatedly generated responses about 'colonial' and 'pioneer' days, with the
nuclear family, snug in their sexually determined roles, bravely forging
westward to build a new life. These stories were clearly based on the web of
myths woven, no doubt for strong social purposes, in the home and in
schools. Those objects which failed to conform or find a place within the
established myth structure (for example, a photocopy of an 1850
newspaper, a tablecloth or a Wedgwood plate) were ignored or seen as not
relevant. The responses took no note of the real significance of the objects to
hand or any alternative connections the objects might have had.

   Hawes's research would seem to confirm the degree to which our lives are
coded by the objects around us and how these objects can be re-encoded
according to different social needs and pressures. As Hawes points out,
there is a definite 'politics to certain museum artifacts and the tales and
myths associated with them'. This reading of objects according to a

previously encoded pattern is not confined exclusively to the museum. But as a legitimizing institution, the causes and effects hold strong significance. It renders the interpretative processes and techniques of the museum all the more powerful and critical. Labelling, juxtaposition of objects and images, demonstrations, lectures and publications are the means available to the museum to disrupt received views and give context and meaning to the past.

14. Interpretation and Performance

Even in the most visually satisfying of exhibitions, the ordering and labelling of exhibits risks tidying away the past: the knick-knacks of memory settled into a convenient space. The representation of the past as consensual, harmonious and preferable to the present is the inevitable corollary of this. Domestic life is shown without conflict or violence, work without exploitation, transport without risk, seafaring without danger, farming without deprivation, childhood without epidemics, childbirth without death. Life in the past also appears without emotions and feelings. Humour, anger, joy and belief appear to have been banished. Moreover, large areas of human experience are omitted, either because little material evidence remains or because they have been excluded from curatorial interest. In this way evidence of social deviancy, the social nature of work, economic and social relations, popular political activity, the work of the professions and modern industrial practices are under-represented.

There is no reason why museums cannot expand the length and depth of interpretation through wider collecting and through more-imaginative use of the exhibition techniques available. Whereas some exhibition forms are limited by available resources, many of the methods which could enliven and liberate the histories museums present can involve expenses no greater than those already accepted as being standard for exhibitions. This process begins with the museum determining what it is that ought to be said or discussed through the exhibition. Without some central point, there can be no means of developing or evaluating the exhibiton. For example, is the exhibition of a reconstructed Edwardian nursery supposed to be a a way of thinking about the meaning of childhood for a specific income group, childcare and development, or the roles of nursery staff?

Where the subject has an established but narrow appeal, some form of access has to be provided to attract a broader and more-democratic audience. The opportunities are limitless. For example, stamp collections could be more exciting by exhibitions such as that at the Postmuseum in Stockholm, which considers how the postal service has changed and what that has meant for the way people have been able to communicate. Coin collections could be made more accessible by exhibitions which explore the purchasing power of coinage, the changing value of money against common goods, and the availability of such coinage to workers through their earnings. Transport collections could be broadened to look at the social meaning of travel and transport, in the way that the exhibition 'All Stations' which toured London, Paris and Stockholm in the early 1980s explored the social meanings of railway stations (Dethier 1981). This was a thought-provoking and moving exhibition which demonstrated that the standard approach given in transport museums is both soulless and very partial.

Words and labels

Museums have laid great store on the use of words on labels to communicate their ideas to the public. In spite of the fact that the use of labels to interpret objects on display has been a technique employed from the earliest days of museums, until recently little research attention has been directed at museum language; even though labels represent a particular genre of writing and reveal a great deal about the ideas that inform museum developments.

Curatorial attitude towards labelling has undergone several transformations. In a comprehensive paper on the principles of museum administration given at the Museums' Association Conference in Newcastle in 1895, G. Brown Goode repeated his favourite observation that 'an efficient educational Museum may be described as a collection of instructive labels, each illustrated by a well-selected specimen' (1895: 108). By the 1960s and 1970s a different perspective prevailed. It was believed that as objects could speak for themselves, labels were an unnecessary interference. Exhibitions appeared with minimal text, with information confined to peripheral labels and guidebooks. In the late 1980s different trends prevailed. A number of recent museum exhibitions have contained 75–80 per cent text and printed images, and 20 per cent objects, as if faith in the relevance and communicative value of objects has been lost.

Different views are now emerging, based on the study of the use of labelling systems and the language they contain. The Swedish author Margareta Ekarv has questioned whether in modern museums 'loaded with messages of various kinds' visitors can learn all they need from the exhibits, without having to work through labels. Her conclusion to this well-established question is that there is still a need and a place for the written word in exhibitions: 'we can use words to give a new, deeper dimension to our visual experience. Words make us think, and our thoughts conjure up pictures in our minds. Is it not through mental pictures like these that we discover the world around us?' (Ekarv 1987).

Labels should function to add information and perspectives that cannot be provided in any other way. They can be written to help people think and look. They can also be presented to prompt feelings, imagination and questions. The more distant and unfamiliar the theme or object, the greater the need to provide text that jolts the view and enlarges understanding. In sum, they are a key part of the museum dialogue; the voice to which the visitor should relate and respond.

But not all labels work. There are many common problems in museum

Figure 21. No other educative medium expects people to *stand* and read vast amounts of texts. Museum labels need to be sharply relevant, interesting and readable.

texts. Ekarv observed that much museum language used in labels is 'laced with academic grooming, abstract and long-winded'. Undefined, specialist jargon and excessive data can obscure the message. Information provided can be irrelevant or self-evident. The text can be too long and printed illegibly. Interesting facts and observation can be lost if visitors are not alerted to visual details. Established myths can be allowed to prevail. In the space of one gallery, visitors can be offered in excess of 1500 words. Is it little wonder that much is lost in the way people see history in museums?

Label-writing is an essential skill in museum work. In Sweden and the USA, in recognition of the importance of exhibition text, authors are being employed in museums to write labels. Margareta Ekarv has worked on exhibitions for the Swedish State Exhibition Service and the Postmuseum in Stockholm. Her experiences led her to a number of very helpful conclusions about the process of label preparation and styles of language (1987). These include the observation that it is not necessarily a matter of intellect or reading ability that determine the visitor's comprehension of text. All museum visitors view exhibitions from an upright position. As a result, the visitor tires easily and will put less energy into the sections of exhibiton which require effort. There is no other form of educational experience that requires people to read and learn while standing and walking. Therefore, museum texts need to be presented in forms that can be comfortably consumed by people on their feet and on the move.

Content has to be carefully judged in terms of the overall exhibition and the function individual labels play in interpretation. People will dismiss labels not immediately seen as pertinent. So the language used should be full of associations and should provide the reader with food for thought. Moreover, they should fuel an eagerness to learn more.

The style can vary. Ekarv has suggested that a variety of forms could be experimented with, including poetry. Her experience of writing easy-to-read books for the adult literacy movement led her to develop an easy-to-read style of writing for the Postmuseum. Active verbs, direct description and line breaks following the cadences of speech have given her text a sense of liveliness and it easily engages attention. As museum text is often read aloud within groups, for example between parent and child, writing labels according to verbal rather than written styles has benefits. The Boston Children's Museum is another which has provided text in forms suitable for reading aloud. But such an approach is not a matter of writing simplistic text. It requires a specific style which aims for clarity without sacrificing knowledge, or appearing condescending to the reader.

A form of label-writing which has been under-utilized is one that draws directly on the words of the very people who used the objects on display or experienced something of the subject being discussed. Where this approach has been employed, it gives the exhibition a directness and an impact which is unparalleled. In these instances the museum ceases to be overtly interventionist in the view it offers of the past, and goes some way to handing back the narration and explanation of the past to the true experts: the people who lived it. This approach has been adopted by the People's Story Museum in Edinburgh, where the curators have worked with reminiscence groups in the preparation of the galleries (Beevers *et al.* 1988). It will be the words of local people which will be informing visitors as they walk around the galleries.

How a label looks can be as important as what it says. Labels with too small type, located too high or too low will be of little use. Labels that are back-lit or require reading aids before the reader can focus and those that are just too long are easily ignored. Experimentation with script styles, colours and fabrics can yield startling and satisfying results. In 1982 Upplandsmuseet, Uppsala, Sweden held an exhibition on work. It was captioned with brief extracts from the conversations held with the people who used or owned the objects on display. The intimacy of the dialogue was maintained through the labels being written in a flowing, legible handscript on a familiar material, brown, corrugated paper. The basic idea was to create an informal dialogue, which, it was felt, the hard edges and official nature of more formal type and presentation would deny. In Springburn Museum's exhibiton called 'See they young yins', held in 1988, the words of local teenagers appeared in their own handwriting. These were extracts from the questionnaires they had filled in as part of the exhibition's preparation and were used to explore their attitudes and expectations on such subjects as job prospects and music. The teenagers also captioned the photographs they themselves had taken. Again, a directness and impact of message resulted.

Changing styles between formal text, and different levels of information can be achieved by changing typefaces and sizes and by varying the use of formal type and handscript. This creates internal rhythms to the text and allows the reader swift access to the kinds of information required. A very good example of this is found at Västerbottens Museum in Umeå. Here, formal headings and introductory texts are given in formal printed typefaces. shifts to narrative or pieces of oral testimony are indicated by handscript.

Sounds, words and images

Labels are not the only means of adding depth and meaning to an exhibition. Sound has a part to play, too, and can bring a very special dimension. Voices, memories, songs and poems, music and environmental recordings add the human element to the silences of once-familiar objects and images. There are three ways in which museums introduce sound to their galleries: through the use of primary sound collections; through sound effects, including music, to give period atmosphere; and through audio-visual units.

The majority of history museums have holdings of oral history recordings. Some have also recorded musicians and local songs. Others have undertaken dialect studies and collected examples of folklore, stories and local beliefs. The Imperial War Museum and the Welsh Folk Museum were the first history museums in Britain to engage in oral recordings, yet neither museum has a gallery devoted to these collections, although some use of them is made in exhibitions. People interested in the recordings held by museums usually have to make enquiries with the museum and go behind the scenes to listen to material from the collections.

There is a case for treating all recordings, both of voices and music, as collections in their own right and not simply as support material for exhibitions. For example, the Museum of Lincolnshire Life has a folklore section, where stories, beliefs and dialect are discussed and made available through a series of listening stations. At Bohusläns Museum in Uddevalla, Southern Sweden, a whole room is devoted to the oral traditions of the area. Visitors can sit in comfort and listen to local music, stories, memories and dialect. Valuing oral evidence alongside material collections allows some understanding of the depth and variety of human experiences. It leads to a better awareness of objects and the lives which gave them meaning. Opening this up for visitors extends the potential of the museum and adds to the quality of the histories it produces.

In the absence of exhibition areas devoted to oral traditions, a significant number of museums use sound within the galleries to add information, and sometimes atmosphere. Snatches of memory or parts of historic broadcasts accompany formal exhibition area. This has been used, for example, at Somerset Rural Life Museum, where recordings of memories of cider-making are played, and at the Imperial War Museum, where Chamberlain's radio broadcast on 3 September 1939, announcing Britain was at war, has

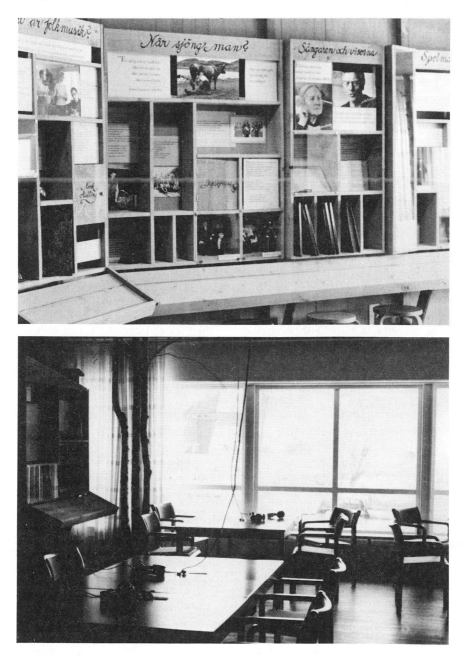

Figure 22. Collections of recordings, especially music, dialect and oral history, are made by the majority of history museums. However, few have a gallery or room where visitors can listen to recordings. One of the exceptions is Bohusläns Museum, Uddevalla, Sweden.

been used in temporary exhibitions. As helpful and evocative as this is, constant repetition on a tape loop is a profound irritation to people working in the museum. Also, failure to soundproof other exhibition areas results in sound carrying, creating an incongruous mixture of images and sounds at other points in the museum. One of the ways that museums could deal with the containment of sound in exhibitions is to increase the use of personal audio-guides. Although a good number of museums have listening posts, at which snatches of verse or speech can be heard, the use of audio-guides is relatively undeveloped in history museums.

Taped music can be more successful in that some variety can be introduced and it can be programmed for different times of day. Music provides context and period and is very useful in unifying different elements of an exhibition. The Museum of London uses period music to designate the chronological stages in the history of London told through its galleries.

Music, dance, story-telling and demonstrations also have a place within a museum's presentation. At the People's Palace in Glasgow use is made of the adjacent Winter Gardens for performances. The museum has taken particular interest in the hammered dulcimer: 'the instrument of the working classes *par excellence*'. Local advertising brought together 20 players, each of whom thought they were the last one. The Glasgow Hammered Dulcimer Society now meets once a fortnight in the museum to discuss and play the dulcimer (King 1988). The museum has also given consideration to having a juke-box in the museum, playing the records of local performers and rock bands. Many of these now have national and international reputations. Just like the objects in the museum they were made in Glasgow and were born of local cultural patterns.

Whereas the People's Palace benefits from the facilities provided in the Winter Gardens, few museums in Britain have been designed to accommodate performance. Open-air museums have been able to use the available space for concerts and demonstrations, yet none has designated all-weather performance areas. In the main history museums have been thought of as silent centres for the passive consumption of the past. As the People's Palace shows, it need not be like that at all.

The architectural design of the new museum at Bohusläns Museum at Uddevalla in Sweden, opened in 1984, has much to recommend it. One of its principal features is the space allowed for performance and demonstrations. It has an auditorium with seating for 150, which can be used for formal presentations and is also available for community use. But the museum's most interesting feature is the organization of the internal spaces around a central point, an intermediate area called 'the shelf', where performances of all kinds can take place. The centre of the museum is, therefore, active and participatory, a lively pivotal point for all the museum's activities and a valuable focus for the people of the area (Adegren 1984).

The combination of words and images in audio-visual presentations has a very valuable place in museums. Programmes, either slide-tape or film, can be used in formal exhibitions to give historical context, illustrate how an activity was carried out or provide social detail that the exhibition cannot contain. Contemporary and archive film and photographs, cartoons and illustrations, oral testimony and sounds can be combined to give extra perspectives to an exhibition's subject. The words can be those of an interpreter or from oral archives. Such presentations can be very powerful means of focusing visitors' attention on the exhibition. Used as a preface, they can pose questions for visitors to ask themselves about what they see, suggest things to look out for and place them in a frame of mind for the exhibition's theme. Used as a conclusion, they can bring the exhibition's strands together, suggest further ideas and pose questions about what happened in the years following the exhibition's elected time-span.

The technology is now available whereby people can be offered a choice of audio-visual presentations, to suit their interests. This happens at Västerbottens Museum, Umeå. Each of the themes explored by the museum in its galleries is supported by an audi-visual station at which visitors can comfortably sit and make a personal selection from a list of programmes, each one on a different aspect of the exhibition's theme. Headphones are provided so that the sound from the programme is not an interference for visitors in other parts of the gallery. The use of audio-visual programmes is one of the means available to the museum to update their interpretation and vary permanent exhibitions.

Interpreters and activities

Interpretation through drama and performance has been employed with enthusiasm, especially in those museums which aim to provide 'living history'. Performance takes many forms. Interpreters and guides are the most commonly encountered performers, although rarely seen as such. Added to their numbers are costumed demonstrators. The ability to slip into role and to repeat information many times over in the course of the day requires an attitude of dramatic presentation, the supersedence of the role of guide or demonstrator over that of self. It also requires both careful work planning, so that activities are varied, and the continual input of new information to enliven and refresh both content and role.

In open-air museums people are employed to add to the image of the site, sell things and show how certain processes were conducted. Blists Hill, part of Ironbridge Gorge Museum, has peopled its 'late nineteenth-century town' until recently through various job-creation schemes. Temporary employees have sold money in the bank, sweets in the shop, and beer in the pub, made candles and run an iron foundry. Blists Hill is a representation of nineteenth-century town life, curbed and adjusted according to present-day health and safety regulations, and permitted through current schemes to alleviate high unemployment and promote tourism. Like many such enterprises, it portrays a life without children, old-age and the continuity of skills and working practices.

Interpretation given in the first person is the most difficult to employ with any marked degree of accuracy and purpose, and has been largely avoided in Britain. The Wigan Pier Heritage Centre opened in 1985 to very mixed feelings about the use to which drama was being put. At Wigan Pier, actors and actresses perform and improvise on storylines around the exhibits, involving the visitors in conversations about events around the turn of the century as if they were happening today. Robert Hewison has described this as 'an effort to create, not so much an informative as an emotional experience, a symbolic recovery of the way we were. The displays, recorded sounds and performances prompt recollections for the pensioners who seem to throng the centre; for younger people they present memories, unexperienced but ready formed' (1987: 21).

While Hewison is prepared to express considerable reservations at the methods employed, he has to concede that 'for schools the centre functions as an educational resource'. The educational potential of performance is undoubted; what Hewison is bringing into question here is the message being conveyed. Is this the past dressed up in fancy clothes, swaying mesmerized to half-forgotten tunes? Or is this the basis from which active discussion and dialogue about the past can be opened up to those long-since dissociated from, or disenchanted with, more formal and 'approved' sources for knowledge of history? As with the use of any formal interpretation, the medium and the message require equal attention.

Figure 23. Plimoth Plantation, Massachusetts, is a re-creation of the first successful English colony in New England and a nearby Wampanoag Indian summer campsite. At Plimoth Plantation, interpreters carry out the daily routines of seventeenth-century life.

Figure 24.   First-perspon interpretation at the Wampanoag campsite is difficult because the Wampanoag language cannot be readily understood by visitors. Instead Native Americans relate the story of the first inhabitants of Plymouth.

The use of interpreters is seen at its most developed and successful at Plimoth Plantation in Massachussets, where a great deal of attention has been paid to the detail and accuracy of the individual portrayals of life in an early American colony. The Plantation is centred on a reconstructed pilgrim village and a nearby Wampanoag Indian summer campsite. In the village, men, women and sometimes children, dressed in period costume and speaking dialect, pursue the daily routines of seventeenth-century life, engaging visitors in lively discussions of politics, economics, home-making, gardening and medicine. A similar approach was adopted at the campsite. But as it was found that visitors could not understand the Wampanoag language, a different approach had to be developed. Today, Native Americans relate the story of the first inhabitants of Plymouth at the Wampanoag camp by talking about their ancestors.

Plimoth Plantation has not only developed highly detailed interpretative techniques on site, it has also developed a whole structure of eduational programmes and support facilities to help visitors make sense of what they see and extend their educational choices. An important element of this is the Visitor Centre which all visitors enter before going into the village and campsite. This briefs people about what they are going to see and recommends how the visit should be used. Workshops for children, lectures

Figure 25. Wampanoag outreach instructor working with a class, building on a experience of their visit.

and publications back-up and extend opportunities for people to discover more about these times and ways of living (Plimoth Plantation 1986).

Performance can also be given in demonstrations. Many museums convey techniques of making and doing: everything from the baking of bread to wood-turning. Such work requires not only an appropriate degree of skill from the demonstrator but also a considerable amount of tact and patience in dealing with visitors' questions while performing sometimes delicate craft techniques. Demonstration in museums helps people to understand how, and sometimes why, things were made or tasks were performed. They are often a means of retaining and fostering scarce or dying local skills and practices.

The use of demonstrators in British museums has a long pedigree. Peate had craftsmen working at the Welsh Folk Museum from the time it opened. Since then the museum has employed craftsmen on a permanent basis, demonstrating wood-turning, coopering, milling, weaving and clog-making. There are now many examples of demonstrators and interpreters at work in museums. At Quarry Bank Mill in Styal and at Big Pit Mining Museum in Blaenafon, skilled workers in these industries (weaving and coal mining) now demonstrate and explain working techniques. Sheffield Industrial Museum at Kelham Island has three workshops built to house and foster the skills of 'little mesters' in the making of fine steel tools and implements.

Dramatic performance is increasingly found in museums, in a variety of forms to suit educational and interpretative requirements. Role-playing, such as that used at Clarke Hall near Wakefield to interpret seventeenth-century life, has established validity in educational work, encouraging children to empathize with their subject and by so doing to open their minds to historic facts and detail. More formal dramatic productions are used, as at Västerbottens Museum in Umeå, as an integral part of an education programme. At Västerbottens Museum, it extends the theme of an exhibition and provides the basis for further activities. Drama can also be used at site museums as a method of visitor management. By attracting visitors to performances in open spaces, pressure in popular areas of the site can be alleviated at peak times. This ensures that the educational qualities of the site are more evenly balanced: it is hard to learn a great deal from a reconstructed house, regardless of the quality of interpretation, if it is overcrowded.

The most exciting interpretative potential of drama is that it can deal with aspects of a subject that more formal exhibition may not convey well. Subjects such as health, debt, industrial accidents, immigration, disputes between neighbours are some of the themes that have been explored through museum-based drama. Dialogue can be built from oral testimony, as in the work of Age Exchange Theatre in London. Contemporary records, such as newspaper accounts and court proceedings, can also be used. The

Figure 26.   Sheffield Industrial Museum, Kelham Island, has built three workshops to house 'little mesters' and foster their skills in the making of fine steel tools and implements. Here Rowland Swinden, blade grinder and finisher, finishes a Bowie knife on a glazing wheel.

Figure 27. Drama group working at Västerbottens Museum, Umeå with a group of schoolchildren. Issues from the play were later explored, using handling collections, in the museum's education room.

potential of drama in museum interpretation must be attributable to characterization which allows the visitor-audience opportunity to think about real-life experiences in a pesonal way (Brown 1982; Schlereth 1984; Age Exchange 1986).

The histories a museum produces are highly ephemeral. Exhibitions can last between five and ten years; a temporary exhibition only a matter of weeks or months. The objects are then returned to store or rearranged in other combinations, reinterpreted and relabelled. Demonstrations and performances, unless recorded on video, are completed in an even shorter perid. Some form of permanence has to be given to the understanding of the past reached by the museum.

Museum publications, catalogues, leaflets, books and learned papers are the obvious answer to this problem. They give curatorial scholarship the opportunity to reach a larger audience and provide a permanent record of the research undertaken. Publication of research relating to an exhibition should be an integral part of its planning. In many instances there is a need for several levels of publication: brief information sheets which sum up the main themes, perhaps using the text of the exhibition itself; a more extensive booklet dealing with the subject in some depth; and a learned paper published in an appropriate journal. Without publications and without the careful and thoughtful use of interpretative techniques, exhibitions will remain ephemeral in themselves and will be of only marginal use in popular understanding of a lived past.

15. Meaning, Learning and Education

The notions that objects can impart knowledge and that the museums which house them are, therefore, learning environments have underpinned the growth of museums since the nineteenth century. Educational potential has been the most influential of arguments for museum development and for continued support from the public purse. But the benefit society derives from museums and the ways in which they are able to use them positively for learning and enjoyment have been contentious areas of debate.

In the late nineteenth century, it was thought that museums could provide opportunities for people to learn about the glory of ancient civilizations: the distant, and by implication culturally inferior, peoples of the Empire; the gradual path of British society from noble but uncivilized beginnings to modern-day sophistication; and the glories of art and manufacture. People were expected to spend their museum visits 'in awe' of what they saw. They were also expected to be humbled by, and grateful for, such experiences and by some form of cultural osmosis to be duly led to a higher social order.

But other ideas have prevailed. These centre on the museum as an institution which stimulates and promotes questions rather than controls them. The basis for such views is that through collections a museum can provide experiences of seeing, and sometimes hearing and touching, evidence about ourselves and the world. The emphasis now is on enquiry, empathy, criticism and discovery. The museum is beginning to be seen as a workshop where people can move and think at their own pace, engaging with the museum through displays, publications and performances. It is also a place for the formal and informal transmission of skills, ideas and narratives through organized educational activities.

Museum language to an extent confuses. Both in established museum literature and common curatorial usage two key words have developed rather restricted applications. The word 'education' has been associated simply with organized educational activities. This risks excluding its far more potent and relevant use in reference to the whole museum and all its activities: the museum as a dynamic system of communication. Similarly, 'interpretation' has come to be associated with the various media used to tell a story or explain a collection rather than the construction of the message conveyed. Thus, how a museum performs has tended to predominate over what is being said.

The museum profession is very well-equipped with research about and arguments for learning in the museum (see in particular Hooper-Greenhill 1989). But a simple truth remains. Those museums which are in Constance Hall's words 'boring and fusty' and indifferent to the public they serve, impart to the visitor feelings of inadequacy and ignorance (1981). In such circumstances learning is frustrated and confined to a privileged minority. But with lively and full understanding of the collections and available interpretative media, the museum has the capacity to bring audiences to new levels of knowledge and promote self-worth and satisfaction through the experience of learning.

History museums and children

Somewhere in the region of one-third of museum visitors are children. A significant proportion of these comes in organized school parties; others come in family groups or with friends. Museums can provide for children in many ways: by involving them in discussion about the past through the handling and discovery of objects, sounds and images; by enveloping them in drama and role-play; by teaching skills, from preparing foods to making silhouettes; and by encouraging them to look and enquire not only through the use of worksheets and puzzles but also through engaging displays and well-written labelling. When these approaches are used at their best, the history museum is a powerful tool in the stimulation of imagination and interest. Touch, sight, sound and story can bring the humanity of the past into focus and confirm its reality. History is lifted off the pages of textbooks and given substance, even a tangibility. The memories of grandparents and elderly friends are given fresh meaning.

There is much awareness that children in museums, especially as part of a school group, need and benefit from directed activities. As a result, a significant number of museums now employ staff members whose principal responsibility is to service education in the museum. This has often meant specifically work with children, rather than a broader audience, and has frequently excluded a more purposeful role in the museum as a whole, especially in the development of new displays. The loss of this valuable input has weakened the effectiveness of some museums and has resulted in suspicion and tension between some curators and education officers.

The education specialist's contribution is one that should facilitate and enlarge the learning environment of the museum rather than restrict it to the 'education room'. In many museums the partnership of skills of the curatorial, interpretation and education staff ensures that the museum has a depth of message and a range and quality of educational provision. This can be seen at Quarry Bank Mill Museum in Styal, Cheshire, where the variety, relevance and standards of educational work with people of all ages sets it apart as one of the best in the country.

Quarry Bank Mill is a Georgian cotton mill belonging to the generation of water-powered cotton spinning mills which marked the start of the

Figure 28. The Apprentice House, Quarry Bank Mill, Styal. Children role-playing a day in the lives of mill apprentices. Here are they inspected for cleanliness.

factory system. Set in a deep valley surrounded by parkland, the mill was producing cloth from 1784 until the 1950s. In its heyday, it employed up to 400 workers, including pauper apprentices, providing them with food, housing, education and places of worship. Quarry Bank Mill epitomized capitalist paternalism, with its expectation of adequate return for its social investments. It is now owned by the National Trust and leased to the Quarry Bank Mill Museum Trust.

The mill succeeds as both a museum and as an educational resource because it has always had very clear ideas about how and why it should develop. It has managed to balance the critical quality of its histories with the need to survive as an independent museum. The one has not predominated over the other, and education has been a central consideration in all its plans. This sense of purpose has translated itself into well-thought out schemes for the use of the museum by adults and children. Educational provision is based on an awareness that the museum can offer a number of different themes and, within these, variable levels of study. Five educational programmes for schools have developed based on a colour-coded system:

Figure 29.   The Housekeeper at the Apprentice House supervises the preparation of food in the kitchen.

Green—How did industry begin and grow? This deals with power, technology and the rise of the factory system. Children can look at early machinery, follow an assembly line process and consider the management and administration of the mill through documents, artefacts and role-play.

Orange—What are textiles today? This programme deals with the property and uses of fibres and fabrics. An extensive collection of samples is used. Children can find out about how cotton grows and is processed.

Yellow—How do we know what happened at Styal? This is a programme for older children, aimed at encouraging historiographic skills. Objects and archival evidence help the children to build a picture of the people associated with the mill and the surrounding area.

Blue—What was it like to live at Styal? This deals with health, medicine, education, working conditions, housing and religion. Costume role-play, the use of demonstrations in the galleries and the handling of objects help to focus attention on the museum's child workers, the mill-hands and the mill-owners. Older children are encouraged to form judgements and reach conclusions.

Red—What was the Industrial Revolution? This looks at the mill within the context of the Industrial Revolution and again uses the handling of evidence for older children and the use of role-play for younger ones.

Each of these can be adapted according to the age range and interests of the audience. The museum has a resource centre equipped to deal with direct teaching, handling, demonstrations and experiment. The mill's galleries are also used, including those where demonstrations of spinning and weaving take place. The colour-code system alerts the demonstrators in the mill to the requirements of individual school parties and they can immediately respond with relevant information that fits into the children's programme. The coding also provides specific routes through the museum which marry into the theme of study. Overall this scheme, while allowing some flexibility, ensures directed, enquiring studies; maximizes opportunities for learning; and allows the management of parties so that they get a full and rewarding programme. In 1988 the mill's Apprentice House, carefully restored to its likely late eighteenth-century appearance, was reopened for educational work. School parties can spend a day at the house and through re-enactment gain an insight into the world of the child workforce at the mill.

Using the museum's workshop, the museum also provides a programme of courses, for adults and children, on textile crafts. These include ones on weaving and braiding, spinning, patchwork and quilting, constructed and experimental textiles, dyeing and printing, embroidery and lace, traditional textiles and handknitting.

Quarry Bank Mill's question-centred, material-based, mixed-media educational programmes exemplify many of the best aspects of educational provision in history museums in Britain. It is successful not only because it can offer choice and different levels of study. The efficient management of resources and the amount of preparation on each of the themes are critical factors. History education work undoubtedly prospers where appropriate techniques in education are matched with ones derived from curatorship.

Many history museums which use methods not dissimilar to Quarry Bank Mill have been able to adapt easily some of their work to fit the needs of the new curricula and learning modules in schools, including the Certificate of Pre-vocational Education (CPVE) and the General Certificate in Secondary Education (GCSE). The GCSE examination system came into effect in 1987 and will have considerable effect on the demands made on history museums by schools. For the first time syllabuses are governed by national criteria. Coursework is a significant part of a pupil's assessment, although assessment and the choices of syllabus remain at a regional level, through five regional bodies. In the criteria for the GCSE in history, the relative importance of 'content' and 'skills' has been acknowledged, and should be accommodated within the course and the assessment procedures. The aims and objectives of history GCSE stress that pupils should develop skills to enable them to use and study a wide variety of historical evidence. They are also expected to be able to deal with concepts such as continuity and change; cause and consequence; similarity and difference (Whincup 1987).

The criteria established for the GCSE in history have provoked some controversy, especially amongst those teachers who feel a content approach is more appropriate for the 14–15-year-old age range. Perhaps the greatest controversy has arisen because one of the objectives to be assessed is the pupil's ability to look at events and issues through the perspectives of people in the past. This requirement for 'empathy' has been questioned on the grounds that our social, cultural and political values are very different from people in the past and, therefore, no pupil can really 'empathize' with historical figures. Further, it has been suggested that even to get close to a moment in history, to work out what people were thinking and experiencing requires a vast amount of original research, outside the requirements of GCSE study. Even then it might not lead to true understanding.

Based on the national criteria, regional examining boards further define coursework requirements and available topics. Many of the available topics directly relate to museum collections and exhibitions. These include: trade unions 1866-1914: urban conditions in Victorian England 1837-1901; education since 1870; women and society from 1870; the Edwardian age 1901-12; Britain since 1945; the history of medicine; communications since 1750; agriculture since 1870; and South Wales mining villages 1840-1980. Only one of the five regional groups responsible for the provision of GCSE, the Northern Examination Association, offers 'local history'. This it does with a statement that it is primarily suited to meet the needs of more mature students (Rees 1987).

Pupils studying these or any other of the topics offered will have to demonstrate an ability to deal with historical evidence including; primary and secondary written sources, statistical and visual material, artefacts, textbooks and orally transmitted material. Museums are tailor-made for this kind of pupil development. Many education officers now see the developments in GCSE as offering challenges and opportunities to museums.

It is a challenge in as much as many museums have hitherto concentrated their efforts on primary school children. GCSE will now bring older children into the museum. There, they will need to work purposefully towards perhaps the most important examination they will take in their lifetimes. Museums will have to meet this challenge through programmes and sessions that are effective and finely tuned to modern needs. This will inevitably extend from the museum's education room into all quarters of the museum, including the galleries. It may be the most rigorous test to date of the 'histories' found in history museums.

It is also an opportunity because, as John Fassnidge, formerly of the National Army Museum, has identified, museums will be promoting their collections to a highly significant section of the population and stressing their vital role in the education of the nation's children (1987: 7-8). For once this will be more than museum hyperbole. The success of museum educational provision will be seen reflected indirectly in pupils' examination results. As a consequence, it is not just children who will be assessed.

GCSE is now well established. The most recent and, indeed, wide-ranging educationl innovation is the National Curriculum. Attainment targets and programmes of study are being drawn up by the National

Curriculum Working Group on History. In their discussions they have continually underlined the relevance of museums, arguing that visits to museums play a central part in the curriculum because they can help reinforce what is being taught in the classroom.

History museum education and adults

The educational interests of adults are often assumed to be catered for through a museum's permanent displays, research facilities and occasional lecture programmes. Therefore, this has not been an area which has attracted much attention in Britain. Exceptions obviously apply. The courses offered by Quarry Bank Mill Museum described above are a case in point. They extend the museum's role through the teaching of skills related to its central subject. The museum provides high standards of tuition and generates an income through its courses.

It is surprising, therefore, that more museums have not developed programmes for adults where skills can be learnt. A great number of history museums have evolved on the premise that they exist to record skills and processes that would otherwise be lost, yet rarely are these handed on through teaching. Admittedly, some are hazardous; for example, chain-making, foundry-work, thatching and knife-grinding; or involve work with animals, for example, ploughing. Others are easier to deal with, such as the preparation of food, weaving of baskets or the mending of nets. But in the main these are all interpreted through demonstration, rarely through courses aimed to transmit the skills.

Some skills are relatively easy to teach but others require long 'apprenticeships', because the skills are complex, or because there are hazards involved. However, there is no reason why the museum cannot be a place where these are handed on. Such work can be as illuminating for curatorial staff as it is for those who study. The experienced Swedish ethnologist Katarina Ågren points to the old proverb 'what you hear you will forget, what you see you will remember, what you do you know'. She asserts that only when tools and materials are used can people understand their shape and function. Katarina Ågren has insisted in her own work that in recording any craft it is necessary not only to collect the tools and record the crafts person at work but also to learn personally the techniques involved. For example, many museums have collections of saddlers' tools, but how many curators or visitors understand how or why a half-moon knife is used on a piece of leather?

The museum is an institution ideally suited for such purposes. It would normally hold collections both of tools and finished products which indicate styles and techniques. Museum archives contain photographs and film of people making and doing things. And usually a museum employs or has contact with people able to teach others. Moreover, as Quarry Bank Mill shows, courses can be a highly satisfying and commercially viable part of a museum's provision for its public.

But only few museums, other than open-air museums, are equipped with the space and facilities to provide adult classes of this sort. It is something that may develop in the future, as museums expand and new ones develop. It is by no means a new idea. During the nineteenth-century many believed that the standards of design and manufacture of products could be improved through the availability of teaching collections and education facilities for the artisan. It is an idea that can be adapted to our modern lives. Without the encouragement and development of skills, many of the old ways will be lost completely or confined to commercial organisations. We will be left to guess how people sailed Norfolk Wherries; managed on a diet derived from the kitchen garden and half a pig; made music in the home, welfare halls or chapels; or made charcoal, clog soles or chairs in the forests.

Other ways of working with adults are opening up. Perhaps one of the most rewarding, for all concerned, has been through reminiscence therapy projects. Reminiscence therapy aims to stimulate older people and instil a sense of self-worth which living in a long-stay hospital or a home may have eroded. The memories generated are often of value to museums.

Sally Griffiths, tutor and organizer of the Prestonfield Remembers Group in Edinburgh, found that books, pictures, music, press-cuttings and photographs were all useful in triggering memories and discussions amongst reminiscence groups. But objects from the more recent past were found to be by far the most evocative: 'everyone had a story about a gas mask, a "stone pig" hot water bottle or a real silk stocking' (Beevers *et al.* 1988: 1). Sally Griffiths's pioneering work led to a project called 'Memories and Things'. This took the form of a partnership between Workers' Educational Association (WEA), a number of working groups of retired people, Edinburgh libraries and curatorial staff involved with setting-up a new museum, the People's Story. The partnership nature of the arrangement was particularly stressed. The first two objectives of the project read:

> (*1*) To find ways of welcoming small groups of older people into the museums and libraries for short visits in which their participation as teachers as well as learners are emphasized.
> (*2*) To develop and publicize handling collections of objects and books that could be lent out to reminiscence groups in the community. [Beevers *et al.*: 2]

The development of handling collections specifically for adults has not been a departure many museums, as yet, have taken. Alongside the sort of partnership arrangement that has developed in Edinburgh, it would seem a valid and profitable educational use of collections.

Museums and messages

Whether for children or adults, using museums to learn about ourselves and the past has often excluded critical analysis of the museum itself. The content of collections, what is excluded and included; the labels that give

Figure 30. A group of objects used in reminiscence work at the People's Story, Edinburgh.

Figure 31. One of the reminiscence groups worked with the museum in the preparation of the People's Story Exhibition.

'the facts'; the organization of space and people; and ways in which visitors are treated—together make museums amenable to analysis as visual ideologies, as manifestations of the schematic order in which we find ourselves. This should be a fundamental aspect of thinking and learning from museums, for curators and public alike.

Dr Jeanne Cannizzo argues:

> Museums are carefully created, artificially constructed repositories; they are negotiated realities. We need to examine the ideology and cultural assumptions which inform our collecting policies, which determine our display formats and influence the interpretations placed upon the objects which we designate as the essence of our cultural historical identity. [1987: 22]

In the light of this perspective, Dr Cannizzo examined the exhibitions and plans of the National Barbados Museum. The museum was controlled by a museum society which, because of high membership fees, had become an exclusive organization with an overwhelmingly white and wealthy membership. The inevitable corollary was that the exhibitions at the museum until the mid-1980s celebrated the products and values of the plantation society. It did not display or celebrate in the same way the lives of the black people of Barbados. Cannizzo argues that by not displaying the cultural heritage of the majority of the population: 'the museum has taken from them by implication, their role as history makers, as active participants in their own past' (1987: 24).

Comparison is drawn with the re-exhibition of the museum in 1985, under the new curatorship of a black Barbadian woman, Alissandra Cummins, trained in museum studies at the University of Leicester, and with the support of a new museum council. The museum now introduces Barbados as a plural society, with a present growing out of its past. There are now no 'primitives', inferior or unchanging people in the exhibition, no natural order springing from the ruling white class. In their place are stories and discussion of the contrasting cultural and historic experiences of the island's free and enslaved settlers: Amerindians, African slaves, Europeans. The museum does not keep history at bay, but brings it up to date with topics at the heart of present-day Barbados, including the success of Barbadian cricket.

The museum, under Alissandra Cummins's curatorship, works from the threefold basis that history is a living thing not divorced from experience; that history is not just about dates but about meaning; and that the act of exhibition is an interpretative art and not just a question of artefact identification. Some of the success of the museum may depend upon the degree to which exhibition techniques can actually facilitate discussion of the past as a process and can present opportunity for active comparison of races, classes and cultures. But, nevertheless, substantial inroads have been made. Human stories of exploration, survival and exploitation now confirm that history there no longer belongs to the rich and powerful.

In Canada Cannizzo's paper opened up discussion of the museum as a symbolic structure which makes visible social myths (Harrison 1987; Janes

1987). In Britain the examination of the museum as a 'negotiated reality' is already underway, through the work of Patrick Wright (1985), Robert Hewison (1987), Bob West (1988) and Tony Bennett (1988). West and Bennett have analysed England's two most expansive museums, certainly ones with well-cultivated public profiles: Ironbridge Gorge Museum, Telford; and the North of England Open Air Museum, at Beamish. Both museums deal with aspects of Britain's nineteenth-century industrial past through reconstructed buildings and streets, costumed staff and demonstrations.

West sees Ironbridge Gorge Museum controlling a view of the past derived from the current dominant political economy. He sees the museum's concentration on local industrial archaeology and the re-presentation of 'urban ways of life' in its constructed village at Blists Hill as a means of celebrating and recuperating capitalist industrialization as a '*positive* moment of historical transformation'. He writes:

> Locating industrial history in a rural setting, and resulting from the inspiration of individual capitalists, is only as invidious as the parallel tendency to represent the labour process as a pleasurable spectacle and deny the presence of class struggle in the work-place. [1988: 59]

West sees the museum as being organized around the moral, political and economic (hegemonic) values of the middle classes, and their men in particular. In total, he sees the museum as a private or 'bourgeois public' space, with its own constraints, preoccupations and perceptions. The museum devises the rules, lays down one version of history and gives permission for its use.

In a museum that has been established and developed by men, largely in what is now called the 'enterprise culture', the deliberate and conscious control of its images has been a part of its strategy to survive. Although it has recently given education a very high priority, the fact remains that Ironbridge Gorge Museum has developed in ways thought suitable to attract people to it and encourage them to spend money. The messages it conveys have been at times subordinated to the demands of survival in a competitive leisure industry. As a consequence, the museum is available to be read as a case study of 'history-making' in the market-place of tourism.

Although the museum has been conscious of its professional and interpretative standards, like all independent museums, it is a self-supporting company and needs a buoyant income to exist. Ironbridge Gorge Museum is a graphic reminder that no museum history comes to us in a state of neutral interpretation. The production of history here has as many economic pressures as political ones. Bob West's conclusions about Beamish have a similar ring to them. He seems the museum as 'providing less of a lesson on industrial or regional history and more of a crash-course in the bourgeois myths of history' (1988: 84).

West and Bennett have identified national myths and preferred stories about the past surfacing in these museums. The images provided by them embody the 'selective tradition' and the predetermined 'significant past'.

They transmit the stories that are allowed, but in so doing neglect many unheard histories to which attention might be directed. Instead, the essential driving force has been the provision of a good day out: the market-place has been served first; history second. Educational work within them has to take into account the forms of history provided and the circumstances of their production.

Alongside efforts to train curators to have a more critical approach to their tasks, two initiatives have developed to open up the 'reading' of museums to museum users. One has been for schoolchildren within the 15-year-old age range, through the revision of a syllabus formally offered as a Certificate in Secondary Education (CSE). In 1987 a General Certificate in Secondary Education (GCSE) in Museum Studies became available.

One of the expressed general aims of the syllabus is that it should promote a knowledge of the concept, range, organization, administration and potential of museums. The first part of the core content is the concept of the museum. Candidates must consider: What is a museum? Why do we have them? What purposes do they serve in society? How are they affected by changing ideas, economic issues, political issues? Museum Studies is not part of the core curriculum and is likely to remain a fringe subject for GCSE. However, a critical and demanding generation of museum visitors may well be the product of such attempts to help schoolchildren think, not only about what they are seeing but also about why they are seeing it.

A similar purpose was built into the Edinburgh project 'Memories and Things', described above. The fourth of the five main objectives reads: 'to establish and run a *People's Story Group* of older people to work in Huntly House Museum, providing information for the new museum, but also learning how a new museum is created and how and why sections of their history are interpreted and presented'.

The reminiscence groups involved in the project have lived up to this objective. They have visited museums in Edinburgh, Glasgow and elsewhere, looking at the displays, the objects in them, and what they say about a past that they themselves knew or at least heard of from parents and grandparents. They have been encouraged to discuss what they liked and disliked about the museums visited, the quality and placing of information offered and what was missing from displays (Beevers *et al.*: 15). One of the members commented on their visits to, and discussions about, museums by saying: 'I think we are all becoming very critical now and that really makes museums more interesting' (Beevers *et al.*: 25).

It seems likely that arguments for history museums will continue to rest on their educational roles, because these give definition to the social and intellectual place of history museums in society. With the new secondary schools curriculum and an ageing population whose needs museums can well serve, the value of history in the museum will inevitably be tested. Indeed, well-held theories about the educational potential of collections and museums are now being assessed and, it is hoped, will be proven. In this, much will ultimately depend, as in all museum functions, on the quality of curatorship and the depth of understanding it brings to collections and their educational uses.

Beyond the content-based educational use of museums, the critical attention addressed directly at the museum itself may increase the willingness of people to think about what it is a museum offers. The development of an informed audience—one that is prepared to question not just the content but the format and substance of museums—is a crucial ingredient in the making of better museums and more-democratic histories.

16. The Future

Museums have undergone revolutionary change in the last 20 years. New attitudes prevail, born of economic pressures and greater incentives to serve the public. Plural funding rather than guaranteed support from the public purse is now well established and represents the greatest challenge to museum management this century. In the light of this development, priorities are being reorganized so that a balance between audience needs and the costs of continued growth and care of collections can be attained. It seems likely that these trends will continue and that the museums of the year 2000 will be very different from the ones we know today. More-imaginative interpretation of collections, wider acquisitions of material and improved visitor services are the obvious components of the ongoing revolutionary process in museums. However, the underlying struggle will be, as now, the maintenance of professional levels of collection management and research.

Much can be achieved by competent, caring curatorship, but this may not be enough. Museums are enabled or restricted by political and economic forces outside curatorial control. To a degree, strong, well-articulated arguments for museums can have some influence, but the conditions have to be right and the times conducive. The ways in which museums develop in future will be influenced by many things, not least being the constitutional form of museums, and popular consciousness of the past.

The radical changes which have taken place in Britain since 1979 have brought revisions in the role and responsibilities of local government. Further reform seems inevitable (Walsh 1989; AIM 1989). As the substantial proportion of history museums in Britain are run by, or receive funding from, local government, the effects of such reforms on museum provision could be profound. Local authority museums are already experiencing revisions in their activities and spread of responsibilities, as established functions are opened for tender and devolved onto outside agencies. In a small number of museum authorities this has led to the situation where only the minimum of core museum functions are paid for directly. In these museums, education, design and outreach services are being offered for tender from the museum staff and outside agencies.

The model used for these developments is the private museum, run as a charitable company. But, since the heydays of the late 1970s, independent museums have experienced considerable difficulties. Few can be said to be secure. There are no figures available for the number of museums that fail each year, although several do and more will. This questions the long-term viability of the museum as a small business, operating according to profit and loss. Even highly successful and astutely run museums, such as Quarry Bank Mill Museum, have to work increasingly hard to raise funds for established functions, let alone growth (*Museums and Galleries Commission Annual Report*, 1987–8). Plural funding, although a fact of life in modern museum management, may prove in the long term too fragile a financial basis. The measure of this will be the changing pattern and scale of museum provision.

Economic and political change will continue to influence how the past is remembered and the degree to which it is of interest to people. The 1980s affected self-perceptions both nationally and locally, throwing into high relief a British past which is believed to have a very different tempo and form from current experiences. Historical awareness has stemmed from the degree of diolocation that appears between the past and the present. If social and economic change becomes even more frenetic, the past will figure more strongly in the popular imagination. This would create further opportunities for museums. But it would also create pressures for specific forms of history in museums.

The market-place

Museums no longer exist in isolation; other forms of history display and exhibition are rapidly emerging. The 'market-place', where 'heritage' and leisure ventures vie with one another for customer attention, is held up as a warning to curators not producing the same proven 'product'. The past has been commodified. Britain's 'priceless heritage' is seen as being quite simply 'a source of future wealth'. In line with this wealth-making attitude, museums are collectively referred to by the Minister for the Arts as the 'museums industry'.

The wealth-producing potential of the past is such that private sector companies are investing what are, in museum terms, vast sums of money in creating historical attractions. Unicorn Heritage floated a £5 million share issue to raise capital for the permanent exhibition 'Royal Britain'. A consortium aims to provide Glasgow with an exhibition called 'Words and the Stones' estimated to cost well in excess of £2.8 million, for its year as European City of Culture in 1990. Both ventures are based on the latest and most spectacular design and audio-visual techniques. Similar plans are underway for heritage exhibitions in Birmingham and Newark. The 'White Cliffs Experience' at Dover, due to be opened in December 1990, is being heralded as 'the first of a new generation of heritage centres in Britain'. Investment on this project is in the order of £13.75 million.

No such investment would be made if there was not some assurance that it would, at the very least, be covered in immediate receipts. Attuned to what is thought to be the public's limited concentration span, reduced by too much television, and a demand for 'entertainment experience', such ventures aim to provide a memorable and exciting visit. With tourism earning a record £11 billion in Britain in 1987, and with a predicted rise to £20 billion in the 1990s, leisure developments, especially those that provide for the whole family, will be on the increase and secure for some time yet. With no overheads in terms of long-term research, temporary exhibitions, public enquiries, the housing of collections and educational programmes, the principal capital outlay remains the major investment. Beyond the original concept, design and production work, all that is needed afterwards are running and maintenance costs. Beyond that, all is pure, taxable profit.

These ventures have to be seen as relatively short term, compared to museums, which are evolving institutions, serving both present-day and future generations. This obvious fact does not prevent museums from being compared with heritage entertainments. But this is the real world in which museums exist and evidence would suggest that astutely publicized and well-organized museums can attract large audiences and generate income. When appropriate attitudes and methods are brought to bear, museums can meet and match challenge from the heritage industry, without eroding responsibilities towards scholarship and collection care. The Armada Exhibition at the National Maritime Museum in 1988 was a good case in point. It did not adjust the balance of its interpretation to meet perceived popular opinion, nor did it fail to recognize marketing opportunities. The museum entered into very useful commercial and sponsorship arrangements with, amongst others, Kodak and Penguin. The exhibition was a great success. Visitor figures met the best of the museum's expectations and the exhibition could easily have lasted longer than the four and a half months planned.

The Armada Exhibition indicated the degree to which museums can exert their position within this market-place without prejudicing any of their well-established functions. Indeed, such involvement might enhance and enable museum developments rather than corrupt them. One of the lessons that the leisure industry has pushed home is that the visitor must count and must be catered for, in Madison's words from 1925, as a 'visiting guest'. This attitude, coupled with the knowledge that history museums can offer forms of knowledge and an interpretation of the past not available from other institutions, places museums in a position where they can develop their own very specific 'industry' and market position. In this, it is essential that museums establish an astute awareness of *how* they are different from heritage exhibitions and the heritage industry in general. Museums need to make their collective identity felt and, it is hoped, this will have been one of the products of the Museums Year, 1989.

It is also critical that museums lift their horizons and plan for the medium and long term. A central part of this planning will almost inevitably involve refinement of curatorial work and the management of change.

Curatorship

The curator has traditionally been a trained graduate, able to carry out all the functions required to create and foster the museum. The curator is, therefore, researcher, collector, manager, intepreter, communicator, teacher and security expert. As museums change and grow, each of these roles has required ever-greater degrees of skill. Yet rarely are they found in equal measure in one person. Even where they do exist in some balance, curators have preferences for some roles over others.

The cost of curatorship and the balance of curatorial functions against other museum activities, especially commercial ones, have led to a reassessment of museum work. In particular, the cost of curatorship is considered in the context of annual expenditure and income. Clearly, those museums which devote over 80 per cent of their annual income to staff costs have very limited resources for research and development. Changes had to come, and they are taking the form of increasing specialization, not just within subjects but also within functions of curatorship. Future museum curators are likely to be not only specialists within their academic fields but also within different museum activities, such as documentation, research and interpretation. The museum worker is, therefore, changing and is beginning to be assessed in terms of the contribution to the museum overall.

This, combined with demographic changes, is creating a situation where future museum provision is highly dependent on the quality of skill and type of ability new staff bring with them. The expected scarcity of young graduates in the years ahead means that the museums profession must be actively prepared to seek out and recruit special talents. Museum work has always attracted the idealist, the person who believes that the museum is an institution of social worth. Idealism may not be enough in the future. Higher rewards, more-attractive conditions of employment, and greater opportunities for training and personal development may be required if museum work is to appeal to the best of young talent and to compete with alternative career opportunities.

But the future of museums is not only dependent on the quality of recruitment and training. It is also dependent on the quality of museum management and museum directors. Museum staff will become increasingly composed of people with diverse backgrounds and skills who will find themselves operating with limited resources but with marvellous opportunities. The ability to find direction, work corporately and respond collectively will be determined by the way a museum is managed. Management for hearts and minds will be the prerequisite of financial and social success. This requires very special forms of museum leadership, based on quality of ideas and relationships rather than on control and power.

As with the intake of new staff, fundamental changes are required, especially in the profile of museum directors and ways in which museums are managed. Developments which could be crucial to the future well-being and development of museums include: a significant drop in the age of museum directors, as people are recruited on the criterion of talent rather than years of experience; more short-term contract posts, where renewal is determined by performance criteria; opportunities for management training, especially in inter-personal skills, time-management and financial affairs; and the adoption of recruitment and selection procedures which draw on the experience of industry rather than administration.

People, services and collections

In the late 1970s and 1980s, museums actively sought to increase their visitor numbers by appealing to day visitors and tourists. They associated themselves very successfully with the idea of the family day out. In the 1990s new audiences may be sought: the early retired; mobile young people; and sections of the population hitherto not attracted to museums, for example ethnic minorities.

In particular, assessment has to be made of whether museums are adequately serving local people, and whether hidden audiences exist on their own doorsteps. Surely, the extent to which local people identify with, and care about, their local history museum is the strongest foundation for its continued existence. If this is so, then questions have to be asked. Do museums give local people adequate reason to visit frequently or are they providing only a one-off visit, something which is exhausted on first encounter? How democratic are their services and are their local audiences a representative cross-section of local people?

Two relatively new projects—Age Exchange and People's Story—are useful models for future museum developments. They indicate how museums can strengthen local community links and improve the quality and range of collections through making more of their recording and collecting activities, integrating them with education and exhibition. The social relevance of their activities provides them with the potential not only to reach local people but also to create histories likely to engage a wider, more democratic audience than other, more-standard history and heritage exhibitions.

Age Exchange Theatre Trust is a London charity, supporting a professional community theatre and publishing company. It is not strictly speaking a museum, although what it does has museum relevance. Age Exchange produces shows, books and exhibitions based on the reminiscences and current concerns of older people. The Trust's expressed aim is to entertain, inform, record, stimulate and create a greater understanding between young and old, through exploring living memory. Age Exchange's activities centre on the musical entertainments they create, but these have to be seen as part of a chain of activities and initiatives.

The shows, of which there are in the region of two a year, have included *Can We Afford the Doctor?*, on health care and sickness from the turn of the century to present day; *From Stepney to Golders Green*, about the early years in the Jewish East End; *What Did You Do in the War, Mum?*, on working women in the Second World War; and, recently, *Good Morning Children*, about school life between the wars. These are directly based on interviews Age Exchange conducts with older people in homes or hospitals. The people whose memories are used in the shows are later involved as advisers in the rehearsal process.

The productions are designed for touring to community centres, sheltered homes, clubs, schools, hospitals and art centres. Each performance is followed by discussion between audience and actors about the play and the memories invoked. To accompany the productions, edited reminiscences on each of the themes are published, and a touring exhibition of photographs, reminiscences and objects created. In this way, the productions have complete cycles in the coverage of their themes: from the recording of memories through to a final publication.

Beyond its primary role through theatre, Age Exchange has developed a number of ways of encouraging valuable work with elderly people in London. Young people are involved through the Age Exchange Youth Theatre, which mounts its own productions using the methods of the main company. Carers, whether in hospitals or homes, can receive training in reminiscence therapy from Age Exchange, and can use resources they have developed, including a resource pack called *Lifetimes*, and sets of objects.

The Age Exchange Reminiscence Project is a separate venture designed for long-stay hospitals, old people's homes and nursing homes. Experienced reminiscence workers alongside permanent staff work with elderly residents or patients, discussing and sharing their experiences. They participate in music-making, mime and improvization, as well as handling objects and looking at pictures associated with the past. The sessions aim to be fun for the old people and give them a chance to experience success. Such work has demonstrated that reminiscence activity increases their sense of identity and level of communication.

In January 1987 Age Exchange moved into new premises in Blackheath which have been developed into a Reminiscence Centre. This now houses offices, facilities for training activities and rehearsal rooms. It also has space for the temporary exhibitions based on the Age Exchange shows, and permanent exhibitions of objects given to them for their work. It is open six days a week and has an atmosphere which is extraordinarily warm and welcoming.

A regular programme of events includes joint sessions with South Greenwich Adult Institute on autobiographical writing, which aim to encourage people to commit their memories to paper. Reminiscence recording sessions held each week enable people to elect to come to Age Exchange with their reminiscences and have them preserved on tape. Through autobiographical writing and the recording sessions, Age Exchange enables people to say that their memories are important rather than having to wait to be asked. There are regular social events as well, including weekly tea-dances.

The work of Age Exchange differs from that of history museums in that the collections are not an end in themselves nor the principal means through which it operates. Instead, the collections are aids, illustrations, props, language, keys to the sometimes closed door of memory. They are primarily concerned with communication through theatre. Long-term research, critical use of sources, learned publications, collection management and more formal exhibitions are characteristics of museum work which are largely absent from their activities.

However, there is much in common with the intentions of history museums: the advancement of knowledge and understanding; close and reciprocal contact with the public; the valuing of human experience; detailed recording, where accuracy and balance is important; the creation of long-term archives of former ways of living and working; and the provision of environments in which people can be stimulated by, learn about and discuss the past—are present in Age Exchange's work and are history museum ideals, too.

If all this were achieved and well-documented collections of relevance were created in a museum, there might be totally different perspectives on the place and value of museums in modern life. It would lift history museums out of uncertainty about whether they are leisure, academic or a social service. The intellectual quality and leisure uses of museums would be more strongly founded if the essential social and cultural components of their activities were more fruitfully explored.

The People's Story in Edinburgh is one museum that has whole-heartedly involved itself in reminiscence work, particularly through the joint project 'Memories and Things', described in previous chapters. The museum is due to be opened in the Canongate Tolbooth in the centre of Edinburgh's Old Town. The museum has a commitment to ensure that it becomes a genuine part of Edinburgh, a place where local people feel a sense of participation and a pride in their past. To ensure direct local involvement from the earliest stages of the museum's development, the curatorial staff opened all possible channels to local people. These included oral history work, publicity campaigns, and talks and appeals on local radio. Two People's Story groups were established out of the project 'Memories and Things'. The groups have worked on themes underlying the displays, reviewed collections and advised on the content of the 'sets' through which the museum tells the 'People's Story'. They have made a substantial impact on the sort of history the museum conveys.

Each week the groups discuss a theme set by the museum: 'trigger material' is used to jog memories. At the end of the session, each member takes home a questionnaire so that more-detailed responses can be recorded. These complement and extend the museum's own research, assisting curators in the development of historical perspective. The themes have generated a constant flow of objects and photographs which have either been copied or added to the museum's collection. Further, members of the groups have been able to identify and rectify gaps in the collections; for example, a 'tinny' taken on picnics, a co-op washbag, a wrap-around overall and a selection of packets and washing powders. The groups advise on displays, which has proven especially helpful. For example, a model 1938 Electrolux vacuum cleaner was rejected from the display of a 1930s council house kitchen. The groups were able to point out to the museum, 'why would you have a vacuum cleaner if you had no carpets?' (Clark 1988: 6).

The People's Story groups are not only providing information and enjoying the process of involvement, they are also helping to ensure that the museum tells the story and histories of real Edinburgh people. Their words will appear in the text of the labels and in a video, alongside the interpretative comments of the curators and extracts from other oral history recordings. Some of this will be used by Winged Horse Touring Productions in a play which will tour Edinburgh.

The work of Age Exchange Theatre and the People's Story provide inspiration. Much livelier museums, more in touch with the past, could develop if note were taken of the opportunities available and the ways in which museums could be more active and in touch with local people. The effectiveness of any museum must lie, in significant part, with the quality of what it offers and the generosity of its spirit. This is rooted in how the museum sees its task, the genuine efforts it is prepared to make, and the enthusiasm and care it invests in all it does. The more successful a museum is in its own locality and region, the stronger the basis for attracting people from further afield.

In conclusion, the future of history museums is as bright and as fraught with difficulties as it has ever been. Material and oral evidence will always fascinate and inform, confuse and mislead. But through the steady development and improvement of museums such evidence can be opened to enquiry and greater public understanding of the past. If the challenges are seen as opportunities and more-democratic means are found to develop collections and services, much will be gained. However, the history museum's future, as with its present, will ultimately be determined by the social need to remember and the political will for remembrance.

Bibliography

Adegren, A. (trans.). 1984. *Museiboken Sveriges Länsmuseer*, Borås, Sweden.

Age Exchange. 1986. *Annual Report 1985-6*. London.

——1988. *Age Exchange Theatre Trust Report 1986-8*. London.

AIM, 1989. 'Local authority-influenced museums affected by new bill', *AIM Bulletin*, 12(2): 1.

Airey, V., 1980. 'The Nordic Museum and research', *GRSM Newsletter*, 8: 6-12.

Alexander, E. P., 1983. 'Artur Hazelius', *Museum Masters*, Nashville: 241-75.

Allen, R. E., 1984. 'Research: social history—a case study', in Thompson, J.M.A. *et al.* (eds). *Manual of Curatorship*. London: 179-86.

Almqvist, B., 1979. *The Irish Folklore Commission: Achievement and Legacy*, Folklore Studies Pamphlet 3, Dublin.

Ames, M. M., 1977. 'Visible storage and public documentation', *Curator*, 20: 65-79.

——1985. 'De-schooling the museum: a proposal to increase public access to museums and their resources', *Museum*, 145: 15-31.

Anon. 1966. 'Folk parks: report of a seminar held at the Institute of Advanced Architectural Studies, University of York', *Museums Journal*, 66(3): 220-4.

Atkinson, F., 1967. 'Regional and site museums: relation to the work of the industrial archaeologist', *Museums Journal*, 66(4): 254-6.

——1968. 'Regional museums', *Museums Journal*, 68(2): 74-7.

——1975. 'Presidential address', *Museums Journal*, 75(3): 103-5.

Beevers, L., *et al.* 1988. *Memories and Things: Linking Museums and Libraries with Older People*. Edinburgh.

Bell, C. and Newby, H., 1971. *Community Studies*. London.

Bennett, T., 1988. 'Museums and the people', in Lumley, R. (ed.). *The Museum Time Machine*. London: 63-85.

Bennett, T., *et al.* (eds). 1981. *Culture, Ideology and Social Process*. London.

Blackburn, M., 1987. 'Polar bears in the community—a new role for a traditional museum', *MPG News*, 25: 1-3.

Blake, Lord., 1979. *Report of the Committee to Review Local History. Standing Conference for Local History*. London.

Bloch, M., 1954. *The Historian's Craft*. Manchester.

Board of Education, 1931. *Museums and the Schools: Memorandum of the Possibility of Increased Co-operation between Public Museums and Public Educational Institutions*, Educational Pamphlet 87. London.

Brears, P. C. D., 1980. 'Kirk of the castle', *Museums Journal*, 80(2): 90–2.
Brown, A. C., 1942. 'Colonial Williamsburg, Virginia: the historical background and restoration', *Museums Journal*, 42(7): 157-60.
Brown, G. Baldwin, 1901. 'Industrial museums in their relationship to art', *Museums Journal*, 1: 93-106.
Brown, M., 1982. 'One museum's drama experience', *Museums Journal*, 81(4): 208-9.
Brigden, R. D., 1984. 'Research: social history collections', in Thompson, J.M.A., *et al.* (eds). *Manual of Curatorship*. London: 170-8.
Brunskill, R. W., 1970. *Illustrated Handbook of Vernacular Architecture*. London.
——1981. *Traditional Buildings of Britain*. London.
Burke, P., 1981. 'People's history or total history', in Samuel, R. (ed.), *People's History and Socialist Theory*. London.
Calder, A. and Sheridon, D., 1984. *Speak for Yourself: A Mass Observation Anthology 1937-49*. London.
Cannizzo, J., 1987. 'How sweet it is: cultural politics in Barbados', *Muse*, Winter: 22-7.
Carlsson, G. and Ågren P.-U., 1982. *Utställningsspråk. Om Utställningar för Upplevelse och Kunskap*. Stockholm.
Carr, E. H., 1964. *What is History?* London.
Cheape, H., 1978. 'Questionnaires and the grain harvest in Scotland', *Folk Life*, 16: 27-41.
——1986(?) 'Dr I. F. Grant (1887-1983): The Highland Folk Museum and a bibliography of her written works', *The Review of Scottish Culture*, 2: 113-25.
Clarke, H., 1988. 'Community involvement in "The People's Story"', *Scottish Museum News*, Autumn: 4-6.
Clifton-Taylor, A., 1965. *The Pattern of English Building*. London.
Collison, D., 1978. 'Making money from your museum', *Museums Journal*, 77(4): 169-70.
Condell, D., 1985. 'The Imperial War Museum 1917-1920' (unpublished MPhil thesis), University of London.
Cossons, N., 1980. 'The museum in the valley, Ironbridge Gorge', *Museum*, 32(3): 138-53.
Cumming, V., 1985. 'The role of training in managing change', in Cossons, N., (ed.), *The Management of Change*. London.
Davies, S., 1985a. *By Gains of Industry: Birmingham Museums and Art Gallery 1885-1985*. Birmingham.
——1985b. 'Collecting and recording the twentieth century', *Museums Journal*, 85(1): 27-9.
——1985c. 'Specialists groups: review of the year. Social History Curators Group', *Museums Journal*, 85(3): 153-5.
Dawson, J. A., 1982. 'The growth of service industries', in Johnson, R.J. and Doornkamp, J.C., (eds). *The Changing Geography of the United Kingdom*. London: 203-26.
Day, L., 1987. 'A short history of the Science Museum', in Nahum, A., *Science Museum Review*. London: 14-18.

Deetz, J., 1987. 'A sense of another world: history museums and cultural change', in Hall, P. and Seeman, C. (eds). *Folklife and Museums. Selected Readings.* Nashville: 88–98.

Dellheim, C., 1982. *The Face of the Past: The Preservation of the Medieval Inheritance in Victorian England.* Cambridge.

Dethier, J., 1981. *All Stations: A Journey through 150 Years.* London.

Dicken, P., 1982. 'The industrial structure and geography of manufacturing', in Johnson, R.J. and Doornkamp J.C., (eds). *The Changing Geography of the United Kingdon.* London: 171–201.

Ekarv, M., 1987. 'Combatting redundancy—writing texts for exhibitions', *Exhibitions in Sweden,* 27–8. Stockholm.

Elton, G. R., 1968. *The Future of the Past.* London.

Emery-Wallis, F. A. J., 1979. 'The value of museums to the economy', *Museums Journal,* 79(3): 115–16.

English Tourist Board, 1982. *Visitors to Museums Survey 1982.* London.

Evans, G. E., 1971. *Where Beards Wag All.* London.

———1976. *From Mouths of Men.* London.

Fassnidge, J., 1987. 'History', *Museums Journal,* 87(1): 7–12.

Fägerborg, E., 1981. *Arbetsliv: En Handledning i Dokumentation av Arbeysplatser.* Stockholm.

Fenton, A., 1985. 'Material culture in local history studies', *The Shape of the Past 1. Essays in Scottish ethnology.* Edinburgh: 2–13.

Finch, K. and Putnam, G., 1977. *Caring for Textiles.* London.

Fitzgerald, R., 1987. 'Right to reply', *Social History Curators Group News,* 15: 5–6.

Fox, C., 1934. 'Open-air museums. Presidential address to the Museums Association Conference: July 1934', *Museums Journal,* 34(4): 109–21.

Frankenberg, R., 1969. *Communities in Britain. Social Life in Town and Country.* London.

Gailey, A., 1986. 'Creating Ulster's Folk Museum', *Ulster Folklife,* 32: 54–77.

Glover, J. M., 1984. 'Conservation and storage: textiles', in Thompson, J.M.A. *et al.* (eds). *Manual of Curatorship.* London: 333–55.

Goa, D., 1979. 'The incarnation of meaning: approaching the material culture of religious tradition', *National Museum of Man Material History Bulletin,* 8: 43–52.

Goode, G. Brown, 1895. 'The principles of museum administration', *Museums Association. Report of proceedings at sixth annual general meeting:* 69–148.

Greenaway, F., 1984. 'Research: science collections', in Thompson, J.M.A. *et al.* (eds). *Manual of Curatorship.* London: 142–6.

Greenhalgh, P., 1988. *Ephemeral Vistas. The Expositions Universelles. Great Exhibitions and World's Fairs, 1851–1939.* Manchester.

Group for Regional Studies in Museums, 1975. 'The newsletter: some introductory remarks', *Group for Regional Studies in Museums,* 1: 1–2.

Hall, C., 1981. *Grandma's Attic or Aladdin's Cave: Education Services for Children.* Wellington, New Zealand.

Harrison, R. J., 1987. 'De-colonizing museum classification systems: a case in point—the Metis', *Muse*, Winter: 46–50.

Harrison, S., 1986. *100 Years of Heritage*. Douglas.

Hawes, E. L., 1986. 'Artifacts, myths and identity in American history museums', *Museology and identity: ICOFOM Study Series 10*. Stockholm: 135–40.

Heighton, M., 1987. 'Museums as a community enterprise', *Museums Journal*, 87(2): 61–4.

Henley Centre, 1985. *Leisure Futures*. London.

Hewison, R., 1986. 'Museums are one of our few growth industries', *The Listener*, 26 June: 11–12.

——1987. *The Heritage Industry: Britain in a Climate of Decline*. London.

Higgs, J. W. Y., 1963. *Folk Life Collection and Classification*. London.

Hooper Greenhill, E., 1980. 'The National Portrait Gallery: a case study in cultural reproduction', (unpublished MA dissertation), University of London.

——1988. 'Counting visitors or visitors who count?', in Lumley, R. (ed.). *The Museum Time Machine*. London: 213–32.

——'Museum Education' in Thompson, J.M.A. (ed.). *Manual of Curatorship* (3rd edition forthcoming).

Hopkin, D. W., 1987. 'Railway preservation: railways, museums and enthusiasts' (unpublished MA dissertation), University of Leicester.

Hoskins, W. G., 1955. *The Making of the English Landscape*. London.

——1967. *Fieldwork in Local History*. London.

Hudson, K., 1965. 'The taming of industrial archaeology', *Museums Journal*, 65(1): 36–41.

——1986. 'Problems in museum presentations of the westernisation of other cultures', unpublished paper given at a conference held at the British Museum on 'The Limits of Objectivity in Representations of Other Cultures'.

——1987. *Museums of Influence*. Cambridge.

Impey, O. and MacGregor, A. (eds), 1985. *The Origins of Museums: The Cabinets of Curiosities in Sixteenth and Seventeenth Century Europe*. Oxford.

Ivanov, N., 1980. 'The twentieth-century heritage and museums of heritage', *ICOM: Proceedings of the 12th General Conference* (not paginated).

Janes, R. R., 1987. 'Museum ideology and practice in Canada's Third World', *Muse*, Winter: 33–9.

Jenkins, J. G., 1969. 'Folk life museums: some aims and purposes', *Museums Journal*, 69(1): 17–20.

——1972. 'The use of artifacts and folk art in the folk museum', in Dorson, R.M. (ed.). *Folklore and Folklife*. Chicago: 497–517.

——1974. 'The collection of ethnological material', *Museums Journal*, 74: 7–11.

——1987. 'Interpreting the heritage of Wales', *Folk Life*, 25: 5–17.

Jenkinson, P., 1988. 'Material culture, people's history and populism: where do we go from here', in Pearce S.M. (ed.). *Museum Studies in Material Culture*. Leicester: 139–52.

Johnson, E. V. and Hogan, J. C., 1980. *Handbook for Museum Collection Storage*. Paris.

Kavanagh, G. E., 1985. 'Museums and the Great War' (unpublished MPhil thesis), University of Leicester.

——1987. 'Ah, yes, but . . . A few thoughts on the objects vs. people debate', *SHCG News*, 16: 7.

——1988b. 'Museum as memorial: the origins of the Imperial War Museum', *Journal of Contemporary History*, 22: 77–97.

——1988b. 'Objects as evidence, or not?, in Pearce, S.M., *Museum Studies in Material Culture*. Leicester: 125–38.

Keuren, D. K. Van, 1984. 'Museums and ideology: Augustus Pitt-Rivers, anthropological museums and social change in late Victorian Britain', *Victorian Studies*, 28: 171–89.

Kinard, J. R., 1985. 'Neighbourhood museums as a catalyst for social change', *Museum*, 148: 217–24.

King, E., 1986. 'The cream of the dross: collecting Glasgow's present for the future', *Social History Curators Group*, 13: 4–11.

——1987. 'Case study: People's Palace Museum, Glasgow', in Ambrose, T.M. and Kavanagh, G. (eds). *Recording Society Today*. Edinburgh: 20–7.

——1988. *The People's Palace and Glasgow Green*. Glasgow.

Klein, B., 1985. 'Swedish ethnology in the 1980s', unpublished paper presented at the annual meeting of the American Folklore Society.

Knowles, L., 1987. 'The portrayal of labour history in museum displays', *Bias in Museums: Museums Professional Group Transactions*, 22: 9–10.

Kusamitsu, T., 1980. 'Great Exhibitions before 1851', *History Workshop Journal*, 9: 70–87.

Leene, J. E., 1972. *Textile Conservation*. London.

Levykin, K. G., 1980. 'World heritage and museums of history', *ICOM: Proceedings of the 12th General Conference*, Paris: unpaginated.

Lewis, I. M., 1985. *Social Anthropology in Perspective: The Relevance of Social Anthropology*. Cambridge.

Lickorish, L. J., 1979. 'Value of museums to the economy', *Museums Journal*, 79(3): 117–18.

Lord, B. and Lord, G. D., 1988. 'The museum planning process', *Museums Journal*, 84(4): 175–9.

Lumley, R. (ed.), 1988. *The Museum Time Machine*. London.

MacDonell, M., 'Glasgow heads for 1990', *Museums Journal*, 89(1): 19–22.

McDaniel, G. W., 1982. 'Something of value: preserving a people's culture', *History News*, 37(2): 12–16, Nashville.

MacFarlane, A., 1977a. 'History, anthropology and the study of communities', *Social History*, 2(5): 631–52.

——1977b. *Reconstructing Historical Communities*, Cambridge.

McKendrik N. *et al.*, 1983. *The Birth of a Consumer Society: The Commercialization of Eighteenth-Century England*. London.

McManus, P., 1988. 'Good companions: more on the social determination of learning-related behaviour in a science museum', *International Journal of Museum Management and Curatorship*, 7: 37–44.

Madison, H. L., 1925. 'Tentative code of museum ethics', *Museums Journal*, 25: 19-23.

Marsh, G. D., 1987. 'The development of social history museums in Britain with particular reference to the London area' (unpublished MA dissertation), University of Leicester.

Marwick, A., 1981. *The Nature of History*. London.

Mattingley, J., 1984. *Volunteers in Museums and Galleries*. Berkhamsted.

Merriman, N., 1988. 'The social basis of museum and heritage visiting', in Pearce, S.M. (ed.), *Museum Studies in Material Culture*. Leicester: 153-71.

Miers, Sir H., 1928. *A report on the Public Museums of the British Isles (Other than the Nationals)*. Edinburgh.

Montagu, Lord, 1979. 'Enterprise in museums', *Museums Journal*, 79(3): 118-19.

Museum of English Rural Life, 1954. *Museum of English Rural Life Report 1951-54*. Reading.

——1955. *Museum of English Rural Life Report 1955*. Reading.

Myerscough, J. et al. 1988. *The Economic Importance of the Arts in Britain*. London.

Nahum, A., 1987. *Science Museum Review*. London.

Noble, R. R., 1977. 'The changing role of the Highland Folk Museum', *Aberdeen University Review* xxvii, z: 142-7.

Nyström, B. and Cedrenius, G., 1982. *Spread the Responsibility for Museum Documentation: A Programme for Contemporary Documentation at Swedish Museums of Cultural History*. Stockholm.

O'Neill, M., 1987. 'Quantity vs quality or what is a community museum anyway?', *Scottish Museum News*, Spring: 5-7.

O'Suilleabhain, S., 1942. *A Handbook of Irish Folklore*. [Dublin.]

Parker, A. C., 1966. *A Manual for History Museums*. New York.

Patmore, J. A., 1983. *Recreation and Resources: Leisure Patterns and Leisure Places*. Oxford.

Pearce, S. M., 1986a. 'Thinking about things. Approaches to the study of artefacts', *Museums Journal*, 85(4): 198-201.

——1986b. 'Objects, high and low: a further examination of the way we think about things', *Museums Journal*, 86(2): 79-82.

——1986c. 'Objects as signs and symbols', *Museums Journal*, 86(2): 131-5.

——1987. 'Objects in structures', *Museums Journal*, 86(4): 178-81.

Peate, I. C., 1941. 'The place of folk culture in the museum', *Museums Journal*, 41(3): 45-50.

——1948. *Folk Museums*. Cardiff.

——1949. 'The folk museum', *Journal of the Royal Society of Arts*. 97: 794-806.

——1972. *Tradition and Folk Life: A Welsh View*. London.

——1976. 'Some thoughts on the study of folk life', in Danachair, C. O. (ed.). *Farm and Farm: Essays in Honour of A. T. Lucas*. Dublin: 229-34.

Percival, A., 1979. *Understanding our Surroundings*. London.

Philipp, J., 1983. 'Traditional historical narrative and action-orientated (or ethnographic) history', *Historical Studies*, 20: 339-52.

Plimoth Plantation, 1986. *Annual Report*, Plimoth, Massachusetts.

Porter, G., 1987. 'Gender bias: representations of work in history museums', *Bias in Museums: Museums Professionals Group Transactions*, 22: 11-15.

——1988. 'Putting your house in order: representations of women and domestic life', in Lumley, R., *The Museum Time Machines*. London: 102-27.

Prince, D. R. and Higgins-McLoughlin, B., 1987. *Museums UK: The Findings of the Museums Data-Base Project*. London.

Ramer, B., 1989. *A Conservation Survey of Museum Collections in Scotland*. Edinburgh.

Rees, P., 1987. 'Local history', *Museums Journal*, 87(1): 13-14.

Rosander, G., 1980. *Today for Tomorrow: Museum Documentation of Contemporary Society in Sweden by Acquisition of Objects*. Stockholm.

Rose, C., 1985. 'A code of ethics for registrars', *Museum News*, 63(3): 42-6.

Ross, E., 1983. 'Survival networks: women's sharing in London before World War 1', *History Workshop*, 15: 4-27.

Rosse, Earl of, 1963. *Survey of Provincial Museums and Galleries*. London.

Samuel, R., 1988. 'What is social history?', in Gardiner, J. (ed.). *What is History Today?*. London: 42-8.

Schlereth, T. J., 1980. *Artifacts and the American Past*. Nashville.

——1981. 'The history behind, within and outside the history museum', *Curator*, 23(4): 255-74.

——1984. 'It wasn't that simple', *Museum News*, 62(3): 61-5.

——1985. 'Causing conflict, doing violence', *Museum News*, 63(1): 45-62.

Scottish Museums Council, 1987. *Research Series No. 1: Public attitudes to Scottish Museums*. Edinburgh.

Sheppard, T., 1935. 'Hull's "Old Times" street', *Museums Journal*, 35(7): 245-52.

Silvester, B., 1981. 'The genesis of a labouring museum', *History Workshop*, 11: 160-5.

Skinner, G. M., 1986. 'Sir Henry Wellcome's Museum for the Science of History', *Medical History*, 30: 383-418.

Stacey, M., 1969. 'The myth of community studies', *British Journal of Sociology*, 20: 2.

Standing Commission on Museums and Galleries, 1963. *Survey of Provincial Museums and Galleries*. London.

——1971. *The Preservation of Technological Material*. London.

Stavenow-Hidemark, E., 1985. *Home Thoughts from Abroad: An Evaluation of the SAMDOK Homes Pool*. Stockholm.

Stevens, C., 1986. *Writers of Wales: Iorwerth C. Peate*. Cardiff.

Summerfield, P., 1985. 'Mass-Observation: social research or social movement?', *Journal of Contemporary History*, 20: 439-52.

Szabó, M., 1986. *Some Aspects of Museum Documentation: Methodological Questions No. 1*. Stockholm.

Thomas, K. V., 1963. 'History and anthropology', *Past and Present*, 24: 3-24.

Thompson, E.P., 1965. 'The peculiarities of the English', *Socialist Register*.
——1972. 'Anthropology and the discipline of historical context', *Midland History*, 1(3): 41–55.
——1977. 'Folklore, anthropology and social history', *Indian Historical Review*, 3(2): 247–66.
Thompson, G., 1985. 'The social significance of folk museums', *Museums are for People*. Edinburgh: 26–39.
Thompson, J. M. A. *et al.* (eds.). 1984. *Manual of Curatorship*. London.
Thompson, P., 1988. *The Voice of the Past*. Oxford.
Tosh, J., 1984. *The Pursuit of History*, London.
Turner, S. and Yates, B. (eds.). *Taken into Care: The Conservation of Social History and Industrial History Items*. London.
Wallace, M., 1981. 'Visiting the past: history museums in the United States', *Radical History Review*, 25: 63–96.
——1987. 'The politics of public history', in Blatti, J. (ed.). *Past Meets Present: Essays about Historic Interpretation and Public Audiences*. Washington: 37–53.
Walsh, K., 1989. 'Competitive tendering', *Museums Journal*, 89(1): 23–9.
Waterer, J., 1972. *The Conservation and Restoration of Leather*. London.
West, B., 1988. 'The making of the English working past: a critical view of the Ironbridge Gorge Museum', in Lumley, R. (ed.). *The Museum Time Machine*: 36–62.
Westerlund, S., 1986. 'Twenty years of travelling exhibitions', *Museum*, 152: 206–12.
Wheeler, R. E. M., 1934. 'Folk museums', *Museums Journal*, 34: 191–6.
Whincup, A., 1987. 'GCSE for curators', *Museums Journal*, 87(1): 26–8.
Wiener, M. J., 1985. *English Culture and the Decline of the Industrial Spirit 1850–1980*. London.
Williams, R. (ed.). 1981. *Contact: Human Communication and its History*. London.
Wright, P., 1985. *On Living in an Old Country: The National Past in Contemporary Britain*. London.
Yavtushenko, I. G. and Markov, V. B., 1982. 'Halography serves Ukrainian museums', *Museum*, 34(3): 168–72.

Index